The Poets of Rapallo

The Poets of Rapallo

How Mussolini's Italy Shaped British, Irish, and U.S. Writers

LAUREN ARRINGTON

OXFORD
UNIVERSITY PRESS

Great Clarendon Street, Oxford, OX2 6DP,
United Kingdom

Oxford University Press is a department of the University of Oxford.
It furthers the University's objective of excellence in research, scholarship,
and education by publishing worldwide. Oxford is a registered trade mark of
Oxford University Press in the UK and in certain other countries

© Lauren Arrington 2021

The moral rights of the author have been asserted

First Edition published in 2021

Impression: 1

All rights reserved. No part of this publication may be reproduced, stored in
a retrieval system, or transmitted, in any form or by any means, without the
prior permission in writing of Oxford University Press, or as expressly permitted
by law, by licence or under terms agreed with the appropriate reprographics
rights organization. Enquiries concerning reproduction outside the scope of the
above should be sent to the Rights Department, Oxford University Press, at the
address above

You must not circulate this work in any other form
and you must impose this same condition on any acquirer

Published in the United States of America by Oxford University Press
198 Madison Avenue, New York, NY 10016, United States of America

British Library Cataloguing in Publication Data
Data available

Library of Congress Control Number: 2020949672

ISBN 978-0-19-884654-3

Printed and bound in the UK by
TJ Books Limited

Links to third party websites are provided by Oxford in good faith and
for information only. Oxford disclaims any responsibility for the materials
contained in any third party website referenced in this work.

For Nura and Sara, with the hope of a better world

The Making of *The Poets of Rapallo*

In the early years of the fascist regime, an unlikely assortment of poets from the United States, England, and Ireland gathered in a small town on the northwest coast of Italy. An array of quasi-friendships brought them together, in the orbit of the one poet who went to Italy for the politics: Ezra Pound, the fiery American who had already lit up London drawing rooms and Parisian cafes. Pound left his mark on literature in English for three reasons: his instigation of two important movements in the early twentieth century, Imagism and Vorticism that were both driven by his commitment to "make it new," and his master-work *The Cantos*, most of which was written in Italy. In Rapallo, Pound hoped to "make it new" again. From 1928 to 1932, he undertook this work alongside the mature poet and elder Irish statesman, W.B. Yeats, with whom Pound had a long and complex set of poetic and personal relationships.

Pound and Yeats's presence in Rapallo oriented their literary networks from Paris, Dublin, and even New York onto a small town on the Italian Riviera. There, they were joined by two veterans of the First World War, Richard Aldington (an Englishman and associate of Pound and Yeats from London) and Thomas MacGreevy (an Irishman and close friend of George Yeats, married to W.B.). Pound and Yeats also drew to Rapallo an even younger generation—the self-identified Northumbrian poet Basil Bunting, and the cosmopolitan New Yorker Louis Zukofsky, son of immigrant Russian Jews. Bunting and Zukofsky, Aldington and MacGreevy forged friendships that lasted far beyond their time in Rapallo. As they became important twentieth-century poets in their own rights, they confided in one another while they tussled with the problem of how to account for Ezra Pound, and—to a lesser degree—for W.B. Yeats, with whom they lived closely in Italy in a period that was marred by the rise of Mussolini's regime.

This book is about the poets' relationships with one another, their collaborations as literary artists, and their intersections with Italian fascist politics, especially wider debates in Italy about what might constitute a fascist aesthetics. Most of the writers and artists who feature in this book did not support Mussolini's regime, and none was always in agreement with Ezra Pound. Yet even writers who were later explicitly anti-fascist were willing to overlook—or at least to diminish—the severity of what was happening around them in Italy. The importance of some poets' complicity in everyday fascist culture—such as Basil Bunting's role in the production of the literary supplement to the local newspaper *Il Mare* and his involvement in Rapallo's concert series that was sponsored by the fascist state—has been elided by a critical focus on Pound's support of Mussolini as exceptional. This perception has been compounded by our tendency to read autobiographies and memoirs written by people in the Rapallo group as credible accounts of the poets' proximity (or lack thereof) to Pound. How tempting it is to think that Thomas MacGreevy and Richard Aldington met in James Joyce's apartment, or that Louis Zukofksy's allegiance to Pound was due to poor self-confidence, or that Basil Bunting's poetic style, as he describes his literary genealogy in interviews from the 1970s, developed concurrently to—but not in tandem with—Pound's poetic.

The impulse to sequester Pound and in so doing redeem W.B. Yeats, among others, in literary history is perhaps an attempt to protect some of the most masterful poetry in English from the twentieth century's most toxic politics. But a cloistered literary history obscures difficult questions about poets' civic responsibility, about the relationship of literature to the contexts that produce it, and about ways of mapping the complexities of literary exchange. Through historical and archival research, the close study of drafts of poems and unpublished memoirs, and a nuanced interrogation of what we *think* we know about Pound, Yeats, and the people who visited them in Italy, *The Poets of Rapallo* illuminates the breadth of late modernism's politics of style.

In *The Extinct Scene*, Thomas Davis argues "in late modernism, we see radical avant-garde techniques marshalled for state-sponsored film and liberal norms."[1] While that is the case for a certain body of British writing, exemplified in the documentary and Mass Observation movements to which Davis attends, *The Poets of Rapallo* asks what happens when British, Irish, and U.S. authors are removed from "liberal norms," beyond the "British world-system" and are placed in predominately right-wing contexts.[2] With the exception of Tyrus Miller's foundational book, *Late Modernism*, which attends to Wyndham Lewis alongside Djuna Barnes and Samuel Beckett, studies of late modernism have focused exclusively on centrist and leftist politics.[3] *The Poets of Rapallo* shows how the conversations, collaborations, and disagreements that occurred in Pound and Yeats's Rapallo network from the late 1920s to the mid-1930s were central to the turn from high modernist to late modernist poetics. This book illustrates how the writers' responses—and sometimes enthusiasms—for right-wing politics is integral to a late modernist turn. By identifying the "outward turn" in the work of Yeats, Pound, and others, *The Poets of Rapallo* returns to Miller's more expansive definition in order to advocate our acknowledgement of the degree to which late modernist writing is not the preserve of anti-fascist politics. *The Poets of Rapallo* reveals how some writers who employed late modernist style are deeply indebted to fascist and right-wing contexts and allegiances.

This book began in another book: in conversation with Ben Tate about whether there might be an afterlife of James Longenbach's *Stone Cottage*, a book that gives an account of the three winters that W.B. Yeats and Ezra Pound spent in each other's company in Ashdown Forest in Sussex. Longenbach charts the poets' collaboration, showing how it developed a modernist aesthetic in both of their work. Other studies have also been formative influences on *The Poets of Rapallo*. Any discussion of the nature and degree of W.B. Yeats's right-wing politics must engage with W.J. McCormack's *Blood Kindred*, which makes a strident case for Yeats's fascism and goes so far as to argue that Yeats was complicit in the Nazi regime.[4] McCormack mainly bases his argument for Yeats's fascism in the poet's mythology of eighteenth-century politics and authoritarian political structures. More recently, McCormack's *"We Irish" in Europe: Yeats, Berkeley and Joseph Hone* brings Yeats's reading of Berkeley into relation with Hone's collaboration with the Italian translator Mario Rossi and a wider interest in Berkley among Italian thinkers, including Benedetto Croce and—most damningly—Giovanni Gentile and Giovanni Papini, who were vocal supporters of Mussolini. One reviewer of *"We Irish"* summed up McCormack's books as being occupied with presenting "Yeats as a morally and intellectually worthless person."[5]

As might be suggested by such a bald statement, the question of whether or not Yeats was a fascist is one of the most polarizing debates in Irish and British literary studies. When in 1992 Donald Torchiana reissued his monograph *W.B. Yeats and Georgian Ireland* (1966) with the Catholic University of America Press, he sharply dismissed one scholar's challenge to his representation of Yeats's regard for the eighteenth century as the model for Irish political life.[6] Torchiana writes in the preface for the 1992 edition, "Elizabeth Cullingford, in her *Yeats, Ireland and Fascism* (1981) and her *Yeats, Poems, 1919-1935: A Casebook* (1984) appears to have made a career of attacking me and all of my work. Since her opposition is based on a misreading, there is no point in responding to it here."[7] Where Torchiana criticizes Cullingford for locating a kind of fascism in Yeats's work, the Pound scholar Reed Way Dasenbrook, reviewing Cullingford's book for *MLN*, condemned her for not going far enough:

> *Yeats, Ireland and Fascism*, despite its title, is a book-length attempt to hush things up. For the author, there is no scandal, nothing to explain. Never mind that Yeats consistently had complimentary things to say about Fascist regimes from 1922 until his death in 1939; that he was intimately involved in the abortive Irish fascist movement, the Blueshirts; that in April 1933 he described the "social theory" he was working out for the Blueshirts as "Fascism modified by religion"; that his anti-English statements grew stronger and stronger in the 1930s as war between Nazi Germany and England grew more probable [....] Sweeping aside this history of enthusiasm for Fascist regimes and causes, Cullingford asserts that the label Fascist is inappropriate for Yeats. She does so confidently because she feels she has found the master key to Yeats's political interests.[8]

That "master key" for Cullingford is Yeats's involvement in Irish cultural nationalist movements of the late nineteenth century. *Yeats, Ireland, and Fascism* was written during a period of critical focus on the Irish Revival that was predominately laudatory. That generation of scholarship still holds powerful sway over the way Irish "cultural nationalism" is frequently segregated from political analysis in a manner that is unhelpful for understanding how insidious ideas about "ethnicity"—and its nationalist cultural markers—continue to shape right-wing political movements.

After Cullingford, a potent strand in Yeats criticism spearheaded by Seamus Deane and David Lloyd holds Yeats accountable for the mythological authoritarian structures that he erected in his work. Deane in particular argues that these mythologies underpinned the violence in Northern Ireland and on the Irish border.[9] For Lloyd, there is nothing "to be gained by simple ethical condemnation" of Yeats's poetic strategies.[10] What he offers instead is a complex reading of Yeats's late poetry, including Yeats's use of coercive allegories that make the unwitting reader complicit in authoritarian frames of thinking; as an example he shows how in "Coole and Ballylee, 1931" Yeats's inventive geography fabricates an elemental connection between the river that runs past Thoor Ballylee and the lake at Coole Park.[11] Lloyd identifies a to-and-fro in Yeats's relationship to fascism:

> Though their exultation in violent acts of the will points the way towards a fascist politics, it derives that political solution from a desperation which

is by no means capable of offering the consolatory myths of belonging on which fascism relies for its legitimation. If, as Walter Benjamin put it, fascism is the "aestheticization of politics," Yeats's writings are profoundly antagonistic to the representational aesthetics in which fascism finds its legitimation. And, on the contrary, the very stridency of both Yeats's poetry and his politics derives from the clarity of his recognition of the aesthetic or poetic foundations of the state.[12]

Out of all of the critics to tackle the question of Yeats's fascism, my argument in *The Poets of Rapallo* most closely aligns with Lloyd's, since what emerges from Yeats's interest in Italy in the 1920s and 1930s is an attraction to what has been termed "aesthetic fascism" but a revulsion to overtly fascist political structures.[13]

When it comes to Ezra Pound, the question is not whether he was a fascist—he left no room for doubt—but *when* and *how* he was fascist. Most scholarship on Pound and Italian fascism focuses on his writing from the mid-1930s through the *Pisan Cantos*, with a concentration of interest around the radio broadcasts during the Second World War. While Pound did not publicly engage with fascist debates about culture until the early 1930s, *The Poets of Rapallo* builds on important research by Lawrence Rainey and Catherine Paul, who show how Pound's interest in Italian fascist cultural projects and Italian literary history shaped his fascist aesthetics. What is most admirable in Rainey and Paul is a nuanced historical and theoretical analysis that takes into account international influences and the poet's rapidly shifting field of references. Building on this work, in *The Poets of Rapallo* I show how intricately Yeats and Pound's overtly political responses to Italian fascism are related to their literary styles and methods and how their various engagements with party-political fascism are often at odds with their aesthetic fascism. At times, the language used by the poets— publicly or in private correspondence—is reprehensible. My decision not to excise it stems from the principle of showing the extent of the poets' racist, sexist, or otherwise abhorrent views.

This study of Rapallo's most prominent poets has opened up new ways of reading work by poets whose politics are less contested—Richard Aldington, Thomas MacGreevy, Basil Bunting, and Louis Zukofsky—and a way of uncovering the politics and aesthetics of writers and artists whose work has been marginalized: George Yeats, Dorothy Pound, and Brigit Patmore. Olga Rudge's collaborations with Ezra Pound are more direct than his work with Dorothy, and for that reason—as well as Dorothy Pound's importance in the Yeats/Pound matrix of relationships—this study focuses on the Pounds' marriage. Readers interested in Pound and Rudge's collaborations are referred to David Moody's masterful three-volume biography and to Anne Conover's *Olga Rudge and Ezra Pound: "What thou lovest well—"* as starting points.

The *Poets of Rapallo* offers a way for scholars to take a conjoined approach to writers' work and their public political pronouncements in a manner that does not diminish the seriousness of their politics or the importance of their writing.[14] While *The Poets of Rapallo* contests the positioning of late modernist writing as left-leaning, it is in agreement with Thomas Davis's argument that "late modernism's encounter with everyday life is not primarily aesthetic or ethical; it is simultaneously aesthetic *and* political."[15] Here, two of my greatest influences are scholars who model astute aesthetic *and* political interpretation: Roy Foster and John Kelly, both of whom were generous in their willingness to talk over tricky issues when it came to analyzing this complex period of literary and political history.

In a characteristically acerbic letter, Ezra Pound wrote to W.B. Yeats in November 1935, "no mercy ought ever to be granted to the Oxford Press perverters of truth": another occasion on which I am grateful not to be counted in Pound's company. Jacqueline Norton has guided this project with enthusiasm on its pursuit of "truth" and has been a dream to work with over the three years that the book has been in her care. The bulk of writing occurred during my residency as Visiting Fellow at Trinity College Dublin's Long Room Hub Arts & Humanities Research Institute in spring 2017 and as Burns Visiting Scholar at Boston College in autumn 2017; I'm grateful to both institutions as well as to Christian Dupont, Marjorie Howes, James H. Murphy, and Rob Savage at Boston College, and Jane Ohlmeyer and Caitriona Curtis at the Long Room Hub for their intellectual and practical support, and to Trinity's Manuscripts and Archives for facilitating access to invaluable material on Thomas MacGreevy and Richard Aldington. The Fleur Cowles Endowment Fund enabled my month-long residency at the Harry Ransom Center, University of Texas at Austin, which houses essential collections on all of the people in this book, and the fellowship introduced me to Rebecca Pohl and Marius Hentea, scholars whose conversations were important in my thinking through this project in the early stages. Special thanks to Emily Grover at the Lilly Library and Katherine Alcauskas (formerly of the Wellin Museum, Hamilton College) for their assistance accessing important materials related to Dorothy Pound. The staff at the Widener and Houghton libraries, Harvard University, accommodated me during the two years that I spent between Boston and Liverpool.

The Institute of Irish Studies and the School of Histories, Languages, and Cultures at the University of Liverpool provided essential periods of leave. Giulia Bruna translated selections from *Il Mare*'s literary supplement, and Sophie Dess undertook research at the New York Public Library. Maynooth University's President, Philip Nolan, provided research support that was essential to the book's production; the Dean of the Faculty of Arts, Celtic Studies, and Philosophy, Colin Graham, and my colleagues in the Department of English cheered the book over the line.

I am grateful to the following estates, libraries, and archives for permission to quote from published and unpublished material: to Bloodaxe Books for Basil Bunting's published poetry and to John Halliday for Bunting's unpublished writing; to the estate of Richard Aldington for all of his work that appears here; to Margaret Farrington and Robert Ryan for Thomas MacGreevy's published and unpublished work; to Jeffrey Twitchell-Waas for assistance pertaining to Zukofsky's writing. Work by Ezra and Dorothy Pound appears by permission from New Directions Pub. acting as agent, copyright © 2021 by Mary de Rachewiltz and the Estate of Omar S. Pound. Reprinted by permission of New Directions Publishing Corp. All Louis Zukofsky materials copyright © Musical Observations, Inc. Used by permission.

The ideas in this book were honed by incisive questions from attentive audiences. Thanks to the National Library of Ireland, Sandra Collins, and Joseph Hassett for the invitation to give the W.B. Yeats Birthday Lecture in 2018; to John Kerrigan, Barry Colfer, and participants at the Joyce to Beckett Symposium at Cambridge University in March 2018; to Shawn O'Hare, who directed my undergraduate dissertation and invited me back to speak at the Appalachian Center, Carson-Newman University, in November 2017, and to Gerald Wood, Susan Underwood, Larry Osborne, and Andrew Smith, some of my first academic mentors and friends at Carson-Newman; to Christian DuPont and the Center for Irish Programs at Boston College who supported the Burns Lecture in November 2017; to James Moran at the University of Nottingham who organized the Irish Society for Theatre Research conference in April 2017; to Lloyd (Meadhbh) Houston and the Oxford Modernism and Contemporary Research Seminar for the invitation to give a paper in spring 2018; and to the W.B. Yeats International Summer School, especially Matthew Campbell, for the opportunity to discuss Yeats and Rapallo with friends from the world of Yeats studies. Shorter papers were presented at the Modernist Studies Association conferences in Columbus, Ohio (2018) and Amsterdam (2017), where important conversations with Emilie Morin shaped the book; the International Yeats Society conference in New York in 2017, and the T.S. Eliot and Ezra Pound conference that was held in Rapallo in 2016, where Massimo Bacigalupo, Tony Cuda, Francis Dickey, John Morgenstern, and Jahan Ramazani encouraged my thoughts about the Rapallo poetic matrix. Ideas about Yeats and late modernism began at a roundtable discussion organized with Gregory Castle, Joe Valente, Marjorie Howes, and Margaret Mills Harper at the Modernist Studies Association conference in Boston in 2015.

The Poets of Rapallo has been sharpened by readers who have been in equal parts rigorous and kind. Roy Foster and John Kelly read the entire manuscript; Catherine Paul read "Living History" and helped me get to grips with *A Vision* without it taking over my life; Eve Patten and Lee Jenkins read "Shell-Shocked Walt Whitmans"; Eric Bulson read "Primavera 1928"; Rebecca Beasley advised on Ezra and Dorothy Pound's art criticism and practice for "Living History"; Keri Walsh helped me refine the proposal and tangle with Yeats at the Volta Conference; Lucy McDiarmid lent me books on Aldington and Pound, advised on the poets' pre-history, and read chapters; Warwick Gould invited me to contribute an essay to *Yeats Annual* that formed the backbone for the early chapters and gave helpful advice on the book in its late stages; Mark Scroggins kindly replied to my questions relating to his wonderful book on Zukofsky, *A Poem of a Life*; Meg Harper discussed difficult questions about George Yeats's politics; Corrina Connor read so many parts of *Rapallo*, in so many forms, that she must have read the entire thing several times over. The two readers for OUP spurred me on. This would be a lesser book without all of their critiques.

Contents

List of Figures	xvii
A Brief Chronology of Comings and Goings	xix

1. The Roads to Rapallo	1
A Pre-History of Poets	4
"The north side of the Alps is an error"	10
Yeats, Pound, and Il Duce	14
An "Ezuversity"	19
2. Shell-Shocked Walt Whitmans	27
A Call to Life	31
Songs of Themselves	34
Who ate Pound's heart?	40
The Problem with "War Poetry"	45
3. Primavera 1928	55
Periodical Pound and His Collaborators	56
Making the Public Man	66
Pedagogical Pound and His Disciples	79
4. Singing School	85
Dangerous Bardolatry	86
Condoms and Classics	93
Broadside Ballads and the Outward Turn	99
5. Making Living History	105
Building the Fascist State	108
Writing for Caesar's Eyes	120
6. Accounting for Rapallo	137
Apologia and Amnesia	144
The Totalitarian Man and the Women of Rapallo	153

Notes	161
Select Bibliography	215
Index	223

List of Figures

1.0 Map of Rapallo from a tourist brochure, emphasizing the hospitable climate and outdoor activities. Ezra Pound Collection, Harry Ransom Center, The University of Texas at Austin.   xxii

1.1 W.B. and George Yeats pictured in Hampshire, summer 1930, after his recovery. Snapshot by Ottoline Morrell, © National Portrait Gallery, London.   2

1.2 Ezra Pound and a hollow-cheeked W.B. Yeats at a Rapallo café. Ezra Pound Literary File, Harry Ransom Center, The University of Texas at Austin.   3

1.3 Rapallo from Montallegro, Louis Zukofsky Collection, Harry Ransom Center, The University of Texas at Austin.   14

1.4 Pound, the self-styled "Master of Rapallo." Ezra Pound Literary File, Harry Ransom Center, The University of Texas at Austin.   20

2.1 Richard Aldington taken by Brigit Patmore on an excursion to Verona. Richard Aldington Literary File, Harry Ransom Center, The University of Texas at Austin.   28

2.2 Brigit Patmore with Tom MacGreevy, probably taken by Aldington. Richard Aldington Literary File, Harry Ransom Center, The University of Texas at Austin.   46

3.1 Postcard from Basil Bunting to Louis Zukofsky. Zukofsky Collection, Harry Ransom Center, The University of Texas at Austin.   54

3.2 Envelope of a letter from Ezra to Dorothy Pound on stationary showing Dorothy's design for *Il Mare*'s literary supplement. Pound Collection, courtesy Lilly Library, Indiana University, Bloomington, Indiana.   67

3.3 Postcard from Pisa, illustrating Dorothy's inspiration for the hippogriff design. Pound Family Postcards, Omar S. Pound Archives, Hamilton College, Clinton, NY.   68

3.4 Basil Bunting reclining on W.B. Yeats's balcony, 1933. Bunting Collection, Durham University Library. Reproduced by permission of Durham University Library and Collections and the Estate of Basil Bunting.   76

3.5 A young Louis Zukofsky. Image in the public domain.   80

LIST OF FIGURES

4.1 Postcard with a view of Portofino. Zukofsky Collection, Harry Ransom Center, The University of Texas at Austin. — 86

5.1 Dorothy Pound, circa 1930. With thanks to David Moody. — 109

5.2 Postcard from the Etruscan Museum, Cortona; Pound Family Postcards, Omar S. Pound Archives, Hamilton College, Clinton, NY. — 115

5.3 Postcard from Ascoli Piceno, denoting the Roman-era "twin gates"; Pound Family Postcards, Omar S. Pound Archives, Hamilton College, Clinton, NY. — 117

5.4 Postcard from Teramo, showing the fascist-era "recovery" of the city's monuments; Pound Family Postcards, Omar S. Pound Archives, Hamilton College, Clinton, NY. — 118

5.5 Postcard from Pitigliano, (a) with the name of the town scratched out on both sides, and (b) Dorothy's sketch of the "P" and aqueduct design. Pound Family Postcards, Omar S. Pound Archives, Hamilton College, Clinton, NY. — 119

6.1 Ezra Pound on the rooftop of his apartment, overlooking Rapallo. Photo by James Angleton; with thanks to David Moody. — 136

6.2 Postcard picturing Rapallo. Zukofsky Collection, Harry Ransom Center, The University of Texas at Austin. — 145

6.3 Basil and Marion Bunting in Rapallo. Bunting Collection, Durham University. Reproduced by permission of Durham University Library and Collections Library and the Estate of Basil Bunting. — 150

A Brief Chronology of Comings and Goings

1924   October: Ezra and Dorothy Pound move to Rapallo and establish it as their permanent base. Over the following years, Dorothy makes regular trips back to England, and Ezra spends extended periods of time with Olga Rudge.
December: the Pounds tour Sicily; W.B. and George Yeats join them for the new year, 1925.

1925   Ernest and Hadley Hemingway visit Pound in Rapallo.
George Antheil is in Rapallo, with Osbert Sitwell.

1928   February: W.B. and George Yeats arrive in Rapallo.
Mid-April: the Yeatses return to Dublin.
November: W.B. and George Yeats are in Rapallo.
December: Thomas MacGreevy visits Rapallo at Christmastime.

1929   February: Richard Aldington and Brigit Patmore are in Rapallo.
March: Basil and Marion Bunting move to Rapallo.
April: the Yeatses return to Ireland.
November: W.B. and George Yeats are in Rapallo for the winter season.
December: W.B. Yeats is very ill with Malta Fever in Rapallo; an emergency last will and testament is witnessed by Ezra Pound and Basil Bunting.

1930   April: W.B. and George Yeats are in Portofino Vetta, near Rapallo.
July: W.B. and George Yeats leave Rapallo, and Homer and Isabel Pound move into their apartment.

1933   August: Louis Zukofsky visits Rapallo; Basil Bunting leaves Rapallo.

1934   June: W.B. and George Yeats return to Rapallo for a brief visit, and W.B. and Ezra have an enormous argument.

1935   October: W.B. Yeats attends the Volta Conference on theater in Rome; George Yeats accompanies him.

I have always found Memory to be a cunning and persistent liar.
Basil Bunting, "Yeats Recollected"

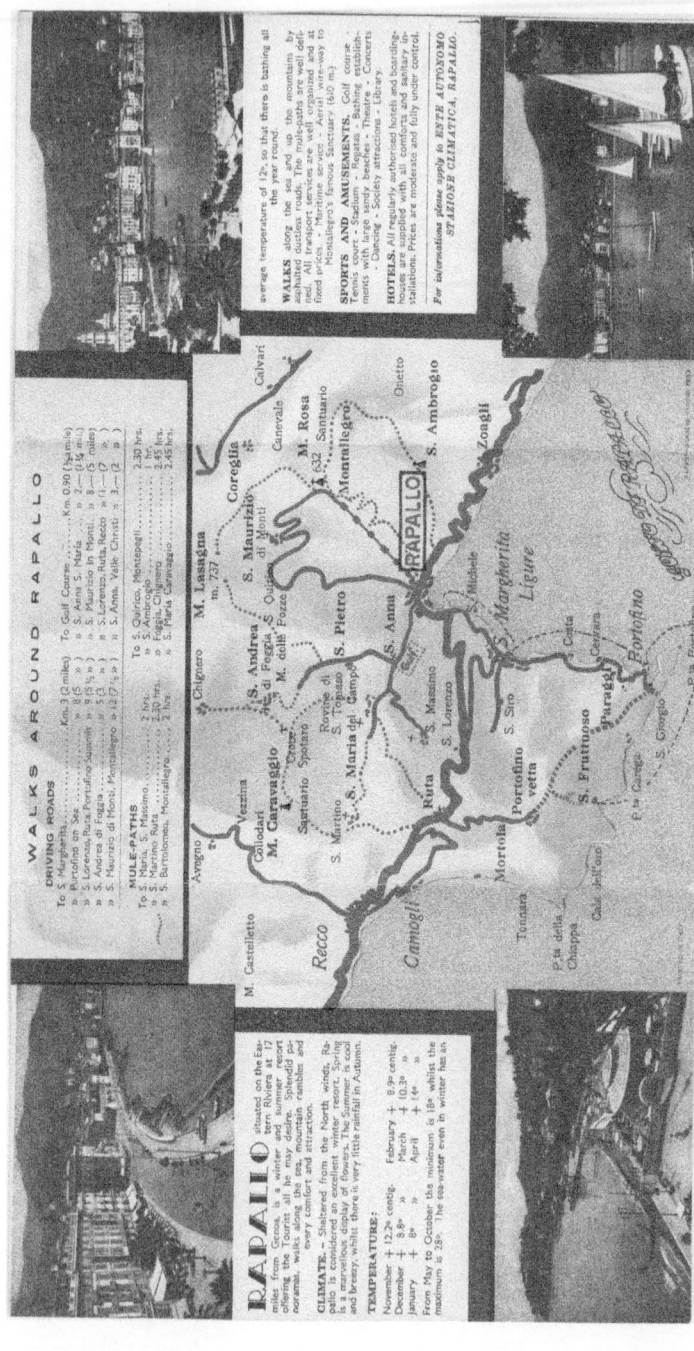

Figure 1.0 Map of Rapallo from a tourist brochure, emphasizing the hospitable climate and outdoor activities

Source: Ezra Pound Collection, Harry Ransom Center, The University of Texas at Austin.

1
The Roads to Rapallo

What began as a case of the flu in October 1927 quickly progressed into an illness so severe that W.B. Yeats's doctors warned he might never write poetry again. He was sixty-two years old, a Senator in the Irish Free State, the founding director of the Irish National Theatre, and a Nobel Laureate. He had recently finished a volume of poetry, *The Tower*, which would be credited with revolutionizing modern literature to the same extent as *Ulysses* and *The Waste Land*. Yeats was exhausted. He was also, as he confessed to his most intimate confidants, extremely bitter.

Worried about the effect that a dark, wet Irish winter would have on his health, W.B. and his wife George left Dublin in November for southern Europe. They traveled by ship to Gibraltar, then up the Spanish coast and the French Riviera to Cannes, where they stayed for Christmas and the New Year. He was full of complaints about the hotel—situated in screeching distance of a train that "passes four times in the early afternoon"—but he had enough humor to remark, "I suppose one shoulndt mind it as it is the only form of self-expression the engine drivers have."[1] There was no doubt that W.B. was suffering from a physical ailment, but George thought that his illness was also psychological. Twenty-seven years younger than him, well educated in the Classics and European languages, and gifted with a dry wit, George could be exceedingly patient with W.B.'s complaints. She tried to distract him with provocative philosophical debates, but her diversions provided short relief. Every now and then, she allowed herself to vent her frustration to her closest friends, one of whom was Thomas MacGreevy, an Irishman in his thirties who had survived the front lines of Ypres and the Somme, was embarking on a career as a literary critic, and would later visit Rapallo. In one exasperated letter, she told MacGreevy, "until he remembers he musnt think, he prances about in bed full of joy, then suddenly flops down 'I must stop. My blood pressure will go up.'" George worried, "if something isnt done he'll sink into awful depths of depression and despair...I hope to get him to Rapallo, in fact well or ill I am going to get him there" (Figure 1.1).[2]

In February 1928, George and W.B. Yeats arrived at the little seaside town, nestled in a placid bay on the Ligurian coast, about eighteen miles

2 THE POETS OF RAPALLO

Figure 1.1 W.B. and George Yeats pictured in Hampshire, summer 1930, after his recovery
Source: Snapshot by Ottoline Morrell, © National Portrait Gallery, London.

east of Genoa. Rapallo had a reputation as a retreat for artists; Kandinsky spent an important period there in the first decade of the century, where his variations on the fishing and pleasure boats that rested on the stony shore show his transition from post-impressionism to the abstraction for which he is best known.[3] When the Yeatses arrived, Rapallo was still "modestly fashionable all year round."[4] WBY took pride in the town's unpretentiousness; in his essay "Rapallo" that was published in *A Vision* (1937), he boasted, "As there is no great harbor full of yachts, no great yellow strands, no great ballroom, no great casino, the rich carry elsewhere their strenuous lives."[5] Rapallo's permanent residents included the German dramatist and novelist Gerhart Hauptmann, with whom Yeats would make acquaintance as Rapallo's other Nobel Laureate, and the English essayist and caricaturist Max Beerbohm, whom Yeats would see very little.[6] In fact, Hauptmann and Beerbohm's presence was incidental—Rapallo, for Yeats, revolved around Ezra Pound (Figure 1.2).

Strident, quarrelsome, with a knack for saying the wrong thing and getting away with it, Ezra Pound burst onto the London scene in 1908 and changed poetry in English irrevocably. His confidence was a centrifugal force, and his Americanness was a masquerade for critiquing "dead convention" and

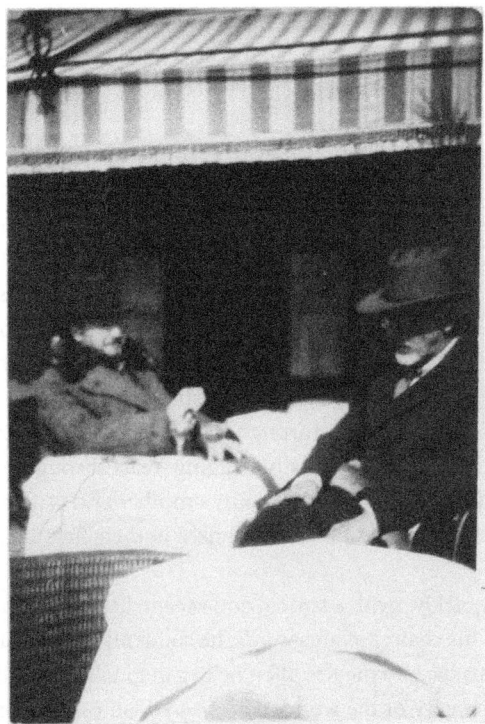

Figure 1.2 Ezra Pound and a hollow-cheeked W.B. Yeats at a Rapallo café
Source: Ezra Pound Literary File, Harry Ransom Center, The University of Texas at Austin.

making literature new.[7] Pound's performance of eccentricity—in London he sported semi-feral bouffant hair atop a carefully waxed and trimmed angular moustache—excused what was otherwise, even in the view of many of his friends, inexcusable behavior.

At the end of the Second World War, after the Allied liberation of Italy in the spring of 1945, Pound was detained at a U.S. prison camp at Pisa, tried for treason, and sent to St. Elizabeths psychiatric hospital in Washington, D.C., where the pioneering scholar of thirties poetry, Samuel Hynes, visited him in 1953. Hynes found Pound "dressed in an open-necked shirt, floppy pants, sandals, and a broad-brimmed straw hat, as though he were still in Italy," and the poet spoke in a

> twanging American slang, and a dated slang at that [....] The language and twang were part of him, the role he played of American Sage, descended in a direct line from Walt Whitman [....] His favorite role, the Plain

American, speaking in his own version of the national barbaric yawp [but he was also] the generous man, giving his words away to a young writer because he needed them.⁸

At sixty-eight years old, Pound gave the impression of being "worn out," "Only the eyes weren't old or worn out; they peered sharply out of deep, dark sockets. They were the eyes of a man who watched, and judged everything. Distrustful eyes, doubting the world."

In Dorothy Pound's diary from the first years of her courtship with Ezra, she suggests that Ezra learned how to perform the role of poet and sage by observing W.B. Yeats. Pound went to London in 1908 with the express purpose of meeting Yeats, who had by then established himself in fashionable literary circles.⁹ Moving tactically through Bloomsbury's drawing rooms, Pound drew closer to his quarry, eventually bagging Yeats through an introduction from Olivia Shakespear, who was Dorothy's mother and WBY's first lover.¹⁰ In her diary, Dorothy recorded Pound's behavior at their first encounter:

> [Ezra] spoke quickly, (with a strong, odd accent, half American, half Irish) he sat back in his chair; but afterwards, he suddenly dropped down, cross-legged, with his back to the fire; then he began to talk—he talked of Yeats, as one of the twenty of the world, who had added to the world's poetical matter—he read a short piece of Yeats, in a voice dropping with emotion, in a voice like Yeats' own [....] And all the while clasping his ankles on the hearth-rug and smoking.¹¹

A year later, Pound believed that he and Yeats were "in one movement with aims very nearly identical," adding, with uncharacteristic deference to another poet, "There has been no 'influence'—Yeats has found within himself [the] spirit of the new air which I by accident had touched before him."¹²

A Pre-History of Poets

The long, entwined history between the Yeatses and the Pounds helped cushion the inevitable blows that W.B. and George suffered in Rapallo—injuries caused by Ezra's volcanic personality but also by Dorothy Pound's tiring asceticism. In the spring of 1914, Ezra Pound had married Dorothy Shakespear, "a charming young wife who," WBY described, "looks as though her face was made out of Dresden china. I look at her in perpetual wonder.

It is so hard to beleive she is real."[13] Yeats complained to Olivia Shakespear, who also found her daughter's parsimony irksome; she "seems to classify champaigne with stake & onions & badgers flesh, & other forms of the tinsel of this world."[14] The Pounds' long marriage was characterized by an amicable and not-so-amicable to and fro; in fact, Moody speculates that their trip to Sicily may have been Dorothy's attempt to "put more miles between Olga [Rudge] and her husband."[15] The Pounds' friends gossiped about the degree of the couple's intimacy; the U.S. poet and novelist Hilda Doolittle, who published under the initials H.D.—and to whom Pound had been engaged at the time of his proposal to Dorothy—visited London soon after the Pounds' marriage and cattily remarked, "there seems to be a pretty general consensus of opinion that Mrs. E. has not been 'awakened.'...She is very English and 'cold.'"[16] The birth of Omar, whom Dorothy conceived in Egypt in late 1925, gave the lie to that assumption. (Omar followed closely on the heels of Mary Rudge, born to Olga Rudge, on July 9, 1925.) Whatever the nature of the Pounds' sexual relationship, politically and aesthetically, they were bedfellows.

Four years after W.B. Yeats and Ezra Pound met in London, they spent the winter together in a remote cottage in Ashdown Forest, east Sussex.[17] Yeats felt that Pound's company brought balance to his work; he wrote to Lady Gregory in October 1914 from London, "My evenings are a great burden. I hear Ezra and his wife are thinking of going to Stone Cottage with me but Ezra has not said anything yet. I hope they will. Here I cannot get any routine. One day I work too little & the next day too much & I always overuse my sight."[18] Ostensibly, Pound served as Yeats's secretary, but he would also be an instructor, and through his editing of the Sinologist Ernest Fenollosa's writing on Japanese theater initiated Yeats into an aesthetics and philosophy that played a key role in both of their subsequent writing, especially Yeats's interpretation of Japanese Noh theater.

Through Yeats's renewed proximity to the Shakespears, he met George Hyde Lees, Dorothy Shakespear's step-cousin in their expansive, rackety English upper-middle-class family; at times, the women's relationship was as close as sisters on good terms.[19] They became doubly related when they married poets who had a difficult relationship that swerved between subdued collaboration and total denunciation. Pound was best man at W.B. and George's wedding in October 1917; relations between the poets became even more complex the following year when Pound had a brief affair with Iseult Gonne—the same woman to whom Yeats had proposed marriage two years earlier and who was the daughter of Yeats's interminable obsession, Maud Gonne.[20]

When the 1916 Easter Rising erupted, Yeats and Pound were ending their third and final winter together at Stone Cottage. The Rising became a reference point for their subsequent history as poets; Yeats's introduction to Pound and Fennollosa's *Certain Noble Plays of Japan*, published later that year, included references to Irish writer-revolutionaries who had been killed in the Rising and its aftermath.[21] In March 1917, Yeats bought Thoor Ballylee, the Norman tower in north County Galway that became the symbol of his work. He and George moved to a house on Lady Gregory's estate, Coole Park, later the same year; in May 1919—in the midst of the Anglo-Irish War—their daughter Anne was born.[22] Two years later, in August 1921 just prior to the outbreak of the Irish Civil War, came the birth of Michael. W.B. Yeats's immediate family history's confluence with Irish political change seems to have informed his growing emphasis on the individual and the family as the basis for a strong government, ideas that resounded with Ezra Pound's readings in Confucianism and would work their way into some of WBY's most polemical late writing. In "If I Were Four and Twenty," Yeats's essay of 1919, he writes what might have been a manifesto, if he were not a man of "four-and-fifty, indolent and discouraged." He imagines a total culture, encompassing literature, drama, and even economics, all arising from the core principle that "the family is the unit of social life, and the origin of civilization which but exists to preserve it."[23] These pronouncements, expressing a totalizing aesthetic, are all hypothetical; the conditional tense mobilizes the excuse of age for not realizing his vision that "a cultivated nation [...] has related its main interests to one another." Rapallo reinvigorated his work and this vision, although he never returned to what could be regarded, from the point of view of the 1930s, totalitarian rhetoric.

Yeats believed that his poetry from the first years of the twentieth century, and especially his play *Cathleen ni Houlihan* that was written with Lady Gregory, had helped to inspire (for better or worse) the revolutionary impulse. To his mind, the violence of the Irish Civil War and the failures of the early Irish Free State were due to the failure of the Irish majority to fall in step with his vision of Irish social and political order. Yeats's frustration was compounded by his grief for what felt like betrayals by important women in his life—Constance Markievicz and Maud Gonne—and the seemingly meaningless deaths of some of his closest friends, including Kevin O'Higgins, the Irish Free State Minister for Justice who was assassinated in 1927.[24] Heaped upon one another, Yeats's grievances with post-revolutionary Ireland drove him to feel isolated, beleaguered, and embittered—emotions that compounded the illness that sent him to southern Europe in the winter of 1927–8.

Rapallo was not the first period that WBY and George Yeats spent in Italy with the Pounds. In December 1924, Ezra and Dorothy had traveled to Sicily, with a view to leaving Paris and with the idea that Italy might suit them for the long term. In Taormina, Dorothy sketched the views of the Greek theater to the north, the Italian mainland to the east, and Mount Etna to the south. They handed down verdicts on the local cuisine: the "wine & apples good," but the oranges and figs "too sweet & tasteless"; the bread was "made with sesame—otherwise food of southern Europe—cats & pigeons gather fragments in dining room."[25] The Pounds were joined in Syracuse in the first week of 1925 by W.B. and George, who were following advice from W.B.'s doctor that "another country and climate" was needed to bring his ever escalating blood pressure under control.[26] The excursion was a successful revisiting of the poets' collaborations at Stone Cottage. They experimented with the acoustics at the Greek theater; Ezra wrote home to his father, "W.B.Y. tried theatre—I stood it for 14 minutes."[27] Dorothy painted, and George took extensive photographs of the sights, including Palermo Cathedral and Monreale.[28]

George Yeats's *Baedeker's* guide to southern Italy and Sicily parsed the region's long history of cultural decline and reinvigoration, instructing that "the Roman-Byzantine Supremacy gave the death-blow to the intellectual progress of the Sicilians" and that "the Arabs were the first to infuse new life into the island," enlivening the architecture "with new forms of construction" and inaugurating "a new era in the writing of history and geography."[29] The Arabic influence inspired the Yeatses' use of Arabic characters and Islamic history in their collaborative esoteric book *A Vision*, the first version of which was finished in the spring of 1925 after their Italian tour.[30] Five of the six major historic sites that W.B. and George visited are mentioned explicitly in *A Vision*: Syracuse, Monreale, and Cefalù in Sicily, as well as Capri and Rome, where they traveled after their holiday with Dorothy and Ezra.[31]

Pencil marks in George's guidebook show that they took particular interest in Palermo's Palatine Chapel, a twelfth-century "Arabic-Norman" construction with Saracenic arches and Cufic inscriptions, crowned by a Norman tower that was fitted with an observatory that commanded views of the town of Palermo, the harbor, and the Capo Gallo mountains. The most lasting impression was undoubtedly made by the chapel's ornately enameled reliquaries of Byzantine and Arab design and the mosaics that covered the chapel's interior walls. Set on a golden ground, they represented scenes from the life of Christ and the disciples. Yeats had first seen Byzantine mosaics in person in 1907, when he visited Ravenna with Lady Gregory. The 1925 tour provided specific reference points, preserved in the sixty photographs that W.B. and George collected, for Yeats's new philosophical prose and his poetry.[32] Images from the Sicilian tour were remade in poems such as "Sailing to Byzantium," which was first published in *October Blast* (by Cuala Press in 1927) and was included in *The Tower* before it reappeared in Ezra Pound's magazine, *The Exile*, in 1928 soon after the Yeatses arrived in Rapallo.

From Palermo in 1925, Ezra gossiped to his father about Yeats's violation of doctors' orders; he "was supposed to be resting—after struggles in Irish senate—bombs—windows busted by machine guns & other celtic & twilit excitements." Instead, "he was rather exhaustedly trying to finish a book."[33] This was the first iteration of *A Vision*. Pound was also working in Sicily; he borrowed Yeats's portable typewriter to hammer out some of the *Cantos*, getting as far as Canto XX.[34]

The Three Mountains Press, the Parisian enterprise of the American journalist William Bird, had begun production of *A Draft of XVI Cantos* early the previous year, but up to January 1925 Pound was still revising the first three cantos and writing Cantos VIII–XVI.[35] Pound was also in an extended, and at times heated, correspondence with Bird about Henry Strater's design for the large red illuminated initials that began each canto. Pound demanded that twenty copies of the ninety that were printed have no drawings whatsoever—only bold red initials—and these should be sold to specific readers whom Pound knew would object to Strater's more elaborate illustrations.[36] W.B. and George were not among these few; their copy, bearing George's bookplate, was one of seventy highly decorated copies printed on Roma paper with a special watermark, "Ezra Pound Cantos" at the base of each page.[37] In 1928, after catching sight of the next installment of the *Draft of the Cantos* (17–27), Wyndham Lewis wrote to Yeats, "What great ugly red letters! You should persuade him to print his poems, for better or worse, *sans images*—all the imagery, such as there is, should be *inside* the bloody words themselves."[38] Pound eventually agreed with Lewis on the point, when it came to starting his little magazine *The Exile*.

The Pounds and Yeatses were joined in Sicily for a little while by the lone traveler Thomas MacGreevy. He and George Yeats had been friends since at least 1922, when they probably met at Dublin's United Arts Club. They may have been introduced when MacGreevy shared a flat with the lanky, eccentric playwright and Abbey Theatre director Lennox Robinson in 1920, or they might have first encountered one another through the Dublin Drama

League of which George Yeats and MacGreevy were both members.[39] Robinson and MacGreevy were both important people in George's life; she could be candid with them and even freer in conversation than she was with her husband.[40] When George wrote to MacGreevy from Cannes, frustrated with W.B.'s depressive state in January 1928, MacGreevy responded with a charitable letter to Yeats, telling him about his own recent illness (an unshakeable cough) and gossiping about Robinson, who had been to see W.B. and George at Cannes over the Christmas holidays. MacGreevy strove to inspire Yeats with a sense of purpose: "Only you can make Lennox realise that its no good reading Wyndham Lewis (or even Maurras or Eliot who are more dignified exponents...) if he doesn't apply the theory of it to his work."[41]

To some degree, MacGreevy and George Yeats's friendship was unlikely: her unapologetic Englishness was matched against his strident Irish Republicanism. But they had in common a love of languages, and—born just a year apart—an understanding that was sometimes lacking between George and W.B., with their nearly thirty-year age gap. She encouraged MacGreevy's friendship with her husband, and WBY in turn encouraged MacGreevy's literary prospects. Shortly after their holiday in Palermo, WBY wrote to H.J.C. Grierson, Professor of English at the University of Edinburgh, about MacGreevy, predicting "If he keep from drink & poetry he will be an acknowledged expert in a few years."[42] Yeats added a postscript: "As at present he neither drinks nor writes poetry his chances of success in life seem excellent." The summation was partly right: the next year, MacGreevy would meet T.S. Eliot, and in 1927 he would be Samuel Beckett's predecessor at the École Normale Supérieure. Unbeknownst to Yeats, MacGreevy *was* writing poetry and relied on George as a trusted critic; his *Poems* was published ten years after the Sicilian tour, in 1934.

After saying goodbye to the Pounds in Sicily, W.B. and George traveled on to Naples, Capri, and Rome, before returning to London, where he finished the proofs for his collection *Early Poems and Stories* for publication by Macmillan later that year. They planned to return to Italy as soon as WBY's commitments to theater business and government would allow. When Ezra and Dorothy left Palermo, they also parted company with one another—for a while. She returned to Rapallo, and he went to Rome to work on his poetry and to see his lover, the violinist Olga Rudge, who was pregnant with their child, Mary, due that summer.[43] In autumn 1927, Yeats's ill health sent him in a circuitous way back to Italy and to the Pounds. But it was not a wholly unwelcome change of plan.

"The north side of the Alps is an error"

Ezra Pound was a man in desperate need of a change of scene. In late 1920, he left London for Paris, where he established himself as both patron and student, praising the sculptor Brancusi's ovoids, admiring avant-garde composer George Antheil's discordant sounds, and trying to keep T.S. Eliot afloat by way of the *Bel Esprit* project, which would allow Eliot to devote himself to full-time writing.[44] By Pound's own account, he decided to suddenly up sticks, but his correspondence shows that while he was certainly busy when he *was* in Paris, he was hardly there at all. Ernest Hemingway, who toured northern Italy with Pound, remarked at the end of *A Moveable Feast*: "Paris was always worth it and you received return for whatever you brought to it"; by the early 1920s, Pound brought little to the table.[45] Other writers who would soon join Pound in Rapallo admitted to the same disillusionment with what had been an epicenter of modernist innovation. The Imagist poet and veteran of the First World War Richard Aldington confessed, "perhaps my fatigue makes me unjust to that great city—but, upon my soul, it seems to contain more idiotic scribblers than the rest of the world put together."[46] Pound's friend Antheil, who was working on the score for Fernand Léger's Dadaist film *Mechanical Ballet*, was even more frustrated, telling Pound, "Because America is too cheap to pay for anything worth while I am forced immediately to abandon Paris, and in a short time Europe, and even perhaps music."[47]

The extent to which the poets' convergence in Rapallo was a regrouping of Pound's Paris milieu is encapsulated in a letter from Basil Bunting, who worked with Pound in Rapallo for about four years. Unlike jaded Aldington and Antheil, the young Northumbrian writer thought that "in Paris there is no one dull." He went about proving it by getting himself arrested for disorderly conduct. With a mix of sheepishness and annoyance, Bunting asked Pound to act as his advocate; he hoped Pound could explain to the gendarme that while Bunting had indeed been drunk, the knife in his possession was used merely for sharpening pencils and cutting bread and cheese (hardly a deadly weapon); and he asked Pound to make it clear that Bunting's previous incarceration wasn't for criminal activity but for conscientious objection.[48] The appeal worked, and Bunting later repaid Pound with his contributions as linguist to the literary supplement to the newspaper *Il Mare*, on which they worked together in Rapallo. Ford Madox Ford, who arrived in Paris the same autumn as Bunting, would also contribute to *Il Mare*, giving an interview when he visited Rapallo ten years later.

From 1922, Pound made regular trips to Italy, researching his cantos on Sigismondo Malatesta, the fifteenth-century poet, patron, and military leader who led the Venetian campaign against the Ottoman Empire.[49] By 1924, a little over a year after Mussolini's March on Rome, the Pounds began to think about relocating permanently. In fact, Mussolini's rise to power in the early 1920s was of principal appeal. Correspondence between Ezra and Dorothy in the spring of 1923 shows Dorothy remarking on a "big fascist meeting" in Assisi, where she was traveling with the artist Stella Bowen, and Ezra praising humorously the "noble fascist" librarian at Rimini who kept the building open late on Pound's behalf.[50] Pound's biographer David Moody summarizes Pound's vision of Mussolini's regime as achieving a "new energy" and a "civic sense."[51] Early on at least, Dorothy had reservations about the state of European politics and was beset by the feeling that they were living on a precipice; she wrote to Ezra, "'Old Moore' says in 1925 Mars is nearer the Earth than for 100 years so I suppose there'll be another war," but Ezra was flippant—"Let's hope it will be a war between Timbuktoo and the Exquimau."[52]

For the most part, the Pounds' friends were happy to indulge the couple's extremist politics as a temporary flirtation. Hemingway, who with his wife Hadley had visited Sigismondo's battlefields with Pound in 1924, went to Rapallo in early 1925 and again in August 1926, when Antheil was also in town.[53] He reported, "By gad Mussolini is running a disgraceful business. Lead pipe government and everybody that squeals gets bumped off," and he jokingly referred to Ezra as "Signor Duce," occasionally escalating the epithet to "Herr Gott."[54]

By the end of November 1926, Hemingway had his fill of Pound's fascination with Mussolini; he told Pound,

> If you actually and honest to God or what have you admire or respect the gent and his works all I can say is SHIT and if I ever start to see any leanings in that direction, obvious ones, (like say [Nancy Cox-] MacCormick's and the late Mrs. Butler's) yr. secret ones being your own business—I will take practical steps by denouncing you here in Paris as a dangerous antifascist and we can amuse one another by counting the hours before you get beaten up inspite of your probity—which in such a fine country as it must be would undoubtedly save you.
>
> But, in fact, I won't do any of this and I will not mention politics again in a letter. Only don't you ever call me on Dago [i.e., southern European] politics. Yes I know the lire is stabilized and all the improvements in the TRAIN SERVICE.[55]

Despite Hemingway's public and private disavowal of Mussolini, the fascist writer Francesco Monotti later claimed Hemingway *for* the regime, writing in *Il Mare*, "despite all, we still consider Ernest Hemingway a friend of yesterday's Italy at war and of today's Fascist Italy."[56]

Regardless of Hemingway's caution, Pound did take inspiration from the work Nancy Cox-McCormack, an American sculptor who established a studio in Rome and was working on a bust of Il Duce. (In 1925, she would also work on a sculpture of the pro-segregation Governor of Alabama, George Wallace.[57]) Pound wrote to McCormack in August 1923 to explain his vision for Italy as a place for cultural regeneration:

> It would be quite easy to make Italy the intellectual centre of Europe; and that by gathering ten or fifteen of the best writers and artists .... I shouldn't trust anyone's selection save my own. There is no use going into details until one knows if there is or could be any serious interest in the idea; that is to say, if the dictator *wants a corte letteraria*; if he is interested in the procedure of Sigismundo Malatesta in getting the best artists of his time into Rimini, a small city with no great resources. I know, in a general way, the fascio includes literature and the arts in its programme; that is very different from being ready to take specific action.[58]

Pound reported to his father, Homer, who would retire in Rapallo, "the north side of the alps is an error, useful only to make one glad to get to this side."[59]

Although Pound was not immediately "firing on all six cylinders," his writing was re-invigorated by the move south; as he told Wyndham Lewis, he "rejuvenated by 15 years in going to Paris and added another ten of life by quitting same."[60] As Pound intimated in the letter to McCormack, what was so "necessary" about Italy was a political and cultural climate in which the ancient past was eminently visible; the visibility of the past was a priority of Mussolini's government, and it inspired Dorothy Pound's drawings and watercolors, some of which were illustrations for Ezra's volumes of poetry. Although Dorothy was self-taught and regarded herself as an amateur artist, she designed several of Ezra's books and published one of her own: *Etruscan Gate*, in 1971, just two years before her death. Dorothy's paintings from their early marriage display an extraordinary use of color and indicate her place within the Vorticist movement, but the landscape of Rapallo and the Gaudier-Brzeska sculptures that decorated their apartment in Italy are strong presences in Dorothy's work, just as they are in Ezra's.⁶¹ Unlike him, her politics are for the most part encoded, and it is only in her private correspondence and through a close, contextual study of her aesthetics that the degree of Italian fascism's influence on her painting becomes clear.⁶²

In a "psychiatric study" of Ezra Pound published in 1949, Frederic Wertham argued, "What appealed to him, in Rapallo and Rome, was a new kind of estheticism [....] Pound loved Fascist Italy because he saw it as movement, as 'full of bounce.'"⁶³ Pound was so eager to get on "the road to Rapallo" that he abandoned his studio in Paris while it was still under lease; he offered first dibs to Hemingway and second to the highest bidder: "If Hem don't want it," he wrote to William Bird, "can yr. friends find 2000 fr. recompense [...]? Or how much *can* they find? [....] Also do yr. friends want the *cat*?"⁶⁴ On leaving Paris, Pound was honest with very few people regarding his whereabouts. He told Bird that he was leaving "for parts unknown and they've got to *damn well stay unknown*."⁶⁵ All correspondence should be sent to Rapallo's Hotel Mignon, near the center of town. This would give Ezra and Dorothy fair warning in the case of unexpected visitors, since, for the most part, they could be found in a different hotel, in the mountains of Montallegro overlooking the town of Rapallo and the Gulf of Tigullio (Figure 1.3). Pound wrote to his mother about the new vista: "Have been through the last half of Dant's Hell; and acquired a little more greek during the past fortnight; real comforts of idleness, after the hurley-burley or hurloo-burloo of Paris." He continued, "Nearest neighbors being H.D. and the McAlmons, somewhere in Suisse. I suppose this state of tranquility can't last, but it is very comfortable while it does."⁶⁶

Soon after Ezra arrived in Rapallo, he settled into a routine: mornings were spent playing tennis, often with literary friends, and the afternoons playing chess with the café waiters. In between, there was writing, copious amounts of writing. The Pounds took an apartment on the top floor of via Marsala 20, where they had a view of the Gran Caffè Rapallo out to the Gulf of Tigullio, and which provided the "setting [...] and the subject matter" for Yeats's *A Packet for Ezra Pound*.⁶⁷ The apartment also made a strong impression on Brigit Patmore when she visited with Richard Aldington early in 1928. She later remembered the living room's perspective "above the slanting roof of a lower storey," where Rapallo's cats would congregate at mealtimes. Until Rapallo, Patmore "never realized how much Ezra cared for cats, but they knew—those multi-coloured ravenous Italian cats [....] Ezra must have trained them well."⁶⁸

Figure 1.3 Rapallo from Montallegro
Source: Louis Zukofsky Collection, Harry Ransom Center, The University of Texas at Austin.

Yeats, Pound, and Il Duce

When the Pounds moved to Italy, Ezra imagined that he might be literary advisor to Mussolini's regime. Yeats's relationship to Italian fascism was less direct but nonetheless troubling. In August 1924, Yeats quoted Mussolini in his speech on the occasion of the Tailteann Games, an Irish sporting competition that was held to coincide with the Paris Olympics and that aimed to draw attention to the newly independent Irish state.[69] Yeats proclaimed at the accompanying banquet, "as a great popular leader has said to an applauding multitude, 'We will trample upon the decomposing body of the Goddess of Liberty.'"[70] Roy Foster writes that Yeats's remarks were "marvellously at odds with the general tone of the evening."[71] Even so, Yeats seems to have interpreted the Games—which were, after all, the Irish Free State's attempt to use mass spectacle for purposes of cultural unification—as being in alignment with the tactics of the new Italy, where parades and performances were early markers of Italian fascism's attempt to succeed where the Risorgemento failed. Yeats was not alone among Irish writers in his praise of Mussolini; five years after Tailteann, in 1929, George Bernard Shaw spoke to the BBC about "Democracy" and declared, "Who can blame Signor Mussolini for describing it as a putrefying corpse?"[72]

The Irish Civil War had seemed to prove to Yeats that Ireland was suffering from an excess of liberty, and he believed that a "firm"—even "tyrannical"—government was required to bring about a state that would be governed by what he conceived as the best minds. In interview with the *Irish Times* in February 1924, Yeats declared:

> Authoritative government is certainly coming, if for no other reason than that the modern State is so complex that it must find some kind of expert government, a government firm enough, tyrannical enough if you will, to spend years in carrying out its plans [....] The question in Ireland, as elsewhere in Europe is whether the authoritative Government which we see emerging is the short reaction that comes at the end of every disturbance, lasting ten or fifteen years, or whether it is, as I think, a part of a reaction that will last one hundred or one hundred and fifty years. Not always of the same intensity, it is, still, a steady movement towards the creation of a nation controlled by highly trained intellects [....] I am afraid [...] it will be busy with very crude things during my lifetime. I shall be a very old man if I live to see it capable of taking up the tasks for which I care and of which I dream.[73]

Although Yeats was careful not to endorse any contemporary manifestations of "authoritarianism," he was confident that it was a necessary step to bring about the Ireland that he imagined. Pressed to be more specific regarding the tasks for which he cared and dreamed, Yeats enumerated "the best teaching in architecture, in metal work, in mosaic work, establishment of a fine school of building here in Dublin." These ideas would form the core of what Yeats hoped would be a second Revival in Ireland during the 1930s, and the philosophy of Gentile—a philosopher who was at the core of Mussolini's cultural program—was integral to Yeats's vision.

In November 1922, almost six months after the outbreak of the Irish Civil War and just one week after Mussolini's March on Rome, Yeats wrote, "The Ireland that reacts from the present disorder is turning its eyes towards individualist Italy."[74] The adjective "individualist" is puzzling, especially with reference to a regime that would declare at its outset the supremacy of the corporate state, but Yeats's use of it is clarified in the reminiscences of Thomas MacGreevy. In an unpublished draft of an essay on Yeats, MacGreevy recalls, "About 1923 or 1924 he told me he believed that Mussolini represented the rise of the individual man as against what he considered the anti-human party machine."[75] Yeats's opposition to the "party machine" was driven by his residual anger over the abandonment of the Irish parliamentarian Charles Stewart Parnell by his party in 1889. The Parnellite split, as it was known, caused the collapse of the Irish Home Rule movement, and—to Yeats's mind—was a precursor of the divisions of the Irish Civil War. In a late essay, "Commentary on a Parnellite at Parnell's Funeral," which Yeats published in 1935 at the end of his excursions to Rapallo, he described in positive tones Shaw, Wilde, and George Moore as "the most complete individualists in the history of literature, abstract, isolated minds, without a memory or a landscape."[76] For Yeats, these three writers mark a transitional phase between an agrarian political party, which degraded literature with "rhetoric and insincerity" and a new historical phase that Yeats believed was initiated by the death of Parnell, when "we began to value truth."

Yeats's praise of "individualist Italy" at the Tailteann banquet in 1924 and his remarks to MacGreevy about Mussolini signal his belief that Ireland was undergoing another transitional phase and that the Free State might look for guidance from the southern European nation that was also experiencing a period of (purported) consolidation and rebirth. This vision of Italy underpins the first iteration of *A Vision*. As Paul and Harper indicate in their edition of the 1925 text, Yeats "had in common with Mussolini his desire to infuse actual world events with the power of myth"; the first version of *A Vision* and Margherita Sarfatti's biography of Mussolini (also published in 1925) share "a conflation of fascism and myth," and Yeats's study of Oswald Spengler, Leo Frobenius, and Wyndham Lewis—all of whom he discussed with Pound in Rapallo—reinforced Yeats's idea of a totalizing mythological system.[77]

In the 1925 text of *A Vision*, Yeats is at an "idealistic moment in his investment in fascism," and this plays out in his plans for an Italian inflection at the Tailteann Games.[78] He invited Gabriele D'Annunzio to speak at the Games and was so enthusiastic about hosting him that he wrote to D'Annunzio twice: the second time on July 2, just a month before the Games were held.[79] Yeats addressed D'Annunzio as "illustrious poet," but like himself, D'Annunzio was also a playwright, a statesman of sorts, and an architect of his country's aesthetics.[80] In March 1924 (just a few months before Yeats's letter), D'Annunzio had been named Principe di Montenevoso, a title awarded in celebration of his short-lived seizure and dictatorship of Fiume in 1919. During the nineteen months that he governed, D'Annunzio created the mechanisms of political performance that Mussolini would later adopt: the choreography of the crowd (which D'Annunzio directed through call and response), the use of costume (the black shirt worn by Fiume's Legionnaires), the "Roman" salute, and the song "Giovinezza" ("Youth") as a call to action.

Ezra Pound disliked D'Annunzio's oratory, but as Rebecca Beasley comments, Pound "was clearly encouraged by the sight of a writer as a political leader." Pound went so far as to say that "In the main he represents art and literature [....] he represents the individual human being."[81] Yeats had been aware of D'Annunzio since the first years of the twentieth century, although early on he was undecided on the merits of D'Annunzio's creative work.[82] Just why Yeats was so keen on D'Annunzio's presence at the Games is indicated in a draft of his Tailteann speech, where Yeats referred to the "industrial unrest which had nearly sabotaged the opening of the Games." He omitted the following passage from his delivered remarks, but his comments illustrate the parallel that he was drawing between the political crisis in Ireland and what he perceived as an Italian solution: "We have exchanged revolver shots for strikes, illegal violence for the legal violence of a small minority that has claimed the right to deprive of the necessities of life and health many thousands."[83]

The Italian National Fascist Party was formed in 1921 and at its inception banned the right to strike, in reaction against the nearly two thousand industrial strikes and nearly two hundred peasant strikes of 1920.[84] At the same time that it banned strikes, the Party asserted the supremacy of the state over the individual. At the Tailteann Banquet, Yeats referred to these developments when he cited Mussolini's authoritarianism as a cure for "nineteenth-century liberalism," and when he proposed that the task for future generations in Ireland would be "not the widening of liberty, but recovery from its errors: that they will set their hearts upon the building of authority, the restriction of discipline, the discovery of a life sufficiently heroic to live without opium dreams."[85]

Yeats was not unique in his thinking about how early fascist Italy could instruct Ireland. As Clare Nally has observed, drawing on the work of Mike Cronin, "The Blueshirt intellectuals tended to appeal to the Italian system as well as to the papal encyclical, but 'minimised the importance of the dictatorship.'"[86] Yeats developed the idea of constructive authoritarianism in his "Commentary on A Parnellite at Parnell's Funeral," written at the height of his involvement with the Blueshirts and published in *Dublin Magazine* in 1934 and by Cuala Press in 1935. His poem "Three Songs to the Same Tune," intended as a marching song for the Blueshirts, was published in *Parnell's Funeral* as well as in the broadside ballad series that Yeats published with F.R. Higgins in 1935. In Yeats's commentary, he recalls the Huguenot artists who designed tapestries for the House of Lords depicting the Battle of the Boyne and the Siege of Derry:

> they [are] celebrating the defeat of their old enemy Louis XIV, and the establishment of a Protestant Ascendancy which was to impose upon Catholic Ireland, an oppression copied in all details from that imposed upon the French Protestants [....] Armed with this new power, they were to modernise the social structure, with great cruelty but effectively, and to establish our political nationality by quarrelling with England over the wool trade, a protestant monopoly.[87]

The vision of an authoritarian government as a modernizing force—in the social, political, and economic realms—strongly reflects Ezra Pound's writing from the mid-1930s about the United States, especially his book *Jefferson and/or Mussolini: L'idea statele. Fascism as I have seen it*, which was published the same year as Yeats's commentary. Pound also looks to the history of his country with France, writing, "Jefferson participated in one revolution [....] He tried to educate another [....] While fat Louis was chewing apples at Versailles, Lafayette and Co. kept running down to Tom's [i.e., Jefferson's] lodgings to find out how one ought to behave, and how one should have a Franch revolution."[88] He compares Mussolini's plan for a group of advisors, one representing each profession or segment of the workforce, to Jefferson who "guided the ruling class. A limited number of the public had the franchise."[89] The similarities in the poets' political writings in the mid-1930s can be traced back a decade, to the Tailteann Banquet to which Yeats invited Pound.

To entice Pound to Dublin, Yeats promised that he would be a "guest of the nation," would see the Tailteann Games ("probably a great bore"), the annual Horse Show at Ballsbridge ("about the only thing we do really well"), and would "be present when I crown in the name of the Irish Academy certain books." He teased, "You will also probably be invited to certain country houses, and will be generally made much of, and meet everybody who is to be met, and have admirable opportunities for your usual violence and brutality."[90] W.B. and George would offer to host no one else at Merrion Square "in order that your temperament may have full sway and exercise."[91] Pound intended to take them up on the offer, although Dorothy advised against it: "Don't go to Oireland—There's a strike in Dublin."[92] There were problems with Pound's passport, which Desmond Fitzgerald attempted to mitigate by providing extra documents (in the Irish and English languages), and for one of these reasons or maybe a combination of factors, Pound decided against making the journey.[93] Instead, Yeats and Pound met in Sicily a few months later and then again in early 1928, when Pound's sharp-witted conviviality marshaled Yeats out of his malaise and into a new phase of work, heralded by the publication of *The Winding Stair* in 1929.

An "Ezuversity"

In an essay for the *New Yorker*, "A Day with Ezra Pound," published in 1940, Elizabeth Delehanty described the *brivido* that the American poet brought to the Ligurian Riviera:

> I had been walking about five minutes on the boulevard toward the baths when I heard a slight commotion behind me. All around people stopped moving. It was as if a fire siren had sounded and nobody could hear anything or even move until it had stopped. I leaned up against a balustrade and waited. They were all looking at a man advancing with giant strides. He was tall and broad, with a pointed beard. He had on a white suit that, large though he was, literally flowed from him. The spotless trousers wrapped around his legs as he walked, the shining coat billowed in the breeze. There was a towel tied about his waist and the fringe from it

bobbed rhythmically. His hat, which was white too, had been slapped on at a dashing angle. He marched by me, swinging a cane, ignoring the awed Italians, his eyes on an interesting point in space.[94]

Delehanty's description gives the impression of Pound as the "Master of Rapallo," an appellation that he gave himself in 1933.[95] And he behaved accordingly (Figure 1.4).

Pound imagined that *his* Rapallo circle would be an "Ezuversity," but Yeats was an equal, if more reticent, touchstone for the group of younger poets who gathered there and would be known for their left-leaning politics. In a letter to Aldington in 1927, Pound described Italy as "the best governed state in Europe and where the goddam shits least bother one."[96] When the young British aesthete Adrian Stokes and the journalist and aspiring novelist Beaumont Wadsworth "both turned up in Rapallo" in early January that same year, Pound wrote to his mother to say the town was "now

Figure 1.4 Pound, the self-styled "Master of Rapallo"
Source: Ezra Pound Literary File, Harry Ransom Center, The University of Texas at Austin.

becoming licherary centre of yourup"; by November 1927, he was hopeful that "a new generation [was] beginning to sprout."⁹⁷ Yeats was more skeptical; he wrote to Lady Gregory the same month, "I do not yet know whether this is inclined here for a social circle apart [from] occasional travellers—Ezra says know but he is exacting. We think of going to church to inspect the material."⁹⁸

During the early months that Pound and Yeats were both in Rapallo, the poets corresponded with many of the writers who would visit the city over the next six years. "We are restarting civilization, and have devised a new modus of making art and lit. possible," Pound wrote to Aldington in 1924.⁹⁹ He wished he could save Aldington as well as Eliot from drudgery and perhaps even bring them to Rapallo: "I should like to remove you both and leave your sodden island to its natural destinies, which are darkness and again darkness and again darkness in the midst of stenches [...] save this for publication after my death."¹⁰⁰ From his new base in Italy, Pound revisited the idea of patronage that had fallen flat with *Bel Esprit*, and he began to think about patronage in more corporate terms.

Whereas Sigismondo Malatesta, who featured in the early cantos, was a model of a singular patron, Pound thought that a "group" was necessary for the cultivation of literary culture in the contemporary moment. He advised the twenty-four-year-old bespectacled poet Louis Zukofsky, born to Jewish immigrants to New York, and who was interested in organizing a similar "group":

> To keep the group pure in heart, I think one must avoid tired and worn out personalities. I won't invidiously give a list. But some of my contemporaries have so institutionalized themselves, and make <dignity> rather than their mental activity <etc ___>. Fill in the blanks to suit yourself. Must make a NEW grouping. and the older elements must be the uncompromised (either toward mediocrity or popularity).¹⁰¹

For Pound, the "group [was] very useful for gathering information, etc. both enlightenment and stimulus to action."¹⁰² Those qualities had been lacking in the Parisian coterie; by contrast, Rapallo's location on the Ligurian coast—a place accessible from Genoa, a major city, but not a tourist hub like nearby Portofino with its cruise ships—made it an ideal place for the careful cultivation of a group.

Out of all the Rapallo poets, Zukofsky had the hardest time accounting for his proximity to Pound during the troubled thirties. Pound and he began discussing a visit to Rapallo in 1931, when Zukofsky was helping Pound obtain information on the history of U.S. democracy, including procuring books on topics including Thomas Jefferson, Roman history, and "whatever book you think I need fer my generl enlightenment."[103] Zukofsky, naïve about how he was assisting Pound's nascent *Jefferson and/or Mussolini* (1935), imagined that he might write his own essay on Jefferson—"How Jefferson Used Words"—which Zukofsky later listed among the abandoned works in his long poem, "A."[104] Whether he was flattered by Pound's patronage, blithe, or simply ignorant, Zukofsky took Pound at his word and disregarded the fascist flares that Pound was sending up. In October 1931, Pound sent him the poem "Yiddisher Charlestown Band" along with the qualifying statement, "The yittisher by itself might give the deleterious impression of antisemitism which I am far from"; in May 1932, Pound reported having an "amiable jaw with Marinetti in Rome and have come back loaded with futurist and fascist licherchoor"; in April 1933, when Pound asked Zukofsky to send Franklin Roosevelt's economic writings, he added, "And fascist ideas moving apace in America, while in Deutschland the pseudo-fascist rages."[105] A casual remark that Zukofsky made to Carl Rakosi in January 1931 would come back to haunt him: "a Jewish ethics—I aint got it myself—it's purely a family affair."[106]

By 1933, the arrangements for Zukofsky's visit to Rapallo were underway, and Pound helped to plan his itinerary.[107] Zukofsky should come via Paris, where Pound could arrange introductions to the city's luminaries—Cocteau, Aragon, Elouard, Dali, and Max Ernst.[108] Zukofsky's trip was undertaken with a degree of awareness of what was happening to Jews in Europe. When Pound wrote to him in April 1933 offering to front the fare for the steamship from New York, Pound advised:

> Mittle and Nord Europa less seasonable for Semites than they wuz lass year. HAVE just seen THE most perfect specimen here on the sea front. Bet HE got out in a box car. Nooz iz that H.D. is consortin with Siggy Freud. Have axd her to ax F. to hexplain it, but bet ten bx [bucks] or biscuit she dont ax him. (I mean the outburst toward pogrum in boscheland).[109]

William Carlos Williams gave Zukofsky one hundred dollars toward the trip, urging him to "Make notes. Learn whatever there is to learn over there [....] Lord knows what you'll see in Europe. My guess is that it won't be poetry."[110] After Bunting and Zukofsky both left Rapallo, Bunting kept his friend in the U.S. apprised of Pound and of the situation in Europe—but with the kind of jocularity that showed no foresight of the horror to come. In October 1935, he reported "Certain German towns having ordained that

Jewish cars may not park in their streets, [Karl] Drerup [who had left Germany and then Madrid for Tenerife] is trying to think out a process for circumcising cars."[111] He introduced Bunting and Drerup by post, telling Zuk, he was "a decent bloke who wont heil Hitler."[112]

Rapallo would be the making of the friendship between Bunting and Zukofsky: introduced by Pound, their relationship soon took on its own exchanges, influences, and intimacies. Bunting wrote to Zukofsky care of Thomas Cook in Paris, to be sure of their arrangements, sending a postcard of Rapallo harbor and conveying the expectation that Zukofsky would be a willing passenger on Bunting's sailboat: "Marion has put forward the miserable excuse of seasickness."[113] The young poets met at the bookstall in Genoa station and planned to spend two or three hours in the city before making the journey down the coast.[114]

From Pound's perch at the Albergo Rapallo, a large hotel on the waterfront, he described his daily routine to George Yeats:

> The 'terrase' of the Rapallo is where we normally sit from 11.30 till after lunch. Hauptmann sits on the other side of the shrub box, ten feet off at the Aurum (i.e., the jazz hell in our basement). Probably the slight va et vient will provide Wm with mild object of observation. The 'gardens', are against the hill side, with dampish rocks at strategic points.
>
> At any rate the foci of solar heat are at 'Albergo Rapallo', on our elevated terazza, and on a tin bench the other side of a bathing pavilion to the north of the Chris. Colombo monyment. Does Wm know, like, dislike or what Hauptmann. My present relations with same are limited to ceremonious bow.[115]

Beerbohm later quipped about Pound that any "treacle of admiration" he had for his friends "was always strongly tinctured with the vinegar of envy."[116] The Yeatses would feel this keenly, since Pound was guaranteed to "condemn" any new visitors to Rapallo to whom "the WBs," as he dubbed them, took a shine.[117]

George left after the first week in Rapallo, in order to convey their son Michael to boarding school in Switzerland, but the couple had already decided that the place would be a fixture in their new life. W. B. sent a long letter to Olivia Shakespear, explaining their vision:

> We have made great changes of plan & intend now to take a flat here & move over some of our furniture, & let all but one floor of 82 Merrion Square. We can then spend say from August to April here & the rest of the

year in Dublin, with passing visits to London. Doctors tell us the Dublin climate will no more suit Michael than his father so we think to keep both children at a Swiss school & fetch them here for summer & winter holidays (hence August is included in our time here). George is longing for the freedom of flats & daily help & all heavy meals out. We have the refusal—George decides on her return from Switzerland—of a large flat—9 or 10 rooms—with balconies & the most lovely view imaginable [....] We shall live much more cheaply & this change of place & climate at my time of life is a great adventure one longed for many a time.[118]

Yeats refused to move in until mosquito nets were hung, but by mid-March they were settled in the flat, on the fourth floor of the via Americhe near the road to Portofino. The expansive balconies, which wrapped around the corner of the building, gave views of the mountains above the town as well as the Gulf of Tigullio. They took the lease while it was still unfinished, so George was able to "dictate where electricity switches went," choose plain tiles throughout, and "veto Italianate ornamentation and glass doors."[119] There was central heating and electric radiators, and in addition to a quantity of bedrooms, the space allowed for a schoolroom for the children and a study each for W.B. and George. It was sparsely furnished, with a large bookcase, a round table, and three upright chairs in the sitting room, with a few engravings hung on the walls.[120] The overall impression it made on W.B. was of a "pleasant place," "clean and luminous," a retreat "with great balconies to sleep in on the sun."[121] Although he craved the quietude, George wasn't ready to retreat from sociability; at one stage she "relieve[d] her boredom" by painting the furniture "Chinese red."[122] In mid-April, they returned to Dublin, but by August he was yearning for Rapallo, in order "to get away from damp and political agitation."[123] "I am tired," he admitted to Olivia Shakespear: "I want nothing but the sea-shore & the palms & Ezra to quarrel with, & the Rapallo cats to feed after night fall."[124]

Soon after W.B. and George arrived in Rapallo, he wrote to Lady Gregory: "This is an indescribably lovely place—some little Greek town one imagines [....] Here I shall put off the bitterness of Irish quarrels, & write my most amiable verses. They are already—though I dare not write—crowding my head. 'The Tower' astonishes me by its bitterness."[125] He wrote similarly to Olivia Shakespear,

> this change of place & climate at my time of life is a great adventure one longed for many a time. Once out of the Senate—my time is up in

September—& in obedience to the doctors out of all public work there is no reason for more than 3 months of Dublin—where the Abbey is the one work I cannot wholly abandon. Once out of Irish bitterness I can find some measure of sweetness, and of light, as befits old age—[126]

As Yeats anticipated, his poetry underwent an important change in Rapallo, although it was hardly reflective of the sweetness and light that he predicted. The poems of *The Winding Stair*, his first volume after *The Tower*, show him working to purge "bitterness" from his work. This process required, first of all, an inward turn, which involved the reading of Buddhist philosophy, which he explored with Pound. An "outward turn" soon followed; Yeats's essays and poems began to engage again with their political and social contexts, not only with the Ireland with which he was so disillusioned but also with the new Italy and the concerns of the Rapallo group.[127]

As late as 1932, Yeats was positive about the potential of Italian fascism; by 1934, when he left Rapallo for the last time, he was equally disillusioned with the regime, a distaste that is evident in his derogatory, multiple references to fascism's "bundle of dry sticks" in his writing and speeches from the mid-1930s. The importance of Yeats's seasons in Rapallo and the diversity of his collaborations and influences in Italy have been occluded by his most well-known reflection on the period: "A Packet for Ezra Pound" in *A Vision* (1937), where he qualifies his proximity to Pound in what is ultimately "an attempt to account for himself."[128]

All of the poets who traveled in and out of Pound and Yeats's Italian orbits made dubious claims about the significance of their time in Rapallo. In their private letters, unpublished memoirs, and discarded drafts of work-in-progress, the lineaments of their conversations, creative collaborations, and their attitudes to the fascist regime are most discernible. What follows is a new story of Rapallo that recovers an intense period in which friendships were made and broken, and of poets who responded to political change in a way that most of them, in the years that followed, preferred to forget.

2
Shell-Shocked Walt Whitmans

On a particularly cold night in January 1929, W.B. Yeats arrived for a dinner party at the Albergo Rapallo wearing wool socks pulled up over his gloved hands as a prophylactic against the frigid air. He was aloof for much of the evening, turning to Brigit Patmore and Richard Aldington on one occasion to ask the impossible question, "How do you account for Ezra?" Yeats responded to his own riddle:

> "Here we have in him one of the finest poets of our time, some erudition and a high intelligence and yet he is sometimes so—amazingly clumsy— so tactless and does what one might call outrageous things [....]"
> "And those little books of poetry by new writers he shows me." He slanted his head back and said firmly. "They are just shell-shocked Walt Whitmans!" Then down sank the noble head. "But we are all just pebbles on the beach in the backwash of eternity."[1]

Across the table, George queried under her breath, "Willie talking poppy-cock?"

Brigit Patmore probably hoped so, since it was at Pound's urging that she and Richard Aldington had gone to Rapallo in the first place. At forty-seven years of age, Patmore was best known as a literary hostess, but she also aspired to her own career as a writer. Her first book, *This Impassioned Onlooker*, had been published two years before her visit to Rapallo and is eerily prescient about the way she would be dragged around by Aldington (with whom she took up in 1927): "In their damnation men have further damned women: to drag a creature into hell by its love...it is funny and damned, isn't it?" (Figure 2.1)[2]

Pound had reserved rooms for Aldington and Patmore at a hotel on "the left of the bay" (probably the Hotel Mignon), and as soon as they arrived, he immediately took them to tea at the English Tennis Club, "which was funny," Patmore remembered, since "we had come to Italy to be with him away from England, both climate and people."[3] They were surprised by the

Figure 2.1 Richard Aldington taken by Brigit Patmore on an excursion to Verona
Source: Richard Aldington Literary File, Harry Ransom Center, The University of Texas at Austin.

cold weather but stayed long enough to experience "the miraculous spring with the mimosa in flower and tulips everywhere. And Richard began to write with a new inspiration."[4]

Patmore and Aldington arrived in Rapallo shortly before W.B. and George landed for their second season, and Pound advised that after Yeats had rested for a few days, they would "have permission to see him." Under her authorial breath, in *My Friends When Young* Patmore remembered wondering "how long Yeats would allow Ezra to arrange his life."[5] She was speaking from experience. Her fraught love affair with Aldington was entangled with her history with Pound; she had introduced the poets over tea in London in 1911.[6] At that time, Patmore was married to the philandering grandson of Coventry Patmore, who wrote the long poem *The Angel in the House* about the Victorian ideal marriage.[7] She used the Patmore reputation and wealth to establish herself on the literary scene, securing her place through her friendship with Violet Hunt, who was a client in Brigit's husband's insurance business. Patmore first met Pound at one of Hunt's tea parties.[8]

When Pound left the United States in 1908, he was engaged to be married to H.D., whom he had met while he was a student at the University of Pennsylvania. In London, he fell in love with Dorothy Shakespear, to whom he privately proposed marriage on his return to England in 1911. His proposal to Dorothy was issued fewer than two weeks after H.D. arrived in London on a European tour with her friend Frances Gregg.[9] When Gregg went back to the United States, H.D. stayed. Pound had tried to delay the awkward consequences of his double engagement for as long as possible. He introduced H.D. to Patmore in the hopes of distracting his first-betrothed so he would have time for liaisons with Shakespear. Patmore in turn introduced H.D. to Aldington, and H.D. took Aldington to Italy.[10]

Aldington followed on H.D.'s heels when she went to Genoa in December 1912 on holiday with her parents; he trailed along, ostensibly writing a series of articles for the magazine *The New Age*. Also in Italy, but traveling separately, were Dorothy Shakespear and George Hyde Lees who were chaperoned by Dorothy's mother, Olivia.[11] Pound was there too, but because he was—at that point—considered to be an ineligible suitor, a rendezvous with Dorothy never occurred. Instead, he caught up with Aldington, H.D., and H.D.'s mother in Florence and spent a May evening on the canals, with H.D. and Aldington in one gondola and Mr. Pound and Mrs. Doolittle in another.[12]

Aldington and H.D. were married later that year, after what Pound described as "their unofficial honeymoon in Italy."[13] Over the next decade and a half, Aldington's friendship with Patmore persisted while his marriage to H.D. did not. A baby girl was stillborn near the beginning of the First World War (events that H.D. depicted as concurrent in her novels and memoirs), and a string of infidelities followed. By 1928, Patmore had left her husband, published *This Impassioned Onlooker*, and rekindled her relationship with Aldington, accelerating his break-up with the Lady in Waiting, Dorothy Yorke.[14] In a bid to keep Patmore from Aldington, her deposed lover Stephen Haden-Guest inscribed a copy of Yeats's *The Tower* with a declaration of love that ran to seventeen pages, surrounded the poems "Sailing to Byzantium" and "The Tower," and included such desperate effusions as "Richard, for his own loveableness, as much as you and he and nice Paris can manage: enjoy nice Paris: but do not Flee from me, nor the past, nor London [....] cast out fear of me, and memories of bitterness and sordidness. 'Action, not reaction,' said Richard."[15] In 1927, Patmore was pulled between two controlling personalities, and Aldington was intent on winning her over. He enlisted Pound: "Help me Unkil Ez, I'm kinder going crazy over it. Can't you send her a letter & tell her to cut free?"[16] And she did, for one reason or another. A further directive from Pound sent Patmore and Aldington to Rapallo, on January 9, 1929.

Gossip from Rapallo also had a hand in influencing Aldington and Patmore's visit. Osbert Sitwell, himself a veteran of the Battle of Ypres, sent Aldington "the most amusing letters [from Rapallo] about Ezra," including reports on sartorial developments and personal animosities: Ezra "bought a new overcoat with a tiger-skin collar out of the Dial Prizemoney," a handsome sum of £2000 he was awarded from the American literary monthly in 1927. "On the other side of Rapallo lives Max [Beerbohm], so between the two (and it is a question whether Max hates Ezra more than Ezra hates Max) our friend Osbert is having a merry time."[17]

Aldington and Patmore soon had a dose of Rapallo's other entertainment; Patmore reported Aldington's first sighting of the looming figure of WBY:

> There's Yeats walking by the sea. He's so tall...in his black coat & large black hat...obviously a disguised god visiting these short bumbling Italians. He stops to gaze at something on the beach: his hands behind his back he ponders long. Wonder what it *could* be...it's such a treasureless strand. He moves on. He would never stop to stare, but is clearly interested in a girl...she's very brightly coloured...probably too much dazzle on his glasses. Ah! There's George. She takes his arm, he seems surprised and a little startled. Who is this stranger? Can it be?...It is! It's my wife! Relieved, he allows her to lead him to the Savoia for the café Belge he loves.[18]

Two days later, Patmore and Aldington realized that Richard had observed the composition of Yeats's new poem, "Three Things," after Yeats "chanted" the poem to them over tea on the fourth floor of the via Americhe: "after every two lines, he raised his head a little and, over his spectacles looked at me and then, after the next two lines, at Richard." It was an occasion of restrained hilarity.[19] Pound later joked, "Mr. Yeats probably would distinguish between a *g* and a *b flat*, but he is happy to think that he doesn't, and he would certainly be incapable of whistling a simple melody in tune. Nevertheless before writing a lyric he is apt to 'get a chune in his head.' He is very sensitive to a limited gamut of rhythms."[20]

Patmore's willingness to endure Yeats's offhanded insults and her commiserations in terms of the difficulty of a friendship with Pound meant that she and Yeats struck up a friendship between themselves, inspiring as well as amusing one another. On one of her visits to the Yeats apartment, he remarked on the "energetic young American girls who come over to study with Freud [...] and talked about the phallus as if it were no more than a carrot."[21] All this was delivered with a dry wit; Patmore recalled never seeing Yeats smile. In unpublished memoirs, she reflected, "the great poet had in him what I love & have found only in a few people—something I can simply call an ambience of being at home with the saints, and this has nothing to do with religion or churches."[22] Their friendship had unintended effects: Yeats inadvertently had a hand in one of the most acerbic critiques to come out of the First World War, Richard Aldington's *Death of a Hero*, and Aldington, in turn, is present in one of Yeats's most powerful late poems.[23]

A Call to Life

Patmore described *Death of a Hero* as "a call to life," and she thought that its completion marked Aldington's return to health after the ruin of the war she had witnessed only second-hand: the "disappearing lives [...] horror & [...] ceaseless imagination of worse horror, in a continual shriek in the mind."[24] Aldington had begun and abandoned the novel on three occasions, largely on the advice of D.H. Lawrence who had "told him to destroy what he had written if he wished to preserve what little reputation he had."[25] Away from Lawrence's overbearing instruction, and with the encouragement of Patmore and Frieda Lawrence, Aldington began the novel again, in Paris during the autumn of 1928. In the new year, he took it with him to Rapallo, where he and Patmore worked in the mornings before meeting the Pounds to socialize over coffee or cocktails in the afternoons. By the time they returned to Paris in late February 1929, Aldington had written about 30,000 words, enough to secure his contract with a publisher.[26]

Aldington was keenly aware that the book broke ranks with the genre of the war novel as well as the conventions of the novel more generally. In a preface addressed to his friend, the playwright, novelist, and veteran of the First World War, Halcott Glover, he describes the book as "not a novel at all" or perhaps "a jazz novel": "To me the excuse for the novel is that one can do any damn thing one pleases."[27] In Thomas MacGreevy's book *Richard Aldington: An Englishman* (1931), he dismisses Robert Graves's *Goodbye to All That* (also published in 1929) and designates *Death of a Hero* as the book that "broke the silence" and "opened the floodgates" for truthful accounts of the travesty of the Great War.[28]

What marks *Death of a Hero*'s difference is its wholesale refusal of the heroic; Aldington's narrator declares, "The death of a hero! What mockery, what bloody cant! What sickening, putrid cant!"[29] Aldington's soldiers are not lionized martyrs or hapless victims of trench-foot: they're hospitalized for venereal disease as frequently as for war wounds. His protagonist, George Winterbourne (whose story is told through an unnamed narrator) dies "soon after dawn on the 4th November 1918, at a place called Maison Blanche." But George's death is not heroic:

> The whole of his company were lying down, waiting for the flying trench-mortar squad to deal with the [German] machine-gun, when for some unexplained reason George had stood up, and a dozen bullets had gone through him. "Silly ass," was the Colonel's comment.[30]

At the funeral, Winterbourne's grave is surrounded by a "mourning party of Tommies and N.C.O.'s from his company on one side, and, facing them, the officers of his battalion." The narrator observes, "I was on the extreme left of the line." This positioning signals the perspective of the entire novel, most of which is not about the events of the First World War but the corrupt society that produced it and will produce the "Next War" and the next.[31]

In relaying Winterbourne's history, Aldington's narrator blurs the line between the home front and the battlefront, demystifying the landscape of the war by transposing it onto London's "Sabbath ennui." His stroll along Church Street on a Sunday is a sally through "that dismal communication trench which links the support line of Kensington High Street with the front line of Notting Hill Gate." In one of the novel's jazz riffs, the narrator interrupts George's story to muse,

> How curious are cities, with their intricate trench systems and perpetual warfare, concealed but as deadly as the open warfare of armies! We live in trenches, with flat revetments of house-fronts as parapet and parados. The warfare goes on behind the housefronts—wives with husbands, children with parents, employers with employed, tradesmen with tradesmen, banker with lawyer, and the triumphal doctor rooting out life's casualties. Desperate warfare—for what? Money as the symbol of power; power as the symbol or affirmation of existence. Throbbing warfare of men's cities! As fierce and implacable and concealed as the desperate warfare of plants and the hidden carnage of animals. We walk up Church Street. Up the communication trench. We cannot see "over the top".[32]

No one is exempted from Aldington's satire, especially not the so-called avant-garde. In *Death of a Hero*, George, Elizabeth, and Fanny's modern sexual entanglements are pilloried along with their artistic pretensions. Winterbourne can't paint in Paris because he finds it too intimidating: "It was easier to feel important in the comparative desert of London."[33]

The pre- and postwar disillusionment that Aldington expresses in the novel is similar to the sentiments that Antheil expressed in a long letter to Pound in the spring of 1924, when he wrote,

> the splendid machine Rossini war of 1914–1918. Trata…da ….Curtain! Grand Fancy Gallop of the Machine Guns ….bless their hearts! Fantasy overture of Airplanes [….] Nothing has changed. When I go to the Garden Luxembourg I see that nothing has changed in the human being…he is just the same…BUT HIS SENSE OF TIME HAS ALTERED.[34]

When the war finally erupts in the novel, Aldington describes it with an unrelentingly fast pace that alternates between horror and anxiety; the war is, he repeats, "a timeless confusion."[35] Just as the geography of the war extends beyond the battle lines of Continental Europe in the novel, so do the war's aftereffects. Winterbourne "looked unaltered; he behaved in exactly the same way. But, in fact, he was a little mad. We talk of shell-shock, but who wasn't shell-shocked, more or less?"[36] The change manifests itself in "an anxiety complex" and in "a profound and cynical discouragement, a shrinking horror of the human race…."[37]

Throughout *Death of a Hero*, scholarship is scorned as grossly irrelevant. In the novel's preface, Aldington takes a clear swipe at Pound (and maybe Yeats too) when he says that he "disbelieve[s] in bunk and despotism, even in a dictatorship of the intelligentsia."[38] Neither Aldington, Winterbourne, nor the unnamed narrator identifies any redeeming qualities in contemporary society or in the idea of "civilization." Winterbourne, home on leave, finds on his bookshelf Thomas de Quincey's *Murder Considered as One of the Fine Arts* and is overcome by feelings of disgust.[39] Near the end of *Death of a Hero*, shortly before his suicide, Winterbourne stands "Alone in the white curling mist, drifting slowly past like wraiths of the slain [….] and contemplate[s] the last achievements of civilised men."[40]

Yet the novel is not overwhelmed by a disillusioned mood. In the epigraph, Aldington returns to classical tropes in a poem that evokes the sun-drenched terraces where the Rapallo poets took their leisure: "Eleven years after the fall of Troy, / We, the old men—some of us nearly forty— / Met and talked on the sunny rampart / Over our wine, while the lizards scuttled / In dusty grass, and the crickets chirred."[41] Throughout his postwar work, Aldington's classical training provided a foothold for his emotions, giving him a lexicon that enabled him to write about his experience of the war. In his memoir, *Life for Life's Sake*, he recalled,

> Just after the war, in the confusion and reaction against everything pre-war and war, there was an almost unanimous belief among artists and writers of the vanguard that all art of the past was so much dead stuff to be scrapped. They were wilfully trying to make themselves barbarians. I felt unhappy about this, for my instinct was to do just the opposite. After the long hiatus of the war I thought we should for a time at least steep ourselves in the work of the masters; but nobody would agree with me.[42]

Nobody but T.S. Eliot, Aldington argues, before conceding, "Eliot was not the only one."[43] Pound is the unacknowledged other here, consigned to the margins because of Aldington's unwillingness to admit how much he owed to a proponent of one of the regimes over which the next war would be fought. In addition to his ethical motives, Aldington harbored more personal resentments. Soon after *Death of a Hero* was published, Aldington wrote to Patmore complaining that Francesco Monotti's review of the novel repeated Ezra's mistaken claim that the name "Winterbourne" was derived from Henry James's *Daisy Miller*, whereas Aldington claimed to have taken the name from a village in South Gloucestershire. Aldington thought that Monotti's entire article was "all to the glory of Ezra!"[44] In *Life for Life's Sake*, instead of owning up to Pound's directive that he and Patmore go to Rapallo, Aldington implies that he went on the basis of a vague rumor that the weather would be good. Pound and Yeats just happened to be in town at the same time—Yeats, Aldington remarks sardonically, "one was given to understand," having been drawn "into the orbit of the greater genius."[45]

Songs of Themselves

On one of Patmore's visits to W.B. and George's Rapallo apartment, she browsed their bookshelves and—despite WBY's genial protest that she'd never return it—borrowed the first volume of Peter Cunningham's edition of Horace Walpole's letters.[46] Walpole, a Whig politician, was the author of the gothic novel *The Castle of Otranto*, which purported to be a translation of a sixteenth-century Neapolitan text. The Yeatses owned all nine volumes of the letters, and it isn't clear whether in the winter of 1929 it was Walpole's novel with its Italian connection, his constitutional-monarchical politics, or the verve of the letters themselves that was the principal draw.[47] In any case, the books were there; Yeats acquiesced to the loan, and Patmore found the perfect epigraph for Aldington's *Death of a Hero*:

> See how we trifle! but one can't pass one's youth too amusingly; for one must grow old, and that in England; two most serious circumstances, either of which makes people grey in the twinkling of a bedstaff; for you know, there is not a country upon earth where there are so many old fools and so few young ones.[48]

Walpole's observation may have spoken to Aldington's sensibility as a writer of the so-called Lost Generation; the image of the fool probably also struck a chord, since it evoked the title of Aldington's long poem, *A Fool i' the Forest*, which had been published in 1925, and which MacGreevy described, in a backhanded compliment, as "ambitious" and "a statement in ideal terms of the theme of post-war disillusionment that was treated more realistically and elaborately in *Death of a Hero*."[49]

Even if "Willie" was "talking poppycock" at the Rapallo dinner party, could he have been talking about Aldington's *Fool*? The mock epic takes its title from one of Jacques's lines in *As You Like It*: "A fool! a fool! I met a fool i' the forest."[50] Shakespeare's cynical outsider serves as a reference point for Aldington's poem's trifurcated self: the "I" that Aldington intends "to be typical of a man of our time."[51] The unmitigated display of the self is what Yeats found so objectionable in Walt Whitman; the problem was not merely the focus *on* the self ("I celebrate myself, and sing myself") but the egotistical looseness of form that went along with it, undisciplined and individualist in the worst sense: cut off from the tradition that Yeats believed sustained the highest art.[52] In *Fool i' the Forest*, Aldington's severance from tradition is mimetic: "O break the silver trumpet and the lyre, / Sully the marble, cut the crisped bronze; / Byron is dead."[53] While he maintains a tenuous connection to tradition with his references to Homer, Virgil, and Byron, his form is chaotic, justified—perhaps—by his subtitle "A Phantasmagoria." For example, the tenth movement is described as "The Vision of Hell," but does not pay homage to the *Inferno*:[54]

> That made me think of Hell.
> It was like a crematorium
> Or rather a Kadaver-factory

> Where every day
> Millions of persons were consumed to smoke.
> Out of ten thousand towering chimneys
> Gushed black greasy smoke
> That whitened to a cloud of bank-notes.
> [...]
> By the throne stood policeman-lictors
> Bearing fasces made of golf-clubs.
> [...]
> All the angels drove to work in tanks.[55]

The image of chimneys emitting noxious smoke from incinerated bodies is a terrifying premonition of how the industrial mass-destruction of the First World War would lead to the Holocaust. While the ovens in the poem are a matter of tragic coincidence, the images of the "lictors" and "fasces" are not.

In September 1922, John Halcott Glover (to whom *Death of a Hero* is dedicated) lent Aldington his apartment on the Piazza Margana in Rome, where Aldington stayed for three weeks. The March on Rome took place on October 22, by which time Aldington had left Italy. Even so, Aldington would have witnessed the increasing power of the National Fascist Party (PNF) after Mussolini broke the General Strike led by socialists that August. The party's co-option of the iconography of the classical Roman fasces evoked for Aldington the "lictors" or guardians of the rulers, who are depicted in *Fool i' the Forest* as policemen, guardians of the leisured middle class.

In the next movement of *Fool i' the Forest*, Aldington's "I" clambers "back from Hell." But the return of the self is not accompanied by the recovery of form:

> I saw that Hell is the consequence of the hellish mind
> And that anyone who will risk his life
> Can escape from Hell.
> It is useless to denounce the hellish mind
> And no one yet has quite explained it.
> Moreover, Hell is sometimes useful.
> If only to reveal its opposite.
> If Hell disappeared we might disappear with it.
> Perhaps Hell is the only reality
> And we are its parasites?[56]

The lines are typical of what MacGreevy identified as "the quality that was to mark [Aldington's] verse more and more during the years that followed [the war], absolutely direct statement devoid of every kind of poetic 'trimming.' It was furious verse, at times becoming too personal, at times not personal enough."[57]

MacGreevy's judgment is a gentler version of Eliot's admonition in his introduction to Pound's *Selected Poems* (1928): "One cannot write poetry all the time; and when one cannot write poetry, it is better to write what one knows is verse and make it good verse, than to write bad verse and persuade oneself that it is good poetry."[58] Eliot goes on to say, "Whitman was a great prose writer."[59] But Whitman's "originality" (by which Eliot meant "development" within a tradition) was "spurious in so far as Whitman wrote in a way that asserted that his great prose was a new form of verse."[60]

In the same essay, Eliot identifies contemporary free verse as developing from three points of origin: "my own type of verse, that of Pound, and that of the disciples of Whitman."[61] He dismisses Whitman for many of the same reasons that Yeats does, writing, "I did not read Whitman until much later in life, and had to conquer an aversion to his form, as well as to much of his matter, in order to do so." (He is "equally certain—it is indeed obvious—that Pound owes nothing to Whitman."[62]) It was probably a draft of this essay that T. Sturge Moore heard and mentioned in a letter he sent to Yeats in Rapallo on March 1, 1929, shortly after Aldington had left town: "I heard T.S. Eliot compare Tennyson and Whitman this afternoon. Very acute and quite sound as far as he went, but he evidently does not appreciate good Tennyson more than bad."[63]

Did Pound show Yeats Aldington's *A Fool i' the Forest*? The only book by Aldington that survives in the Yeats library is a presentation copy of *Images, 1910–1915*, which is inscribed simply "To W.B. Yeats from R.A."[64] The title of that book proclaims Aldington's role in the Imagist movement, which he had initiated along with Pound, H.D., and F.S. Flint, urging poets to escape the confines of meter and to base their compositions on musical phrasing. This "Natural 'rhythm'" was deemed to be superior to "codified 'metre.'"[65] Imagism developed from the symbolist movement (which was important to Yeats's development), but Imagism was antithetical to Yeats's poetic mode, as illustrated in "Sailing to Byzantium"—a poem with close ties to Rapallo, since it was published in Pound's magazine *The Exile* in spring 1928. In "Sailing to Byzantium," the poet anticipates taking his place in "the artifice of eternity": "Once out of nature I shall never take / My bodily form from any natural thing, / But such a form as Grecian goldsmiths make /

Of hammered gold and gold enamelling." The regularity of the iambic pentameter stumbles briefly at the word "bodily" where one syllable has to be shed in order to keep the meter perfect; this imitates the casting-off of the physical body with which the poem is concerned, enacting the rejection of the "natural."

Aldington's rebellion against lyric form is only partially related to his involvement with Imagism. During the First World War, questions of poetic form were politicized. Discipline in form was perceived to be reflective of physical and mental discipline; Rupert Brooke's "The Soldier," a Shakespearean sonnet in iambic pentameter, epitomized patriotic verse, while as Raphael Inglebien shows, "free verse was the territory of idlers, deserters or potential traitors."[66] Breaking form often also meant breaking rank in wartime Britain.

For Yeats, the ordering power of meter was both technical and metaphysical; in *A Packet for Ezra Pound*, he reflected on Pound's "praise of writers pursued by ill-luck, left maimed or bed-ridden by the War .... Was this pity a characteristic of his generation that has survived the Romantic Movement...some drop of hysteria still at the bottom of the cup?"[67] Unbridled emotion—the same "hysteria" that is condemned in Yeats's poem "Parnell's Funeral"—had to be governed in the crafting of poetry, and by attaining the right structure, the poem gained power that elevated it beyond the individual's experience. For Yeats, Whitman—along with the other "shell-shocked" poets—was too raw. But for Pound, Whitman's free verse was associated with a patriotic idea.

In "What I feel about Walt Whitman" from 1909, Pound went so far as to say, "He *is* America. His crudity is an exceeding great stench, but it *is* America."[68] Pound admitted that he "might be very glad to conceal my relationship to my spiritual father and brag about my more congenial ancestry—Dante, Shakespeare, Theocritus, Villon, but the descent is a bit difficult to establish. Whitman is to my fatherland [...] what Dante is to Italy." Even so, Pound negatively compared Whitman to Villon in *The Spirit of Romance* (1910), where he explains that Whitman's fault is static self-obsession:

> Villon never forgets his fascinating, revolting self. If, however, he sings the song of himself he is, thank God, free from that horrible air of rectitude with which Whitman rejoices in being Whitman. Villon's song is selfish through self-absorption; he does not, as Whitman, pretend to be conferring a philanthropic benefit on the race by recording his own self-complacency.[69]

Pound follows this assertion with a parody of "Song of Myself" in which Whitman's democratizing atom is replaced by the stereotypically American—and in Pound's hands, racist—image of the watermelon:

> Lo, behold, I eat water melons. When I eat water melons
>   The world eats water melons through me.
> When the world eats water melons,
> I partake of the world's water melons.
> The bugs,
> The worms,
> The negroes, etc.,
> Eat water melons.
> All nature eats water melons.
> Those eidolons and particles of the Cosmos
> Which do not now partake of water melons
> Will at some future time partake of water melons.
> Praised be Allah![70]

Almost two decades later, Pound was still sharpening his wit against Whitman. Writing from Rapallo in 1928, he queried Zukofksy's conjugation of "frero" in "Poem Beginning 'The'," suggesting that Zukofsky might have meant "hermano / fratello, frate / (I forget the portugoose of it) / or perhaps Whitmanian, like Comerado."[71] Zukofsky, probably remembering *The Spirit of Romance*, admitted: "frero—Whitmanian, I am afraid." Nonetheless, Zukovsky changed "frero" (which loosely translates as "bro") to "frate" (brother) when the poem was published in the third issue of *The Exile* (alongside Yeats's "Sailing to Byzantium") in spring 1928.[72]

Zukofsky, almost always eager to appease Pound, was apologetic; Aldington, who felt himself more Pound's equal, was unrepentant in his admiration of Whitman. He later wrote that *Specimen Days in America*, Whitman's collage of diary entries and essays focusing on the Civil War, "made an unforgettable impression" on him as a university student, and when he later "re-read [the poems in] *Drum Taps*" he had "a totally different viewpoint. Up till then, the killings, the maimings, the sufferings and miseries of war had been as unreal and conventional to me as the murders in a detective story. Whitman made me see the reality; and I believe he has the honour of being the only poet of the 19th century to tell the truth about war."[73]

Who ate Pound's heart?

In addition to writing *Death of a Hero* in Rapallo, Aldington was working on his translation of Boccaccio (begun while he was visiting D.H. Lawrence at Port Cros) as well as a separate retelling of one of the tales in the *Decameron*, which he would publish as the long poem *The Eaten Heart* with Nancy Cunard's Hours Press later in 1929.[74] Pound remarked on the visit: "Aldington here, doing new (unnecessary) translation of Decameron for that ass [Pascal] Covici."[75] Pound had been the first person in the Rapallo group to write about the legend of the eaten heart, discussing it briefly in his chapter on Provence in *The Spirit of Romance*. There, he gives a free-verse translation of a song of the troubadour poet Sordello, who appears in the sixth canto of Dante's *Purgatorio*. Sordello mourns the death of his friend Lord Blacatz and grotesquely advises all other rulers to eat of Blacatz's heart, so "the Barons who live un-hearted, for then would they have hearts worth something."[76]

Pound returned to the legend of the eaten heart in Canto IV, published in *A Draft of XVI Cantos* in 1925, after W.B. and George Yeats's visit with the Pounds in Sicily. In the canto, the incident is presented briefly as an association from a story from Ovid, which also deals with a revenge-killing: Philomela's murder of her son, Itys, whose heart she serves to her husband, Tereus, in revenge for Tereus's rape of Philomela's sister, Procne.[77] Scholars have noted that the accusative form of Itys's name, Ityn, sounds like "eaten," a homonym that precipitates Pound's segue to the Provençal story.[78]

> [...] Ityn, Iyn!
> And she went toward the window and cast her down,
> All the while, the while, swallows crying: Ityn!
> 'It is Cabestan's heart in the dish.'[79]

Aldington, like Pound, read medieval French, but the prose summary that prefaces *The Eaten Heart* suggests Pound as Aldington's source, especially as the story is presented in Canto IV.[80]

Aldington describes the characters in the legend as Guilhem de Cabestanh, "a knight and troubadour" and the lover of Margarida, who is married to Count Raimon. In Aldington's translation of the *Decameron* (1930), the characters are named Messer Guiglielmo Guardastagno (the lover) and Messer Guiglielmo Rossiglione (the husband), "two noble knights of Provence." Margarida goes unnamed in Aldington's *Decameron*, where she is described only as a "lady" and Rossiglione's "wife."[81] By giving his two male characters the same forename, Aldington creates a kind of doubling, similar to the plurality of the self that he explored in his *Fool*.

The geography of Aldington's *Decameron* is vague; the knights are simply Provençal, and the dead lovers are buried "in the church of the lady's own castle." However, in *The Eaten Heart*, the location is Roussillon, and Guilhem and Margarida are "buried together in the church of Saint John in Perpignan."[82] The specific geography of Provence was important to Pound's studies of the troubadours, so the precision of people and places in Aldington's *Eaten Heart* further indicates that Pound was a mediator for the tale and suggests that the poets may have discussed the legend during Aldington's visit to Rapallo.

In Aldington's preface, Count Raimon slays Guilhem de Cabestanh and has Cabestanh's heart prepared as a delicious dish, which Raimon serves to Margarida. When she realizes what she has done, Margarida declares (in Aldington's words), "That which you gave to me to eat was so good that no other food or drink shall ever pass my lips," and she throws herself out of the window to her death. In this retelling, the King of Aragon then summons "all good knights and lovers and troubadours" to make war on the murdering husband, who has his lands seized and is cast into prison. Aldington adds a qualifying final paragraph: "scholars will tell you that this could not have happened [....] But these things are as they may be."[83]

Aldington's *The Eaten Heart* is a counter to Yeats's wry aside about the "shell-shocked" generation at the Rapallo dinner party the previous year, which would be elaborated in his critique of the war poets in his edition of the *Oxford Book of Modern Verse* (1936).[84] Aldington answers Yeats in two important ways: by explicitly rejecting the idea that the First World War is to blame for all that is wrong with European civilization, and by exploring tragedy as an ennobling idea (in contrast to the passivity that dominates *Death of a Hero* and *A Fool i' the Forest*). Although Aldington avoids addressing the question of "undisciplined" lyric form, his explicit use of the Provençal myth as a structuring metaphor provides cohesion. The legend, as Aldington reinterprets it in the poem, is a means for him to move beyond Whitmanian "self-complacency" (as Pound had it) into tradition as Eliot and Yeats understood it.

The Eaten Heart opens with Aldington's assertion of a collective "we" that is wholly subject to external forces, and this carries with it the melancholy mood that dominated *A Fool i' the Forest*:

> Under the reign of Mr Bloom[85]
> When the loud machines beat on our minds,
> We, that are children of despair,
> Who see or think we see so clearly
> How all hope's vain, all effort null;
> We that tremble between two worlds,
> Half-regretting the old dead Europe
> Crumbling and melancholy as a deserted palace
> When the last king of the line has long been dead,
> Frightened yet moulded by the cold hard patterns
> Beaten upon life by the loud machines—
> What do we know of love?

The lines that follow express disgust with the baseness of physical desire and assert, in response to the legend of the eaten heart, "the tragedy of thwarted sexual desire is nothing, / The true tragedy is that of inner loneliness."[86]

At first, it appears that *The Eaten Heart* will linger in a passive mood, but there is a sudden shift when Aldington describes the destruction of the old order in positive terms: "We were right, yes, we were right / To smash the false idealities of the last age."[87] While "We were right to question and to destroy," having "faced the facts" that the previous generation would not face, Aldington asks, "I wonder if we have not rejected too much, / If we have not hardened ourselves too much, / Making it impossible to break out of our self-prisons[?]"[88] He goes further, admonishing, "Of course, you can say it is the War / But you cannot put everything down to the War / Nor to the machines either. / We have mistaken the problem, overlooked the tragedy."[89] Rather than succumb to melancholy, Aldington radically reinterprets the idea of tragedy for his generation through an innovative recourse to myth: "Then I remembered the old Provence tale of the Eaten Heart."[90]

In "the last variety of this tragedy," Aldington uses terms that evoke Yeats's dialectical poetics: the tale

> [...] has the savage desire which can only grasp or kill
> And the other love which is the complete exchange of two natures,
> And in the dreadful symbol of the eaten heart
> It shows perhaps how a woman devours a man's life,
> But it also shows how the man's gift of himself is total,
> And the manner of her death shows how her response is total.[91]

In Aldington's poem, the "total" response of man and woman does not produce the transcendence that brings about completion as it does in Yeats's poetic; interference from the "brutality of the world of men / (Who always envy the happiness of others" prevents perfect communion.[92]

Love is not mystical for Aldington as it is for Yeats, and this marks an important difference in the way that each poet uses the legend. For the troubadours, whom Aldington invokes with his description of *The Eaten Heart* as a "Provençal tale," courtly love (the love between a worthy man, usually a knight, and an unobtainable woman) does not enable lovers to commune with the divine.[93] Aldington stakes this position at the beginning of *The Eaten Heart* where "A man or woman might die for love / And be glad in dying; / But who would die for sex? [....] Better turn monk / And keep your sperm for God / And hard despair. / Will you die for a blind hot instinct, / [....] Two breasts and a curled slit?"[94] Sex and love—including courtly love—*were* mystical for the Neo-Platonists, on whom Yeats bases so much of his philosophy. Love and its physical consummation could liberate the soul from the materiality of the world and allow communion with the source of all beauty.[95] George Yeats also shared this view, telling her cousin Grace Jaffe, in 1954, "You know Grace, that all human love is a reflection of Divine Love."[96]

The legend of the eaten heart reappears in Yeats's poem "Parnell's Funeral," where it is used as a metaphor for political power, divorced from love or sexual desire. Two early commentators, Peter Ure and F.A.C. Wilson, observe Yeats's indebtedness to *The Spirit of Romance*.[97] Pound's translation of Sordello's enumeration of various lords has the same pattern as Yeats's condemnation of Ireland's contemporary political leaders: "Had de Valera eaten Parnell's heart / No loose lipped demagogue had won the day, / No civil rancour torn the land apart. // Had Cosgrave eaten Parnell's heart, the land's / Imagination had been satisfied [....] // Had even O'Duffy—but I name no more—"[98]

To see Sordello in "Parnell's Funeral" is to look at the poem in its final version. "Parnell's Funeral" as we now read it began as two poems. The first movement was published as "A Parnellite at Parnell's Funeral" in *The King of the Great Clock Tower: Commentaries and Poems* (1934), where it ends with the couplet, "To this bare soul, let all men judge that can / Whether it be an animal or a man."[99] The three stanzas of the second movement were published in *The Spectator* on October 19, 1934 under the title "Forty Years Later," and the two poems were brought together as a single work in *A Full Moon in March* (1935).[100] Reading the imagery of the first and second parts of the poem against each other, Ure suggests that "at some stage in the composition of the two poems [...] Yeats refreshed his memory of the more arcane meanings of his dominant image by looking up the Pound version of Sordello in *The Spirit of Romance*."[101] In that book, just a few lines before Sordello appears, Pound refers to Yeats by name, which may have provided an impetus for Yeats to look again. Pound writes, "Mr Yeats gives me to understand that there comes in the career of a great poet, a certain time when he ceases to take pleasure in riming 'mountain' with 'fountain' and 'beauty' with 'duty.'"[102]

Drafts of "Parnell's Funeral" suggest that Aldington's *The Eaten Heart* also influenced Yeats's poem, but these inflections were edited out as the poem evolved. Yeats's earliest work on the first part of "Parnell's Funeral" interprets the poem's events as a "tragedy," evoking Aldington's gloss of the legend. Yeats ultimately rejected the lines, "Exit comedy; tragedy walks the stage," but he kept the metaphor of the theater as public arena, substituting "tragedy" for its opposite; the final version of "Parnell's Funeral" begins, "Under the Great Comedian's tomb."[103]

The image of the hunt also connects Aldington's and Yeats's poems. In the seventh movement of Aldington's *The Eaten Heart*, a prayer to the gods—and to the moon—pleads for salvation from "those // Hot hounds of disaster / Swift steel of despair / Launch at us freely // Grant us clean shrift O gods / Pity us never."[104] In the final version of "Parnell's Funeral," the image is reduced to half of a line, "*Hysterica passio*, dragged this quarry down," but Yeats explored it at length in drafts for the third stanza:

> We are the hounds   We have pursued the deer
> We ber bury our teeth in side of flesh [....]
> We hunting when the stranger tarred us on
> To kill the we had brothers And tarred on about our rage [....]
> The whole pack shudders in its [?woeful] blood[105]

Writing about Aldington's *The Eaten Heart*, Victoria Whelpton has commented on its "distinctive form of address," which, while appearing to be in the first person, "actually situates the addressee as *subject* of the poem."[106] She argues that through a clever, second-person form of narration, Aldington can write about "spiritual hunger and distress without the note of self-pity."[107] In "Parnell's Funeral," Yeats similarly labored to purge emotion, in his case not self-pity but "bitterness"—the emotion that overwhelmed him during the illness that sent him to Rapallo in the first place. In drafts of the first stanza of "Parnell's Funeral," the poet stands among the hounds baying for the leader's blood: "We drove him to his death. We [?killed him] ourselves. / Henceforth a bitter people / That is why we have become a bitter people."¹⁰⁸ On the page where these lines appear, the word bitter or bitterness occurs six times. Similar to the poems of the *Winding Stair* (1929), which occupied Yeats during his first season in Rapallo, drafts of "Parnell's Funeral" show how he remade negative emotion into a positive aesthetics, opposed to his idea about the reactive poetry of the "shell-shocked Walt Whitmans."

The Problem with "War Poetry"

In *Life for Life's Sake*, Aldington meditates on his state of mind during and after the First World War. The memoir was published in 1941, by which time, he wrote, the Great War "no longer haunts me against my will, as it did for years [....] Certain smells, sounds, and sights are the battering rams which suddenly demolish the wall and let the memories escape."¹⁰⁹ Immediately following the armistice, he had "slept badly, was subject to meaningless but unpleasant moods of depression, and was in a frenzy of impatience to get out of the army."¹¹⁰ He thought that his "mind had deteriorated," since he struggled to concentrate "on mental work." It was a state, he generalized, that "was not uncommon with men who had been in the war a long time."¹¹¹ The experience of war and the incommunicability of it was the making of the lifelong friendship between Aldington and Thomas MacGreevy, whom Aldington describes as "five hundred per cent Irish" and who, as an officer in the British Expeditionary Force in France, was "well disposed towards my little efforts at reviving common memories."¹¹²

Although they had moved in similar orbits in London and Paris, Aldington and MacGreevy had never met; they barely missed each other again in Rapallo in the winter of 1928-29. Even so, it was Rapallo that finally brought them together (Figure 2.2). MacGreevy visited the Yeats family at Christmastime 1928 and stayed with them in their apartment until the new year, when W.B. and George traveled to Rome for a short holiday, when WBY fell ill again.¹¹³ MacGreevy was eager not to impose on the Yeats family, but George assured him that she had arranged a "daily," so as long as he was content to eat "eggs for our supper" on Christmas afternoon, when "the 'helps' will like to be off duty," he would be most welcome.¹¹⁴

Figure 2.2 Brigit Patmore with Tom MacGreevy, probably taken by Aldington
Source: Richard Aldington Literary File, Harry Ransom Center, The University of Texas at Austin.

Much to WBY's disparagement, while MacGreevy was visiting Rapallo, he "made great friends with Ezra."[115] Yeats grumbled in a letter to Lady Gregory, "I thought him [MacGreevy] solider & richer in all his thought."[116] On MacGreevy's return to Paris, he reflected in a letter to George on the effect that meeting Pound had on him:

> I've had lots to think about as a result of my visit to you. It was terribly worth while to me and, needless to say, enjoyable as well. Needless to say I am upset as a result of it too. I want to be "nothing so much as" a starving poet and am making all sorts of secret plans with a view to achieving that ambition [....] There is no one at the moment only Ezra—my latest hare. But if I had done nothing at Rapallo but get hold of your copies of the cantos it would have been worth the voyage. I also wrote to Geoffrey [Phibbs Taylor] and told him it was his urgent business to read them [....][117]

He concludes, "cordial remembrances and respects to the Pounds. I'll write to Ezra when I have seen his friends."[118] These "friends" almost certainly were Aldington and Patmore, who were due to visit Rapallo in a few weeks. In the essay "Richard Aldington As Friend," MacGreevy writes that it "was probably 1928" that they met, but 1929 seems to be a more correct dating, since his correspondence with Aldington begins with conversations about the sales of *Death of a Hero* and the progress of Aldington's next novel, *The Colonel's Daughter*.[119] In MacGreevy's and Aldington's recollections, they give different settings for their first encounter; Aldington puts it in a Parisian café, while MacGreevy lends their friendship an even stronger modernist genealogy, citing its beginning in the hospitable surrounds of James Joyce's apartment.[120] MacGreevy's probable infelicity is more than a simple matter of establishing literary credentials; it gestures to his sense that Joyce and Aldington were the novelists he aspired to be. Under Aldington's tutelage, he worked on at least one semi-autobiographical novel, the drafts of which bear a strong resemblance to both *The Death of a Hero* and *Portrait of the Artist as a Young Man*.[121] MacGreevy's novel was never published—or finished for that matter—despite no shortage of words: Aldington reported to Patmore that MacGreevy was "doing 3000 words a day [....] I keep warning him not to be literary—and yesterday he casually remarked that he refers to chateaubriand on [the] first page! Query: Can a professor leave his vomit?"[122]

The professor could, given the right medium—but fiction wasn't it. A schema laid out in an early draft of a novel shows MacGreevy attempting to map his protagonist's struggle along the lines of the aborted ambitions of the Irish state: "He gives himself to no woman—personal repression / Irish repression [...] He leaves at the end & goes over to foreign life / Does not work out life from within himself / Ireland similarly goes over to English ideas after shaking off England in one way. Free State is not Irish life worked out from within [...]"[123] MacGreevy planned a novel in two parts, the first dealing with "return of hero to Ireland & his home after war" and the second from "Dublin up to Armistice" through the Civil War, "church domination" and ending with "Home Departure."[124] The most successfully written passages strongly evoke Aldington's *Death of a Hero*.[125] There is also a compelling preface in which the narrator gives his appraisal of the "hero" (here, Jack Madden), which explains Jack's various romantic entanglements in terms nearly identical to Aldington's: "The balance of things between the sexes went wrong for our generation." The narrator blames Jack's failure on the state and social structures that are estranged from the people they are intended to serve: "Ireland broke him in the end as England broke him in the beginning. Official Ireland and official England, that is."[126]

Seven drafts of what was probably intended to be a different novel show MacGreevy fighting his tendencies as an essayist, philosopher, and poet, failing to bring the idea of the novel, its characterization and emotional affect together in a way necessary for good fiction. But MacGreevy excels in his writing about the war directly, although he can only sustain this for short bursts. Most of the short story "Tor Emma" (originally titled "Trench Warfare") deals with the soldiers' seemingly interminable waiting at the front and the awful bureaucratic machinations regarding who would be detailed to the trench mortars. The dialogue is stilted, but one scene is exceptionally vivid: "The drone went on steadily overhead, the searchlights played beautifully through the night, the anti-aircraft guns went off with a swanking vindictive crack and occasionally one saw a burst of shrapnel amidst the searchlights but bomb after bomb came crashing down."[127]

MacGreevy's difficulty in constructing a convincing prose narrative of the war seems less a problem of mastering mechanics than of psychological repression. In order to assimilate into Irish life, especially Catholic Irish society, soldiers had to suppress their service in the British Army, part of a general cultural amnesia about Ireland's involvement in the imperial war.[128] MacGreevy's problem was not just that he had joined up; the problem of his voluntary enlistment was compounded by his feeling that the war was necessary, desirable, and even imaginatively productive. In one fragment of a draft, MacGreevy's narrator reflects on his military service: "now he wouldn't if he could be without those very occasional hours of anguished agonised suspense which had come his way when one was imaginately imaginatively at least as good as killed dead dead killed."[129] (His vacillation over "killed" (active) and "dead" (passive) is unresolved, or perhaps left as an inversion of the vernacular emphatic "killed dead.") MacGreevy thought that the war was essential to knowing, although "it was hard to say [knowing] what." His narrator is certain that "being of the generation that one was one could not afford to be ignorant of its major experiences."[130]

MacGreevy's poetry shows a strong influence of Aldington and the Imagists, but he also learned about poetry from George Yeats, an astute critic whose sensibilities were more "modern" than her husband's.[131] She read several drafts of a long poem (probably "Crón Tráth na nDeíthe") and replied, "I still feel that each variation is its own theme and the main theme is built up out of all the variations instead of vice versa. WB. of course thought it too modern, too difficult, too Ezraic, and was intolerant of it because it hadnt the tightness of Red Hugh."[132] While George could mediate, to an extent, between her husband and her friend, the nearly thirty years' difference was at times unresolvable. Through MacGreevy, George grew closer to Aldington and Patmore; in November 1930, Aldington wrote to MacGreevy, "We were sorry indeed to miss George Yeats—she's a good soul, and I'd greatly have liked to see her. Remember me fondly to her if you write, and add dittos from Brigit."[133]

"Winter," MacGreevy's poem dedicated to Richard Aldington, evokes Yeats's "The Wild Swans at Coole," which was written at Coole Park in the midst of the First World War—a wider context that is entirely absent from Yeats's pastoral autumnal scene. In MacGreevy's verse, "The swans on the leaden coloured water / Look like hostile ghosts / Of kings / Who resent our presence." Where Yeats's poem meditates on the passage of time and in the penultimate line posits death as an awakening, MacGreevy's poem rejects aestheticizing death, asking baldly, "Are they not right? / How should we / Whose hearts are with the dead / Come here / And not die?" The raw emotion and free verse illustrate what Yeats thought was the problem with "war poetry": its lack of restraint.

As Yeats explained in his introduction to *The Oxford Book of Modern Verse* (1936), "This loss of self-control, common among uneducated revolutionists is rare—Shelley had it in some degree—among men of Ezra Pound's culture and erudition. Style and its opposite can alternate, but form must be full, sphere-like, single."[134] For Yeats, total form cannot be reactive; it cannot have edges that bind it to a temporality:

> If war is necessary, or necessary in our time and place, it is best to forget its suffering as we do the discomfort of fever, remembering our comfort at midnight when our temperature fell, or as we forget the worst moments of a painful disease [....] Ten years after the war certain poets combined the modern vocabulary, the accurate record of the relevant facts learnt from Eliot, with the sense of suffering of the war poets, that sense of suffering no longer passive, no longer an obsession of the nerves; philosophy had made it part of all the mind.[135]

As a concession to popular expectations that an anthology should include poetry from the Great War, Yeats includes Herbert Read's "End of a War." Read's preface binds his poem tightly to a very specific time and place, but his afterword explains his intention "to present the universal aspects of a particular event. Judgement may follow, but should never precede or become embroiled with the act of poetry."[136] Ultimately, Read's framing is in keeping with Yeats's ideas about what poetry should and should not do.

Yeats praises Hemingway's *A Farewell to Arms* in his introduction to the *Oxford Book of Modern Verse* because, he writes, Hemingway had created a character who was "a mirror," but "When man has withdrawn into the quicksilver at the back of the mirror no great event becomes luminous in his mind."[137] Yeats believed that the retreat into self-absorption, however much it may be justified by the pain of immediate experience, could not produce writing that reflects outward; this outward reflection was necessary to complete the "sphere-like" form that was Yeats's ideal. He believed, "Generations must pass before man recovers control of event and circumstance." For that reason, MacGreevy's poem "Aodh Ruadh O Domhnail" about the sixteenth-century folk hero was suitable for inclusion in Yeats's anthology; this is the poem "Red Hugh" whose "tightness" George Yeats remarked on in her letter to MacGreevy. MacGreevy's "Homage to Jack Yeats" was also appropriate for the book, since the image of the tower in the poem is a conduit for questioning heroic myths. Aldington—known to Yeats for his Imagism, his association with Pound, and his writing about the war—was omitted from the anthology. Yeats included writers generally thought of as "war poets," but the specific poems he chose for the *Oxford Book of Modern Verse* didn't reflect the work for which they were best known: there is one poem by Rupert Brooke, "Clouds," and—remarkably—four poems by Siegfried Sassoon, a substantial presence that may be owing to Sassoon's visit to Rapallo.[138]

Sassoon and his lover, Stephen Tennant, met W.B. and George Yeats in the autumn of 1929, when they stopped in Rapallo to see Sassoon's friend Max Beerbohm.[139] After the visit, George wrote a gossipy letter to Lennox Robinson: "Damn all the rich young men prancing round the world beautifully existing remote from a gross world by money & money & money."[140] Tennant had left a lingering impression:

> so very tall, incredibly slim, with that pale delicate Ninetyish complexion, large sad hazel eyes surrounded by the long dark up-turned eyelashes that so admirably match blond cendrée hair with a deep wave in it from brow to nape of neck—long and small boned hands ending in marvellously polished pointed nails issue from 3 inches of beige silk cuffs (no turn-back; one large, individual, button) which in their turn emerge from brown suiting. But I didnt care for his taste in scent. He had just spent a week in Paris and had I am afraid been misled by one of these new Parisian

Perfumes which disdain association with any flower—'La Songe' 'Rêve d'amour' 'Pour troubler' and how it troubled the flat!

She wrote more charitably about Sassoon: "the same as ever, as nice as always, full of very incoherent conversation and nerves." Just over a year earlier, in July 1928, Sassoon had published *The Heart's Journey*, but it seems probable that the Yeatses didn't acquire a copy until 1935, when WBY was preparing the *Oxford Book of Modern Verse*.[141] On the inside cover of the copy that now rests in the Yeats Library, Yeats made notes on possible poems for inclusion in the Oxford edition, eventually settling on "When I'm alone," "Grandeur of Ghosts," "The Power and the Glory," and, remarkably, "On Passing the New Menin Gate," about the memorial to the Commonwealth soldiers killed at Ypres:

> Who will remember, passing through this Gate,
> The unheroic Dead who fed the guns?
> Who shall absolve the foulness of their fate, —
> Those doomed, conscripted, unvictorious ones?
> [....]
> Well might the Dead who struggled in the slime
> Rise and deride this sepulchre of crime.[142]

Yeats's avowed "distaste for certain poems written in the midst of the great war" did not extend to an emotional response to the war's *memorial*, even when written by Sassoon who had been hospitalized for actual "shell-shock." Yeats's selection of "On Passing the New Menin Gate" for his anthology seems to be justified by the ten years that separated the end of war and the poem's composition. But that explanation is only partially satisfactory, since the poem's acerbic tone seems hardly less immediate. The structure of the New Menin Gate seems to be the key to understanding Yeats's decision; unveiled in July 1927, the monument mediates between the suffering that Sassoon experienced first-hand and the generalized suffering of war. The materiality of the gate enables its universality, circumventing the "passive suffering [that Yeats believed] is not a theme for poetry."[143] The idea that a monument, museum, or other material object had the power to convey a metaphysical idea is a powerful stream in Yeats's thought from the mid-1930s, when he was also writing about the need for museums filled with objects to bring to life the grandeur of the eighteenth-century Irish past.[144]

In a reminiscence published a quarter of a century after W.B. Yeats's death, MacGreevy recalled "a night in Merrion Square when A.E. rambled on for a while in praise of Walt Whitman. Yeats remained silent and then suddenly cut in with oracular finality, 'No, Russell! No!' he said firmly, 'Whitman is one of the errors of our youth.'"[145] Decades later, Aldington arrived at a similar conclusion. In *Life for Life's Sake*, he admitted that *Death of a Hero*, and by implication his other work from the same period, was full of "passion and indignation," feelings that he had to work "out of my system," purging "stuff which had been poisoning me for a decade."[146]

During the First World War, Aldington had written to D.H. Lawrence, "There are two kinds of men, those who have been to the front and those who haven't"; reflecting on this, he surmises in his memoir, "That was true then, and after the war also. And there seemed no way at first of bridging the gap."[147] In MacGreevy's book about Aldington, he put it a little differently: "If you have been placed suddenly on the other side of the grave and left there for months and years, you do not forget it. And you do not forget those you left there when you came back. Sometimes you bring back not only a darkened spirit but a maimed body from there, and that reminds you."[148] Yeats, having no experience of war, believed that the disordered mind produced disordered poetry: unstructured language that was inward looking, lacking the form that was necessary to ameliorate the poet's experience, transform it into tragedy (or comedy) and turn outward, incorporating but not restricting itself to a particular temporal context. Yeats's skill in revising his poems transmutes raw, timebound emotions—like bitterness— and in the process disguises the extent to which the outward turn in his poetry is a late modernist attention to social and political contexts. The outward turn can be more clearly discerned in Yeats's essays for *Dublin Magazine* and other periodicals, a genre that was the basis for extensive collaboration between the Rapallo poets.

Figure 3.1 Postcard from Basil Bunting to Louis Zukofsky
Source: Zukofsky Collection, Harry Ransom Center, The University of Texas at Austin.

3
Primavera 1928

"wot are the signs of spring?" Ezra Pound wrote to Richard Aldington in November 1926 about the beginning of the magazine that would become *The Exile*:

> The idea, and curiously enough, the possibility, of having .... on my own, uninterrupted with outer interference, a review, has arose. (groans) I shd. Not compete or attempt to compete with the elder British Reviews; but I shd. not exclude Island authors if there are any. (I mean if there are any who haven't like Mssrs. Lewis and Eliot, reviews of their own wherein to cut their caper.)[1]

Pound wondered if he should invite one of Rapallo's Nobel laureates to contribute: "Hauptmann, whose enormous bald head I refrain from spitting on every morning as he perambulates under our terazza? It is a bee-yew-teeful target. But so long since I have read any of his opusculacchia."[2] But it was Yeats's verse that featured in the "Primavera" issue of *The Exile*, which—when it was coming together in early 1928—brought a sense of elation to Pound, who felt he was entering his own season of spring. He wrote to Aldington, "it seems that I lengthened my life by ten years when I went to Paris, and I added another ten moving here, if not to the length at least I deducted it from the feeling of age at the moment."[3]

It's surprising that Pound's first attempt at his own review came as late as 1927, since as Eric Bulson has summarized, little magazines established "modern critical standards," and attempting to shape those standards was a major part of Pound's life's work.[4] *How* to shape them was the most pressing question for Pound: to his mind, good criticism could not be didactic, even when it needed to be polemical. This was a trait that Pound admired in Adrian Stokes's art criticism; in his copy of Stokes's *Stones of Rimini* (1934), he marked Stokes's lines "The writer is a fool (no poet) who formulates a definition when his whole book is intended as such."[5] Later, Pound advised the English poet Ronald Duncan—who was in the midst of planning his own little magazine, *Townsman* (1938–45)—that the editor should aim for "Indirect criticism[:] talking mostly erbaht somfink ELSE so as to open the alledged mind of reader to supposed subject of the critical discourse."[6] This is precisely what Pound achieves in the opening chapters of *ABC of Reading* (1934), where he indirectly situates himself as an expert in poetry by analogizing the poet-critic's role with the jobs of art critics, philosophers, historians, and more mundane expertise: "No one would be foolish enough to ask me to pick out a horse or even an automobile for him."[7] It was also essential, as Pound told the editors of the little magazine *Contempo*, that an editor "define a program" if a magazine were to be relevant; there was no point in going to print if the contents "don't carry enough weight for anyone to answer anyone else in it."[8] In *Contempo*'s case, he thought the magazine should "edderkate the [U.S.] south."[9]

Pound's first magazine project in Rapallo, *The Exile* (which lasted for just four numbers from 1927 to 1928) was important to the development of his ideas about the role of the critic in civic life; these ideas were advanced in his editorship of the literary supplement to Rapallo's newspaper, *Il Mare* (1932–3). The publication of *Il Mare*'s supplement coincided with the tenth year of the Fascist regime and grew out of Pound's contributions to the Genoa-based *L'Indice*, edited by Gino Saviotti with whom Pound partnered on *Il Mare*.[10] While Pound's writing for *L'Indice* was not party-political, it is notably politicized in terms of marking Pound's shift of focus from the United States onto Italy.[11] Moody suggests in his biography that Pound was "trying to do for Italian literature what he had tried to do for America in his London years," and in the process he "was establishing sympathetic relations" with the Fascist state.[12] Both *The Exile* and *Il Mare*'s literary supplement actively engaged with the idea of a masculine public sphere in which periodical culture played a mobilizing part. Pound, Bunting, and Zukofsky's collaborations on both of these periodicals shaped their ideas about forms of what Pound described as "indirect criticism." This included their ideas about the anthology as a medium, which—through its professed aims and the arrangement of its contents—manifested the criteria for criticism that the poets articulated in their work for Rapallo's little magazines.

Periodical Pound and His Collaborators

"W.B. just been to tea. Full of Life. Suggests that you should set up (some Bourbon remnant) a strong Royalist Party in U.S.A. and use the correspondence column in Exile for letters (possibly faked) from many big U.S.A. cities backing up Royalist. He quite approved by emendation that the Bourbon had much better be a Japanese," reported Dorothy in an energetic letter to Ezra from London in the spring of 1927.[13] The tone is jocular, but Yeats's temper was being emphatically exercised on Pound's behalf over Wyndham Lewis's attack on Pound in his new magazine *The Enemy*, which launched Lewis's new persona of the "professional antagonist."[14] By attacking his close friend and collaborator, Lewis gave an extreme demonstration of *The Enemy*'s manifesto, "Outside I am freer."[15] *The Enemy* serialized *Time and Western Man*, including what would become Lewis's iconic excoriation of Ezra as a "revolutionary simpleton."[16] In short, he reduced Pound's work to that of a propagandist and "parasite," characterizing Pound as an embodiment of the "crowd" mentality that Lewis set himself against.[17]

Lewis's strike coincided with Pound's new venture, *The Exile*, appearing shortly after the first number was published.[18] Pound took the attack personally, and *The Exile*'s contributors as well as Pound's friends were quick to rally. Dorothy and Ezra exchanged dispatches, Ezra from Rapallo: "Stokes deeply furious over 'Enemy' dare say he will do all replying necessary and unnecessary possibly," and Dorothy from London: "The Enemy seems to have penetrated a good deal: Bunting also inquiring—"[19] She told Ezra that Yeats had "asked seriously re Enemy: and debated whether there ought not to be a stodgy and serious reply."[20] While Ezra was content to wait for the storm to pass, Dorothy was quietly eager to put up a lightning rod or two: "Rodker & WBY (independently!) both wishing to answer Wyndham— Don't know whether they can all do anything—not sure it is worth it? & would single attack, or a (impossible!) joint attack be strongest?"[21] Ezra was steadfast: "I do not think it needs an answer—the real one being rather pathetic (economic)."[22]

Even so, Pound's letter "from the Editor of 'The Exile'" in the June issue of Harriet Monroe's *Poetry* was an answer of sorts.[23] He explained the basis for the magazine's inception, both revolutionary and economic, and attempted to show that he, like Lewis, was an "outsider":

> I do *not* want mss. that any other editor will print. I want mss. which, in a moment of abandon I might say, "other editors are too stupid to print" [....] I also want a place where I can speak freely concerning certain superstitions and idols of the American people which, as Molochs and other superstitious fetiches, are deeply reverenced by many, and are for that all the more hideous. In the main these arise from two roots.

The twin evils were the collapse of public and private spheres in American life and the "tendency in most occidental religions and moral systems" to throw water on a neighbor's campfire when one's own roof was burning down. A casually mentioned possible third problem—and the issue that seems to have *really* preoccupied Pound—was "the lack in America of [...] thinking of anything in relation to any fundamental principle whatsoever; the acceptance of ideas based on forgotten origins," that is, the lack of interaction with tradition. This is the germ of Pound's idea of the dynamic interrelationship of the present and the living past, which he thought was essential to the development of both Yeats's "new man" and a "new civilization."

The dynamism of past and present is modeled in Pound's editorship of periodicals and pedagogical texts from the first number of *The Exile* in 1927 right through the 1930s, up to his dogmatic *Guide to Kulchur* (1937). In his public correspondence, including the letter to *Poetry*, Pound established his status as an outsider to U.S. culture by emphasizing his residence in "Rapallo, Italy."[24] In Pound's case, outsider-status was everything; the economic preconditions—from the price of paper to the price of binding—led to the production of "national" literature outside of the nation's economy, a dynamic that fueled his pontifications on social credit. (Put simply, this is the idea that people who produce goods—not middlemen or "speculators"—should reap the greatest rewards for their work.[25]) In *Pound and Italian Fascism*, Tim Redman argues that "Pound's support for Italian fascism [...] was consistent with and developed from his thought about social and economic issues," especially his reading of C.H. Douglas.[26] Moreover, Pound's attraction to Douglas's theory of social credit was strengthened by the decades that Pound had spent trying and failing to put the writer on a par with craftsmen, farmers, and manufacturers in the nation's esteem—its economic esteem, not merely the lip service it paid to "culture." In the pages of *The Exile*, Pound insisted that editing and writing were trades: "goods" were produced that contributed to the life of the nation, and he aimed through the magazine to demonstrate literature's value in real terms.

Pound's ambition for the elevation of writers and editors in the national economy through a culture that materially supported its artists was part of his impetus for moving to Italy. This was *The Exile*'s prevailing concern throughout its two-year run from 1927 to 1928, and Pound continued to insist on the principle a decade after *The Exile* folded. As early as 1922, he had declared, "democracy has signally failed to provide for its best writers."[27] And in "National Culture: A Manifesto 1938" (unpublished until 1960), Pound argued that the quality of national life was *reliant* on its periodical culture: "There is at the moment no periodical giving even rudimentary information on American thought, let alone correlating that thought with live thought in other countries." He asked,

> Do six dozen or six hundred Americans value "a national culture" sufficiently to conserve it
> A. By correlated reprint of proofs of its earlier existence?
> B. By periodical bulletin of its present products?
> C. By keeping sharp the criteria which would prevent a relapse into the narcissism of the U.S. of the late nineteenth century?[28]

The Exile was Pound's concerted attempt to import "enlightenment" into the United States, but the internationality of *The Exile* was not unidirectional.[29] While the magazine was still in the planning stages, Pound offered a platform to Desmond Fitzgerald, who was Minister for External Affairs in the Irish Free State. Fitzgerald was also a devoted Catholic, and his religiosity would be a strong factor in his advocacy of the Irish Censorship of Publications, as well as in his support for the Blueshirts and what appears to be a sympathy for European fascist movements more broadly.[30] Pound wrote to him:

> You onner stan I am perfectly willing to be strictly UNOFFICIALLY the official voice of the State Govt. sfar as Irish affairs are concerned. I mean I wont take a subsidy or be in any way limited; but if there is anything you want printed that wont be printed in the controlled press; let me hav it.[31]

Fitzgerald and Pound had met through Yeats, and the pair had kept up a sporadic correspondence, even after Pound declined one of Fitzgerald's poems submitted to the *Little Review*. (Margaret Anderson's judgment of the piece was "quite good enough to print" but not "unique" enough.[32]) Pound now thought to flatter Fitzgerald's "august official personage" by suggesting he write for an audience who would pay for his work: "the young intellexhuls aren't going to pay forty bucks for volumes of your proceeding [at the United Nations] [....] Damn it all I WANT contemporary history. Inconvenient facts."[33] Pound clarified:

> It is not necessary that a review, mainly literary shd. print politics or economics. BUT the editorial office ought to KNOW. It ought to be able to

drop on the Daily Mail [...] when that disreputable bunk office [...] tries to put over some really TOO STINKING a swindle.

Fitzgerald demurred. He hadn't the time, and besides, "a small Review is to aim at the quintessential and our politics are particularly hum-drum." But he hoped to subscribe to *The Exile*, could recommend Sean O'Casey and Liam O'Flaherty as new figures in the "limelight," and planned a trip to Rapallo for the following Easter: "When I am really depressed & want to call to mind a really happy vision I think of you in Rapallo writing a little in your room, going out to play tennis, and just absorbing the sun at the sea's edge."[34] Fitzgerald's depiction of Pound in a literary idyll was probably a little irksome, especially since Pound was advocating the centrality of the state's writers to its culture and economy. (His heated exchange with Fitzgerald over the Irish Censorship bill would reveal how Fitzgerald was at risk of becoming the kind of bureaucratic fat-cat that Pound despised.)

Albeit short-lived, *The Exile* is important for its literary as well as its economic arguments. Pound's selection of material was innovative, choosing what Jacqueline Vaught Brogan describes as work that "clearly manifest[s] the new poetic possibilities being realized in cubist poetry or, at the very least, poetry influenced and motivated by the cubist aesthetic revolution."[35] Among poems of this kind she includes Pound's "Part of Canto XXIII" and Zukofsky's "Poem Beginning 'The'"—both of which were published in the "Primavera 1928" issue of *The Exile*—and William Carlos Williams's "The Descent of Winter," published in autumn 1928, the magazine's final number. Developing from Vaught Brogan's reading of individual poems, the entirety of *The Exile* can be read as a "cubist composition" or, to use a related term, a collage, which gave the magazine an identifiably late modernist form.

The Cantos have been described as "the master collage poem of the century" that inspired the collage poetics of later twentieth-century writers, including Ronald Johnson who edited *Townsman*.[36] In Ross Hair's study of Johnson's poetry, he sums up Pound's method in the *Cantos*: "For Pound, collage answers a rhetorical and ideological need, allowing for what appears as the direct presentation of impartial facts."[37] Hair identifies two major "collage principles innovated by Pound: quotation and the ideogrammic method."[38] The latter of these is most relevant to a consideration of Periodical Pound (although he also makes good use of quotation in his magazines) while the former is most apparent in Pedagogical Pound: his works of criticism and anthologies from the early 1930s.[39]

Pound began to use the term "ideogrammic method" around 1927, borrowing the term from his edition of Fenollosa's *The Chinese Written Character as a Medium for Poetry*, where the ideogram, or ideograph, crystallizes a means of collapsing the distance between an image and the meaning or meanings to which the image refers.[40] Building on the idea of how pure meaning might be conveyed through one image, Pound began to think about composite meanings and how the juxtaposition of seemingly unrelated elements could reveal—without limiting—another meaning.[41] In this process, it was imperative that the reader did the work. As Peter Makin summarizes, "there is no explaining discourse: for any such discourse would blur, and at the same time simplify the relations between the blocks, and those relations are the meaning."[42] With regard to the *Cantos*, this meant that the reader was actively involved in the making of the poem.

Pound believed that readers should also be active interpreters of other forms of writing, and this idea extends to his periodical projects. Each issue of *The Exile* can be read as an exercise in collage (to use Ross Hair's term) or cubist composition (as Vaught Brogan describes Pound's method). A reader actively engaged in interpreting the relationship between the contents of *The Exile* and Pound's editorials would see how the magazine advocated the centrality of literature to the civic sphere.

Pound's assemblage of the magazine's contents in relation to his editorial glosses is key to understanding how the magazine works as a collage or cubist composition. His editorials—which are the most overtly political components of *The Exile*—are frequently positioned at the very end of the magazine, which upends the conventional placement of an editorial at the beginning of an issue. This reversal has the effect of leading readers to Pound's most explicit (albeit still oblique) assertion of the magazine's program, and the placement also resists situating the poetry, fiction, and other literary contents in a fixed frame since they are encountered *before* the editorial. In Moody's biography of Pound, he argues for a disjuncture between the "literary" content and the editorials: "his prose blasts, which one would expect to have been directed towards bringing his chosen forces into some particular focus or vortex, were directed instead towards other preoccupations and a distinctly non-literary agenda."[43] Yet the contents of the magazine can be read in another way that shows the unity of Pound's periodical project: in collage, the audience has to interpret the relations between the material and its arrangement in a space. There is not a "disjuncture" between the elements of *The Exile*; there is interpretive room. This act of interpretation is what Pound required of his readers.[44]

The first issue of *The Exile* opened with "Part of Canto XX," followed by a travelogue by Guy Hickok on his recent visit to the United States that detailed the economic depression, cultural stagnation, and bootlegging antics that he observed. A short "Neothoemist Poem" [sic] by Hemingway was placed between Hickok's narrative and the first instalment of John Rodker's novella *Adolphe 1920*. The relationship between these constituent parts, which differ generically as well as in their ostensible topics, can be identified by reading each component closely before going on to think about what Pound described with regard to the *Cantos* as "subject rhymes" or overlapping ideas. Pound explained in a letter to his father that the subject of Canto XX is the "lotus eaters, or respectable dope smokers," and the extract selected for *The Exile* focuses on a dream sequence that Pound identified as the "bounding surface from which one gives the main subject of the Cantos":[45]

> Jungle
> > Glaze green, and red feathers, jungle,
> > Basis of renewal, renewals ;
> > Rising over the soul, green virid, of the jungle,
> > Lozenge of the pavement, clear shapes, broken,
> > Disrupted,
> > > Body eternal,
> > Wilderness of renewals, confusion
> > Basis of renewals, subsistence, glazed green
> > Of the jungle.

The imagery suggests a vision of life emerging from the ruins of a civilization; the stones and walls that recur in the poem rhyme across the issue, sounding against the "roads" and "public works" that are listed in Pound's first editorial. The proximity of these particular images is obscured by the distance between "Part of Canto XX," which opens the issue, and the editorial that closes it. Between these pieces, the dream-vision of the "lotus eaters" in the canto chimes with Hickock's depiction of a derelict culture distracting itself with intoxicants, and the hedonism of post-war Paris in the first part of Rodker's novella. Similarly, Hemingway's two-line jibe at Neo-Thomism, the anti-modernist philosophy of the Catholic Church that was gaining a significant following, rhymes in subject with the "fake art" and "pseudo-books" that Pound's editorial condemns.[46] Read together, the disparate parts of the issue establish a field of images that illustrates the ideas in the "non-literary" editorial.

At the very end of the first issue of *The Exile*, Pound states his reasons for starting a new magazine project in Rapallo: to advocate the idea of literature as a public good, an integral part of his vision for the republic: "res publica means, or ought to mean 'the public convenience.'"[47] Furthermore, he argued, literature is a "permanent" good, comparable to "scientific discoveries" and "works of art," which are distinguishable from merely "durable" goods, examples of which included well-constructed buildings, roads, public works, canals, and intelligent afforestation. Pound sets these elements apart from what he regarded as the least valuable "transient" goods: fresh vegetables, luxuries, jerry-built houses, fake art, pseudo books, battleships.[48] While Pound's editorial approach is oblique, his conclusion is unmistakable; he says outright, "America is *the* most colossal monkey house and prize exhibit that the world has yet seen."[49] Over the short lifespan of *The Exile* Pound grew increasingly disillusioned with his ability to speak effectively to an American readership, and he turned his attentions to the Italian milieu— where he would be equally ineffective on the political stage.

Pound's editorial methods were not judged to be entirely successful, even by his closest readers. His first publisher for the *Cantos*, William Bird of Three Mountains Press, teased him privately about his use of extended metaphor:

> Just returned from London, where I made a great discovery. I have puzzled over your "devise"—RES PUBLICA—etc. for many a month without getting any forrader, but the other day as I was approaching Trafalgar Square in somewhat of a hurry, I beheld to my consternation that the pavement was up and I was confronted by a sign reading:
>
> "The nearest PUBLIC CONVENIENCES are at Leicester Square." Here is the key, then, to the enigma, and the explanation of your ferocious fascismo. Happily I reached Leicester Square with my dignity intact, and found the Res Publica ditto.
>
> But now can you, or the American readers of EXILE, explain why Republican America is so destitute of Res Publicae?[50]

Bird signed off, "Yours for the old-fashioned saloon," gesturing to the critique at the heart of his joke: Pound's "fascismo"—his bundle of sticks—was too vague to be intelligible to a public that read literally and was capable only of interpreting surface meaning, not interstitial meaning; the conversations that Pound wanted to instigate in a public forum were better left to the capable minds of the literary salon. For a few more years, at least until he began preparing *Guide to Kulchur*, Pound disagreed. As he explained in his 1934 essay "Date Line": "You can take a man to Perugia or to Borgo San Sepolcro but you can't make him prefer one kind of painting to another [....] *cuistres* [pedants] have been shown up for fools time and again."[51] While he could countenance being taken for a "revolutionary simpleton," pedantry went against his critical sensibilities.

Pound regarded the third issue of *The Exile* as a "very great improvement on early numbers," and his hopes for it were echoed in its demarcation as "Primavera 1928."[52] Pound's "Desideria" went further than his previous editorials, now stating baldly that *The Exile* served as a model for the "new civilization."[53] In the "Primavera" issue, Pound constructs this model through a composite of three different iterations of epic poetry: Yeats's "Sailing to Byzantium" and "Blood and the Moon," Zukofksky's "Poem Beginning 'The,'" and Pound's own "Part of Canto XXIII." The three poems are brought into relation to the continued serialization of Rodker's *Adolphe 1920*.[54]

Anticipating "the signs of spring" in the autumn 1927 issue, Pound announced that "eight poems" by W.B. Yeats would be featured in the next number. In fact, "Sailing to Byzantium" and "Blood and the Moon" both consist of four movements, and the two poems were placed consecutively at the beginning of "Primavera 1928." "Sailing to Byzantium" had recently been published in *The Tower*, on February 14 the same year, despite Yeats's hope that Macmillan might delay the volume in order to incorporate a "new Tower series" of which "Blood and the Moon" was a part.[55] Instead, Pound's magazine provided the juxtaposition of the poems that Yeats envisaged, and under Pound's editorship they would be put into the service of his "ideogrammic method."

The eponymous image in Yeats's volume *The Tower* is a metaphor for the power of the imagination to construct, whereas the tower in "Blood and the Moon" is an emblem of the imagination's failure. On its own, "Blood and the Moon" may be read as a reversal of Yeats's belief in the symbol of the tower, but placed directly after "Sailing to Byzantium," the poems take on a dialectical structure. "Blood and the Moon" articulates Yeats's belief that the poet is capable of transcending time and that this ability provides the poet with a capacity to govern that exceeds the capabilities of the modern state (described in the poem as an "unconquerable labyrinth of the birds"). Here, a continuity of images or subject rhyme is discernible between Yeats's poem and the extract from the *Cantos* that Pound published in *The Exile*'s first issue, as well as the "Part of Canto XXIII" in "Primavera 1928."[56]

Zukofsky's "Poem Beginning 'The'" disrupts the continuity between Yeats's and Pound's contributions, fracturing a high modernist field of Classical reference with a mix of high and low forms and historical and contemporary citations. (Zukofksy's poem includes direct references to "Mussolini" and "The Bolsheviki," to name just two prominent examples.)[57] The poem's central concern is its relationship to its origins. Zukofsky's prefatory index identifies the two concepts out of which the poem is made: "Power of Past, Present and Future (Where the reference is to the word Sun)" and "Symbol of our Relatively Most Permanent Self, Origin and Destiny (Wherever the reference is to the word Mother)." These two parts coalesce near the poem's end, where a voice declares, "O my son Sun, my son Sun! would God / I had died for thee, O Sun, my son, my son!" Zukofksy's index attributes these lines to "The Bible," alluding to David's lament for Absalom, but the imagery also rhymes with the poem's reference to the Bolshevik revolution: "Sun, you great Sun, our Comrade." Within the poem, Zukofsky's image of Sun/son addresses the tension—and also makes available a resolution—between Zukofksy's Jewishness and his communist politics. In this issue of *The Exile* more broadly, the poem's subject rhymes with Pound's, Yeats's, and Rodker's critique of "culture" and engages with the questions that their work raises about the relationship of the contemporary individual and contemporary culture to the past.

Pound's "Part of Canto XXIII," which follows "Poem beginning 'The,'" brings together Yeats's and Zukofksy's solar and lunar imagery with the figure of "Yperionides," that is, Hyperion, the progenitor of the Sun and the Moon. This canto appears to omit any twentieth-century references, but in the *Companion to the Cantos*, Terrell notes that there is a problem with Pound's transliteration of the reference to Hyperion; the name should begin with a U, not a Y.[58] But the "mistake" makes available a new image: an allusion to Ypres, the First World War, and the idea of rebirth after the destruction of western Europe. This is the setting for Rodker's *Adolphe 1920*, to which Pound refers directly in a note at the end of "Part of Canto XXIII" where he writes, "Explicit Canto xxiii / *Adolphe 1920*": "uno degli sforzi piu insigni e spasimosi di questi ultimi tempi per impriginoare nella renitente material dell'arte il mistero della vita." ["One of the most forceful and energetic recent attempts to capture the mystery of life in the reluctant material of art."][59] Pound's "Explanation" of the connection between two works in the magazine—and his proposition that a canto could *be* explained—is remarkable and indicates a blurring of the boundary between Periodical Pound and Pedagogical Pound in *The Exile*: he is instructing his audience in how to interpret the magazine's contents, as they work together as a whole. Yet, as William Bird suggested with his joke about the "public conveniences" near Trafalgar Square, Pound's ambitions were inaccessible to most readers' imaginations; the interpretive space between the magazine's constituent parts is so vast that it verges on an unbridgeable chasm.

The collage or cubist composition that Pound creates in his arrangement of *The Exile*'s contents enables his magazine to broach the question of what to do about a "new civilization" without pedantry. His use of Italian in the third issue—in his dating of the number and in his explanation of "Part of Canto XXIII"—signals his belief that Italy had the means to a solution, not only to Italian problems but to world problems. This conviction led to his ultimate abandonment of the indirect criticism that is exhibited in *The Exile* in favor of the prescriptivism that emerges in *Il Mare* and finds full articulation in *Guide to Kulchur* (1938).

Making the Public Man

Pound argues in his editorials for *The Exile*, in his essay "National Culture: A Manifesto" and many other venues, that the degree of public support for writers indicates the health of a nation, and this health is improved by a very masculine public sphere. Pound joked about masculine power in his letters to the Rapallo poets, sometimes in worse taste than others. He signed off a letter to Aldington, in which he discussed plans for *The Exile*, "May your cock never grow shorter!"[60] Writing to Zukofsky about American magazines, he joked horribly that "German anti/ism is [because of] Hitler's lady luvv who is a mezza," and—disgustingly—advised Zukofsky that "rape" posed a solution to some of his problems: "Sometime you can get an idea into a wummum that way when no other orifice will receive it. // luv to Bhill [Williams]."[61] Pound's racist, misogynistic, and homophobic remarks are important to describe because his editorial practice is deliberately gendered to advocate a masculine periodical culture that directs a homosocial, masculine public sphere.

Pound explained in a letter to Zukofksy: "Then there's the ladies. As I may have omitted to mention Exile omitted the ladies. Several of them are as good or better than some of the inclusions."[62] Women whom Pound regarded as superior writers included Nancy Cunard (whose name he underlines), Mary Butts, Djuna Barnes, and Helene Margaret. But he did not think that *The Exile*—or *Il Mare*—were appropriate venues for their

PRIMAVERA 1928   67

work, since he believed (developing from his reading of Leo Frobenius) that the masculine was the generative element in culture. This elides the fact that women were generative with regard to *The Exile* and *Il Mare*: Dorothy Pound was important to both, and she drew the banner head for *Il Mare*'s literary supplement (Figure 3.2), choosing the image of a griffin (Figure 3.3), which was symbolic of military power in ancient Rome.[63] She was never credited publicly.

In Pound's early criticism, he describes music as a metaphor for poetry ("the poet should behave as a good musician"); in his later writing, the distancing analogy disappears: "Poetry speaks phallic direction / Song keeps the word forever / Sound is moulded to mean this / And the measure moulds song."[64] In the later formulation, song has a hard, masculine quality, a potent means of preserving and transmitting "the word."[65] Yeats identified Pound's correlation of masculinity and poetic power in the version of *A Packet for Ezra Pound* that was published by Cuala Press: "He is not trying

Figure 3.2 Envelope of a letter from Ezra to Dorothy Pound on stationary showing Dorothy's design for *Il Mare*'s literary supplement

Source: Pound Collection, courtesy Lilly Library, Indiana University, Bloomington, Indiana.

Figure 3.3 Postcard from Pisa, illustrating Dorothy's inspiration for the hippogriff design

Source: Pound Family Postcards, Omar S. Pound Archives, Hamilton College, Clinton, NY.

to create forms because he believes, like so many of his contemporaries, that old forms are dead, so much as a new style, a new man. Again and again he breaks the metrical form [...] or interjects some anachronism [...] that he may pull it back not into himself but into this hard, shining, fastidious modern man, who has no existence, who can never have existence, except to the readers of his poetry."[66]

The poets of Rapallo were not in agreement about masculine verse. In F.R. Higgins's 1940 essay "Yeats as Irish Poet," he argues that Yeats's aim to restore poetry's "spoken majesty" was motivated by a resistance to "English poets [...who] lolled their tongues in unmanly verse."[67] In his appraisal, Higgins presses Yeats's similarity to Pound beyond plausibility, especially taking into account Yeats's liberal attitudes to sex and gender. For Yeats it was virility rather than masculinity specifically that was important. Similarly to D'Annunzio, whose libido wasn't limited by Mussolini's heteronormative discourse, Yeats thought that a person, regardless of their sex, could accommodate masculine and feminine elements of selfhood.[68] In contrast, Pound took the Platonic model of the masculine state literally, even arguing that the penis was "the organ governing stability and order and whose emissions, coming as the culmination of the poetic and sexual measure, invest the female, the reader, and the earth with knowledge, law and light."[69] In Pound's *ABC of Reading*, the "classes of persons" who are identified in his inventory of "'pure elements' in literature" are all described as "Men who..."[70] While Pound admired a handful of female artists, and even relied on their skill for his own success, in Italy he used the cultural power of the little magazine as a means of making the public man in a regime that valued performative masculinity.[71]

Just as Pound proclaims masculine generativity, he emasculates wire-pulling pedantic editors, excoriating them in his essay "Date Line" as "Sterile incompetents charged to spend the income of millions no longer even in monuments, where the facts are comparatively easy to discover, but *magari* [maybe, possibly] in CHOOSING the paladins of tomorrow, in PICKING the rising talent."[72] In contrast to these effeminate ineffectuals,

> Mussolini [is] a male of the species, and the author of this year's *consegna* [business, or orders in a military sense]. 'Gli uomini vivono in pochi.'

That is, "living men are few."[73] In Pound's imagination, Mussolini's masculinity is bound up with his authorship and authority.

Pound defined the "biological function of literature" in terms that are orgasmic or, more specifically, ejaculate: "nutrition of impulse," "relieve mind of strain," "give feeling of being alive," "set 'em off = mobilize," "energy—start dynamo."[74] Pound's social-biological idea of literature was primed by his friendship with Leo Frobenius, the German anthropologist whose work also inspired Spengler's *Decline of the West*. Both Frobenius and Spengler were discussed extensively by Pound and Yeats in Rapallo.[75]

Frobenius's most direct line of influence on the Rapallo poets is his idea of "paideuma" (the soul-culture), which he conceived as the distilled core of a culture that remained even when the husk of the culture had degenerated; true artists were the guardians and transmitters of paideuma. This protofascist stream of thought is embedded in Pound and is discernible in Yeats's "Genealogical Tree of Revolution" among other places, but it also surfaces unexpectedly in the work of others. Zukofsky quotes Frobenius in his long poem "A," and—perhaps even more surprisingly—Frobenius appears in Ford Madox Ford's blurb for the *Cantos*: "Nations and individuals arrive at a winter when there shall be no more spring...only waiting. Then the arts alone do good."[76]

Ford appears to have shared with Pound the concept of paideuma, but Ford's idea of cultural spring was not misogynistic; in fact, Ford wondered whether the writing profession was masculine at all.[77] When he visited Pound in Rapallo in July and August 1932, he gave an interview for the first issue of *Il Mare*'s literary supplement. Asked by Pound if there were any writers "at the level of Henry James," Ford replied, "Hemingway, Elizabeth Roberts, Caroline Gordon."[78] He also named Rebecca West and Virginia Woolf as important contributors to his little magazine, *English Review*, which had a small circulation but a long life from 1908 to 1937. Throughout the interview for *Il Mare*, Pound and Ford kept up a tone of comradely disagreement, using their shared past as a focus for their own achievements while expressing significant differences in their respect for contemporary writers. Pound and Ford also had significant differences with regard to the role of little magazines; Pound thought that it was the responsibility of the editor to publish work that would be rejected by mainstream editors.[79] *The Exile* was inspired, in part, by Pound's frustration with what he saw as Ford's shortcomings as the editor of *The Transatlantic Review*.

Pound described journalism as "the history of to-day, and literature is journalism that *stays* news."[80] Andrzej Gąsiorek summarizes, "The little magazine" was a place where editors could "provide a critical redaction of the [contemporary historical] period and its culture," but "*The Exile* was the reverse of eclectic. What it did do, however, was exclude women, thus articulating a misogynistic programme. It was a resolutely masculine affair."[81] *The Exile* complemented the idea of a masculine public sphere as it was being constructed in the early Italian fascist regime and that would be manifested in Giuseppe Bottai's influential publications, *critica fascista* (1923–43) and *Primato* (1940–3), which had the principle of leaving out "Jews and women."[82] This exclusion was not prescriptive within early Italian fascism, as Margherita Sarfatti's role of advisor to Mussolini and her influence on arts and culture testify.[83] In the literary supplement to *Il Mare*, Marinetti praised both a masculine and feminine gendering of literature, arguing that the paintings of Benedetta Cappa (Giacomo Balla's pupil, whom Marinetti married in 1923) showed "her feminine side for the immediacy of her art, the quickness of intuition, the variety of elegant, gracious nuances, yet virile without brutality, and with the power of synthesis that militarizes the most undulating, sprawling, and fluid sensibility."[84] Ultimately, Marinetti's take reinforced patriarchal hierarchies: "In restricting herself to a cutting, precise, and geometric verbalization, without fringes or smudges, Benedetta masterly overcomes her sex."

Pound's ideas about masculinity and culture—derived from Frobenius and others—were pre-existent. In 1917, Pound had criticized William Carlos Williams with the phrase "Your sap is interrupted" and had mocked Williams's "lack of 'robustezza.'"[85] An angry letter from Antheil in 1924 shows how misogynistic ideas were at play in Pound's Parisian milieu:

> children and physical-law is so damn powerful. One has to think straight. I find that all the old whore, demi-mondane [sic] terminology is correct. I find that all of the old problems have been worked out millions of times before with correct viewpoint. It is easing to find these things can be eliminated with a stroke. I hate these damn "moderns." Damn little whores, with a lot of new tricks. Not even interesting, that bunch of "Lesbians" (???????) in the Jockey etc, etcetc, or Leipsig, or wherever it is today [....][86]

Before Pound left Paris, when he wrote to Nancy Cox-McCormack in the hopes of arranging an audience with Mussolini, he was prickly about needing her to mediate, insisting that she should only arrange an introduction: "The matter will be settled man to man between M. and me, or else it will be merely bitched, botched, and bungled, bureaucratized, bastardized, boozled, boggled, and altogether *zum wasser*."[87] "Bitched" seems particularly calculated.

In Rapallo, Pound's chauvinism morphed into a late modernist mode, no longer merely looking inward to the world of poetry but looking outward to conjoin the performance of masculinity with the role of the artist in the state. In *Jefferson and/or Mussolini*, Pound co-opted the dictator in the cultural program that he had articulated in his editorials for *The Exile*: "I don't believe any estimate of Mussolini will be valid unless it *starts* from his passion for construction. Treat him as *artifex* and all the details fall into place. Take him as anything save the artist and you will get muddled with contradictions."[88] The creation of the Fascist National Institute of Culture, the bringing together of Italy's cognoscente through the Confederation of Professionals and Artists, and the conventions and conferences that were organized around these institutions enabled Pound's belief that Mussolini was accomplishing the program that Pound had already laid out in his editorials.[89] In short, Pound perceived the Italian regime as a collection of "permanent" and "durable" goods, bundling together a "healthy" masculine literary culture with the "well constructed" buildings that were monuments of Italy's living history.[90] He commented in *L'Indice* in 1931, "They ask me why I'm in Italy. They believe it's only because of my continued interest in archives and architectural monuments [that don't exist here where I live]. Instead I find a sense of contemporaneity more [I admit] in ideas, in the social *Anschaung*, than in the literature."[91]

Pound's presumptuous advice to Italians in the literary pages of *Il Mare* drew the attention of Marinetti, who published an open letter to Pound in the supplement in February 1933. Pound's ideas about masculine virility overlapped with Futurist imagery ("set 'em off = mobilize," "energy—start dynamo"), but Marinetti argued for an important difference, with Futurism dominating:

> So, today the world is shaken by two parallel forces often brawling with each other, equally bulky, aggressive, and tenacious: the male element made of synthesis, inequality, frontiers, mechanic progress, absolute patriotism, a constructive, simplifying, and heroic optimism (today it bears the glorious name of Fascism) and the feminine element made of contemplative analysis, idolatry of freedom and equality, radical-socialist parliamentarism, and diplomatic, pacifist pessimism.[92]

Because *Il Mare*—like *The Exile*—was pessimistic in tone, Marinetti disparaged it as a feminine enterprise: "One of these people [i.e., *Il Mare*'s contributors] actually praises a periodical because, after having given birth to an important writer, it had the brilliant idea of dying." Marinetti argued that Futurism, with its hyper-masculinity, "would have bestowed immortality upon this periodical, even if artificial" because Futurists were "stubborn builders of ideological, literary, and plastic optimism [...] the fervent propagandizers of an Italian pride which renews and accelerates, which creates and defends."

Marinetti tried to get Pound under his thumb by emphasizing Pound's foreignness: "I wish to the American waves of the spiritual Rapallo's periodical *Il Mare* the accelerated, prancing, bursting and frothing rhythm of the best wine from Asti..."[93] But where Marinetti cast him as an outsider, Pound saw himself as an ambassador. Punning on *terra incognita*, in the essay "Terra Italica" for the *New Review* in the winter of 1931-2, Pound attempted to make Italy known in the U.S. as a place of enlightenment:

> for some time I tried and have tried to stimulate the publication in the outer occident of a series of brochures that would serve as communication between intelligent men, proposing to print such books in America! [....] the conclusion, i.e. that the idea that publishing is a profession not a trade, and the idea of using a publishing house as a focus of enlightenment are both alien to our national sensibility, will come as a surprise to no one.
>
> It is therefore with a certain pleasure that I observe the appearance of such a series in Italy (the country least known in American literary circles and most misrepresented by the lying Brittanic press.) dorado Tinto, editore, publishes his series [...] at one lira a number [...]. Ogni fascicola una lira. This is part of the Italian awakening. It is also the kind of publishing that must happen wherever people are indulging in a life of the understanding.[94]

"*Ogni fascicola una lira*"—every document is a lira—puns on the false cognate, bridging the material text with the iconography of the regime.[95] The line was probably intended to play on his readers' ignorance of the Italian language; Dorothy had advised, "Newspapers here [in Britain] always getting in little jabs v. Italy when possible. 'Fascist' is now, rather suddenly, becoming any damn thing that isn't communism. So remember if you use it ... to specify & that nobody knows what you mean even if you say, the one & only Italian fascism."[96]

The Exile fits the formulation of a little magazine produced "in exile" for a national audience, but Pound's editorship of the literary supplement to *Il Mare*, which ran from August 1932 to July 1933, inverts the equation: he was importing into an Italian provincial city international perspectives and translating authors (principally of British and U.S. origin) for an Italian readership.[97] While Marinetti took issue with the "pessimism" of the supplement's literary criticism, he praised its dynamism and its internationalism: "I taste the fruits of your intimate, mysterious sea of American poetry which becomes a little Italian in the voluptuous embrace of our gulf."[98]

Pound's partnership with Saviotti of *L'Indice* on *Il Mare* involved Pound taking the title of "foreign affairs editor," but in many ways this was a false distinction of the supplement's remit. In *How to Read*, which was also published in *L'Indice*, Pound criticized the delineation of literature according to territorial boundaries: "You do not divide chemistry according to racial or religious categories. You do not put discoveries by Methodists and Germans into one category, and discoveries by Episcopalians or Americans or Italians into another."[99] Or, as he puts it in *ABC of Reading*, "When it comes to the question of poetry, a great many people don't even want to know that their own country does not occupy ALL the available surface of the planet. The idea seems in some way to insult them."[100] Pound's aims for *Il Mare* were trifocal: to inform readers of goings-on abroad (through the supplement's "Foreign Affairs" subsection); to develop theories, forms of criticism, and ideas of tradition; and to promote new writers, through means such as *Il Mare*'s competition for the best novella.[101]

On the whole, *Il Mare* ran perpendicular to party-political Italian fascism. Pound wrote to Zukofsky about the literary supplement's contributors: "trying to get the blighters to STOP discussing abstract ideas, doctrines etc; and learn something about language and how to write [....] politics etc. etc. etc. not what we're in the Mare for."[102] But there were notable points of intersection between ideas about culture that were being debated in the state and the literary aspects of *Il Mare*. An article "Intellectuality at the beach," a subsection of the supplement's "Literary Fortnightly" reported that since the Italian state had acquired Giorgio da Castelfranco's *Tempesta* five years before, "what was once reserved for a small category of refined people—now took over the numerous readers of illustrated weeklies, and the beautiful ladies who come to our beaches have shown their fervor by imitating, if not the dress, then the mysteriously voluptuous pose of the admirable Venus of Dresden." Moreover, "this intellectuality" had reached an even "higher level," indicated by the titles of books being sported by beachgoers: *Textes Choisis* by Girardoux, *Coté de Chelsea* by Maurois, and Mario Sobrero's travelogue *Roma* were all frequently spotted—even if *Lady Chatterly's Lover* did not "have serious rivals among its naughty female readers."[103] A more explicit example of this intersection is Enzo De Leone's article on Angelo Conti, which was part of *Il Mare*'s "Men of Italy" series. De Leone veered toward the gauche in his endorsement of a masculine, fascist aesthetic: he acknowledged Conti's friendship with D'Annunzio, while suggesting that D'Annunzio had miscast the idea of a "great thinker" as a man who was "fervent and *sterile*! Ascetic of beauty." D'Annunzio's androgyny and sexual openness were just two ways that "the first duce" was considered to be a weak point in Italian fascism's genealogy.[104] On the whole, *Il Mare*'s contributors depicted an Italian readership that was responsive to the aims of the state, buttressing Pound and his collaborators' idea of the periodical as an important force in shaping the masculine public sphere.

As the literary supplement moved into its second year, the politics moved to the foreground. An early piece, Salvatore Gotta's contribution to *Il Mare*'s series, "Writers' Confessions" mostly focuses on a reflection on the relationship of his fictional characters to his private family life, but near the end of the article, Gotta swerves abruptly into high-flown political rhetoric:

> Is it possible that this admirable Italy, which has found in itself such lively, strong, and playful spontaneity, is not capable of liberating the minds of the young from the convoluted fashion which comes from abroad, so that their hearts could beat in unison with the one of the great Italian public, and not with the one belonging to a few gloomy gentlemen pompously defined the chosen ones? I don't make it a case of literary schools [...] I never read literary magazines where so much young talent is wasted on a daily basis [....] I cannot but wish that the circle of writers read and loved by the public at large becomes more numerous. Then, we will exist not only individually but also like a critical mass of Italian writers, who will bring with confident faith the unquestionable signs of our recovered Latin joy beyond the borders of our native soil.[105]

Gotta's piece seems subtle compared to later contributions; Bardi's "Fascist Popular Poetry" is a prose poem that opens "You are my Duce, the person who took a white horse and rode it," exhorts "Bring us with you," pledges "At the end of each of our rifle barrels there is a rose [...] we picked for you," endorses the fascist colonization of east Africa, and finally proclaims the dictator's ancient lineage: "there is a Roman arch over there which was made especially for you."[106]

Basil Bunting's extensive involvement in *Il Mare* can come as a shock to readers familiar with his characterization as a pacifist conscientious-objector in the First World War who worked in the British foreign service during the Second World War (Figure 3.4). Yet in Rapallo, Bunting—with Pound and Eugene Haas—organized concerts that were inspired by a performance of Mozart's sonatas that occurred directly "under the auspices of the Fascist Institute of Culture," and Bunting cited this affiliation in *Il Mare*.[107] It was

Figure 3.4 Basil Bunting reclining on W.B. Yeats's balcony, 1933
Source: Bunting Collection, Durham University Library. Reproduced by permission of Durham University Library and Collections and the Estate of Basil Bunting.

only at Mussolini's invasion of Abyssinia and declaration of empire in 1935 that Italian fascism definitely "soured" in Bunting's estimation. Bunting's remarkable naivety evokes the point of view of "literary 'tourists'" in the Third Reich, who saw "what they wanted to see."[108]

As late as 1935, Bunting's ideas about literature and the state are close to Pound's. He wrote to Zukofsky in November of that year about his "observations on Leftwing Papers" coming from the United States. Echoing several of Pound's assertions in *How to Read*, Bunting told Zukofsky that "The effect of literature does not depend on its content. Its function is not propaganda, any more than the function of an analytical chemist is propaganda. Neither is its function to amuse the public. It is to explore the resources of language and make language available for all existing or potential thought."[109] Probably reflecting on *Il Mare*, Bunting thought that political papers didn't need literary sections, but if they had them, they should be free from the political aims of the rest of the paper. In this letter, Bunting unabashedly condemned Hitler and Mussolini and the false equivalencies that were being drawn with Stalinist Russia. A decade later, in the midst of the Second World War, Bunting wrote to Zukofsky again, from a "bad café in a conquered city in Italian Africa," where he was "Sad to find myself among Italians again, in this guise; but I have had some good evenings with peasant families, Sicilians mostly, singing 'Quel mazolin' di fiore' & 'Tu sei la stella' etc; as the Fascists used to say, before they went sour, 'Canta che ti passa [sing to take your mind off it];' And anyway, as you quote from D'Annunzio, 'Me ne frego.'"[110] In other words, I don't give a damn.

In his biography of Bunting, Richard Burton describes him as Pound's "informal secretary," contributing to *Il Mare*'s supplement by publishing "Verse and Version" (a translation of Zukofsky into Latin) and translations of Horace and Catullus into idiomatic English.[111] But Bunting's involvement was more extensive. Ezra wrote to Dorothy in September 1932, reporting, "Basil done a good smash at the Italian section of Mare. Seems to have critical talent, or at least prose Xpression."[112] (Bunting was less talented in visual aspects; Ezra, frustrated with the bad layout asked Dorothy to help his acolyte "see the page."[113])

Bunting's lack of dissent from fascist-sponsored projects in Rapallo is conspicuous since he was not averse to registering his disagreement with some of the aesthetic arguments in *Il Mare*. He was quick to contravene De Leone's opinions in his essay on Conti, calling De Leone's "convictions" "perverse," but this objection was not to De Leone's ideas of masculinity or to the essay's fascist overtones.[114] Rather, Bunting was disappointed by

De Leone's praise of the anesthetizing effects of good art, arguing to the contrary—with a notably Poundian turn of phrase—"Chloroform has the same effect, and it is cheaper." On another occasion, Bunting argued similarly, in "Diagnosi," that "The proper function of literature is to increase the quantity of communicable thought that can be made accessible." The problem with—or "low tension in"—contemporary Italian literature was due to the reign of "The Contemplatives [who] admiringly vegetate in every periodical or publishing house." Bunting thought that Italy needed "a man of action who considered literature a tool to better the world." Not until the very last clause of the article does Bunting even hint at an adverse opinion of the fascist state, when he describes literature as "a safer yet slower tool than politics."[115]

Bunting's definition of literature as a "tool" echoes Pound's *How to Read* (1931), where Pound outlines the "function of literature in the state," repeating his editorial from *The Exile* in which he describes the state as "the *res publica*, which ought to mean the public convenience":

> this function is *not* the coercing or emotionally persuading, or bullying or suppressing people into the acceptance of any one set or any six sets of opinions as opposed to any other one set or half-dozen sets of opinions.
>
> It has to do with the clarity and vigour of "any and every" thought and opinion. It has to do with maintaining the very cleanliness of the tools, the health of the very matter of thought itself.[116]

Pound reiterated this idea in "Nota in luogo d'Appunti" for *Il Mare*, where he argues that the state requires what literature provides:

> a precise value to each word, an in addition to each work group or combination [....]
>
> I did not limit the task of the artist to the valuation of the words the State needs. I am saying that without the cleanness of language, the State would be in need.
>
> Literature has a civic function, which is a literary function, in the same way that medicine has a medicinal function.
>
> The search for precision in expression is not a waste of time.[117]

Bunting's work on *Il Mare* was key to Pound's exploration of these aims; his skill as a linguist was instrumental in helping Pound arrive at the distillation of language that he and Pound both valued. As Pound recalled in *ABC of Reading*, "Bunting, fumbling about with a German-Italian dictionary, found that this idea of poetry as concentration is as old almost as the German language. 'Dichten' is the German verb corresponding to the noun 'Dichtung' meaning poetry, and the lexicographer has rendered it by the Italian verb meaning 'to condense.'"[118]

When Bunting reflected on his time in Rapallo, he underplayed his contribution to *Il Mare*, modestly writing to Massimo Bacigalupo that the literary supplement's official translator, Dodsworth, was "a useful translator of prose journalism for Ezra and Ezra's friends" and "if any translation needed skill, we all turned to Francesco Monotti for it."[119] Despite Bunting's later attempts to estrange himself from the work of *Il Mare* and to distance himself from Pound in Rapallo, Bunting's and Pound's writing from the early 1930s shows a commonality that exceeds their difference. They converged in the politics of their aesthetics: the role of criticism as a tool for "men of action" to shape public life.[120]

Pedagogical Pound and His Disciples

Bunting claimed in an interview from 1978 that he and Zukofsky exerted influence on Pound in Rapallo. He remarked of Zukofsky's visit in August 1933: "I can remember our saying something to Pound...in the days when he used to read in the Yeatsian manner, which we didn't approve of."[121] This claim of authority over Pound's method of reading is one of several measures that Bunting takes, particularly in his late autobiographical accounts, to diminish the visibility of Pound's authority over his work. Bunting's attempt to subvert Pound is also detectible in the abandoned project *Workers Anthology* on which he and Zukofsky collaborated in 1934 and 1935, after *Il Mare* had folded and after they had both left Rapallo (Figure 3.5).

Bunting and Zukofsky's *Workers Anthology* is in dialogue with Pound's *Active Anthology* (1933), where Pound declared:

> The history of literature as taught in many institutions (? all) is nothing more (hardly more) than a stratified record of snobbism in which chronology sometimes counts for more than the causal relation and is often wholly ignored, I mean ignored usually when it conflicts with a prejudice and when chronological fact destroys a supposed causal relation.[122]

Figure 3.5 A young Louis Zukofsky
Source: Image in the public domain.

Active Anthology attempts to extricate poets from their historical relationships in order to create "causal" juxtapositions. (This is also the method of *Jefferson and/or Mussolini* (1935)). In *How to Read* (1931), Pound describes being shocked, when he arrived in England in 1908, by the ignorance of the "British 'serious press'":

> For years I awaited enlightenment. One winter I had lodgings in Sussex. On the mantelpiece of the humble country cottage I found books of an earlier era, among them an anthology printed in 1830, and yet another dated 1795, and there, there by the sox of Jehosaphat was the British taste of this century, 1910, 1915, and even the present, A.D. 1931.[123]

The shelf in Stone Cottage testified to Pound's idea that ever since print culture had been democratized in the eighteenth century, public taste had been hardened into a sentimental canon, a passive reception of the past that was unjustified by any robust criteria. He imagined, "the best history of literature, more particularly of poetry, would be a twelve-volume anthology in which each poem was chosen not merely because it was a nice poem or a poem Aunt Hepsy liked, but because it contained an invention, a definite contribution to the art of verbal expression."[124] *Active Anthology* (1933) and *ABC of Reading* (1934) were Pound's attempt to establish, in freestanding volumes, the history of poetic invention.[125]

Where T.S. Eliot settled on the idea of "poetic inheritance" in "Tradition and the Individual Talent," Pound argued for a "more idiosyncratic, iconoclastic, and interactive sense of tradition." This distinction between Eliot and Pound, Christopher Beach argues, was what "appealed to postwar American poets [...who] saw in Pound's poetry and concerns an alternative model of literary Modernism to what they considered the more rigid and hierarchical set of values and expectations represented by Eliot and the New Criticism."[126] But this appeal can be located earlier, in Pound, Bunting, and Zukofsky's conversations about the aims and methods of criticism that were manifested in their respective anthology projects. Pound bragged to Zukofsky, "I am amused at the fury of [Allen] Tate [...] Our anthologies do seem to annoy, which is the best possible sign."[127]

Similar to the way that he presented his editorials in *The Exile*, in Pound's criticism and anthologies, he diminishes the editor's individual voice through his use of quotation and juxtaposition, two facets of his style of collage. James Longenbach suggests with regard to the *Cantos* that Pound's strategy of quotation is "predicated on the questionable belief that anything we could call a 'fact' exists independently from the interpretive strategy that presents it."[128] Pound disguises the subjectivity of the author—or editor—in order to present the information as absolute, natural, or—as Ross Hair defines it—"totalitarian."[129] In *Fascist Directive*, Catherine Paul writes that *Guide to Kulchur* (1938), which Pound dedicated against their wishes "To Louis Zukofsky and Basil Bunting, strugglers in the desert," is Pound's first prose work to exemplify "a truly Fascist methodology."[130] In Pound's criticism leading up to *Guide to Kulchur*, he removes the subjectivity of the author in his criticism; in *Guide to Kulchur* he goes further, removing the subjectivity of the reader as well and "insist[ing] on an interpretation" where his previous work merely suggested the conclusions that a reader might reach. In short, as John G. Nichols has summarized, Pound's anthologies "increasingly encourage readers to develop and adjust their strategies of reading."[131] But Pound does not stop there: he arrives at a totalitarian methodology that insists on an absolute meaning.

In *How to Read* (1931), Pound wrote, "I have been accused of wishing to provide 'a portable substitute for the British Museum,' which I would do, like a shot, were it possible. It isn't."[132] By 1937, Pound had abandoned the idea that the interaction of writer/editor and reader was vital to the interpretive process; he described the *Guide to Kulchur* to Frank Morley at Faber & Faber as "Wot Ez knows, or a substitute (portable) fer the British museum."[133] Pound's transition to "more explicit forms of interpretive advice" was not unique among anthologies of the 1930s, as "mainstream" anthologies were increasingly using explanatory footnotes and instructive prefaces.[134]

However, the context in which Pound situates his editorial projects shows how this shift in his work embodies a late modernist outward turn that is also right-wing: Paul connects Pound's turn to a dictatorial mode with Mussolini's declaration of empire and the accompanying exhibitions that celebrated it, principally the Mostra Augustea della Romanità. By July 1935, Pound had given up on the prospect of educating readers in Britain and the United States about Italy and was interested in making his work valuable to Italian fascism: He wrote to Dorothy, "I don't think foreign opinion re/Italy matters a damn," and he was glad that *Jefferson and/or Mussolini* was nearly published, since "Abyssinia needs it."[135] As soon as *Jefferson and/or Mussolini* was printed, Pound sent a copy to Mussolini, hoping it would arrive in time for the dictator's birthday.[136] Discerning the "totalitarian" voice in Pound's writing from the early 1930s reveals a late modernist turn in his work: an outward turn that was reliant on context, a turn to a more flexible idea of tradition (and therefore pedagogy) than previously advocated in high modernist criticism, and a method that appealed to Bunting and Zukofsky, as well as poets of the later twentieth century.

In *ABC of Reading*, Pound proposes an analogy between the reader or editor's selection of material and the curation of art: "Any amateur of painting knows that modern galleries lay great stress on 'good hanging,' that is, of putting important pictures where they can be well seen, and where the eye will not be confused, or the feet wearied by searching for the masterpiece on a vast expanse of wall cumbered with rubbish."[137] Bunting parrots Pound's idea in "Open Letter to Louis Zukofksy" in *Il Mare*, where Bunting praises Zukofsky's skill as a poet-curator in his *Objectivists' Anthology*, all the while disagreeing with Zukofsky's formulation of "Objectivist" aesthetics: "Even an exhibition serves its own purpose; chosen examples with sufficient and modest labels, as in good-quality shop windows. I really admired your skill in this job."[138] Here, Bunting is also echoing Pound's essay for *Contempo* magazine, where he chastised "the young literary experimentors, particularly Mr. Zukofsky's Objectivists" for being "so intent on being objective that they have lost all contact with language *as language*." Moreover, in *ABC of Reading*, Pound calls his selections "Exhibits," and he arranges his material in a collage where selections are grouped according to labels that instruct the reader's interpretation.[139]

In his first exhibit in *ABC of Reading*, Pound juxtaposes pairs of lines from Dante, Cavalcanti, and Villon with a single line from Yeats and a quatrain from the Old English poem *The Wanderer*. He follows the excerpts with a note referring to himself in the third person, explaining that the page is an

"Example of the ideogrammic method used by E.P. in *The Serious Artist* in 1913." Pound then switches to the first person to clarify, "I was trying to indicate a difference between prose simplicity of statement, and an equal limpidity in poetry, where the perfectly simple verbal order is CHARGED with a much higher potential, an emotional potential."[140] Pound's layering of editorial and authorial voices buttresses the total authority of the editor, while the author's attempts are recognized as imperfect ("I was *trying* to indicate"). In *ABC of Reading*, Pound's distrust of the reader's capacity to interpret seems to be gaining hold, since interventions like this one, evocative of the cross-referencing of "Part of Canto XXIII" and Rodker's *Adoplhe 1920* in the "Primavera 1928" issue of *The Exile*, are clear signposts for readers clueless about how to proceed from A to B.

Where Pound's criticism becomes totalitarian in its structure, Zukofsky and Bunting's *Workers Anthology* takes a Marxian position. *ABC of Reading*'s totalizing approach extricates works of art from their historical contexts, but *Workers Anthology* is arranged in a chronological progression, explicitly historicizing the contents in a Marxian frame, underscored by the anthology's title.[141] Bunting and Zukofsky begin with Ovid, continue through Apollinaire, and conclude with a poem by Emily Dickinson that opens, "Revolution is the pod / Systems rattle from."[142] This abandoned project anticipates Zukofsky's published anthology, *A Test of Poetry* (1948), which incorporates some of the same selections as *Workers Anthology*, including Robert Burns's "Holy Willie's Prayer," which was discussed among Yeats, Aldington, Bunting, and Pound in Rapallo.[143] *A Test of Poetry* also has a Marxian tone but without the didacticism of *Workers Anthology*. In the published book, Zukofsky refrains from giving the titles of poems or ascribing authorship, which has the effect of removing predetermined cultural judgments and testing each poem's quality against each reader's sensibility.

In *ABC of Reading*, Pound had allowed that "'The ideal way to present the next section [the "Exhibits"] of this booklet would be to give the quotations WITHOUT any comment whatever. I am afraid that would be too revolutionary. By long and wearing experience I have learned that in the present imperfect state of the world, one MUST tell the reader."[144] In *A Test of Poetry*, Zukofsky tries to achieve what Pound couldn't bring himself to do: to trust the reader's ability to interpret without instruction. Even so, Zukofsky's anthology still shows Pound's influence. In *ABC of Reading* Pound "tests" his readers; he specifies exercises for the reader to undertake in order to thoroughly learn his objectives. In *A Test of Poetry*, the challenge is bi-directional: the anthology judges the poem's ability to stand on its own but also the capacity of the reader to interpret it.[145] In a preface that is tinted with Pound's turn of phrase, Zukofsky writes, "desirable teaching assumes intelligence that is free to be attracted from any consideration of everyday living to always another phase of existence. Poetry, as other object matter, is after all for interested people."[146] Uninterested people, Zukofsky implies, lack the skill to read without cultural markers to guide them—a very Poundian sentiment. *A Test of Poetry* also includes an appendix that maps what Pound describes elsewhere as "causal relations" between the poems in the volume, disrupting chronology to locate affinity in poetic innovation and showing the way that the poets are in dialogue with a living past. Bunting thought *A Test of Poetry* was an "exhilarating book" even though "one misses the Ezra which should be there in so many places…." Even though Pound's poetry was omitted from Zukofsky's *Test*, Bunting thought that his ideas were omnipresent: "I think you, like Ezra (and myself-when-young) look on criticism as a branch of pedagogy, in which your book excels all the others I've seen."[147]

In a letter to his mother, Pound described his plans for the book *How to Read* (1931), which he hoped would be "a sort of pivot" that would give "the central idea, or ideas" of the *Cantos*, "and the until-now apparently random and scattered work all falls into shape, and one sees, or shd. see wot is related to wot and why the stuff is not merely inconsequent notes."[148] Pound saw his poetry and prose as complementary, and early on in his work on the *Cantos* he thought that the reader could be relied on for making the necessary connections.[149] Part of his motivation for discarding his method of collage in his criticism and for moving to an unmistakably "totalitarian" mode may be due to the reception of his method among the Italian audience that mattered to him most. In the pages of *La Stampa*, Pound's edition of Cavalcanti (published in Genoa in 1932) was dismissed as "'a mix made of heterogenous things jumbled together incoherently'; the poet-curator shows 'the blissful ingenuity of a self-taught person and of an American who discovers the world by himself.'"[150] It is hard to imagine how the insult could cut more deeply. In "Date Line: Rapallo, 1934," Pound refined his task: "The ordering of knowledge so that the next man (or generation) can most readily find the live part of it."[151]

4
Singing School

In December 1929, Yeats succumbed to Malta Fever, and George worried—again—that the illness would be the end of him. She wrote to Lennox Robinson from Rapallo: "two or three days of panic that William might die *here*. Some day of course he will have to die but I do hope it will be in Dublin or at least London. Here one is absolutely helpless. More than ever I believe that no one should be dependent on anyone."[1] She hired an English nurse out of Florence for night duty, but the days were still exhausting. As soon as she had a respite, she confessed to Robinson, "I shall go down to the Aurum and drink three Luigi's one on top of the other! (A Luigi is orange juice, gin, 5 drops of curacao...)."[2] While George wore herself out, W.B. convalesced on a diet of Hauptmann's champagne, and port and brandy egg flips.[3] In April he was well enough to decamp to Portofino, where it was quieter (Figure 4.1).

It was Yeats's second winter on the Gulf of Tigullio, and his reputation had grown among the residents of Rapallo to the extent that British expats had taken to ringing the doorbell uninvited. George had to give friends "instructions for a coded ring" to ensure some measure of privacy.[4] Even so, whenever Yeats left the apartment, he was overburdened by expectations that he perform the role of poet, to the extent that he was afflicted by "stage fright [...] whenever George brought me to the little Café by the sea." In Portofino, he felt uninhibited: "Here no mountains shut us in; I think three weeks should make me well as ever."[5] By the beginning of the summer, he had recovered, the children had joined them in Rapallo, and George—"tired to death of watering-place life"—was ready to get back to Dublin.[6] They left in early July, traveling by sea via Genoa. It was an early end to their lives as seasonal migrants. W.B. and George would not return to live in their apartment in Rapallo and would sublet it to Ezra's parents who were relocating from the United States.[7] The Yeatses returned briefly in June 1934, to arrange for their belongings to be shipped and for W.B. to have one last spectacular argument with Ezra.

Figure 4.1 Postcard with a view of Portofino
Source: Zukofsky Collection, Harry Ransom Center, The University of Texas at Austin.

Dangerous Bardolatry

In a diary that Yeats kept while he was convalescing in Portofino, he invokes Ezra Pound, and—typically of their relationship—he dismisses the idea of Pound's influence in the same gesture that raises its possibility:

> Pound's conception of excellence, like that of all revolutionary schools, is of something so international that it is abstract and outside of life. I do not ask myself whether what I find in Elizabethan English, or in that of the early eighteenth century, is better or worse than what I find in some other clime or time. I can only approach that more distant excellence through what I inherit.[8]

The allusion is to Pound's essay "The Hard and Soft in French Poetry," which had been published in *Poetry* in 1918 and which surveys "a certain gamut of styles" from the "good Chaucerian" through the "the bad, or muzzy, Elizabethan."[9] In this essay, Pound uses "textural terms" to describe poetry: "hardness" denotes "close-cut lines and stanzas," an "orderly method," a texture "like weather-bit granite." Later, in 1935, Yeats and F.R. Higgins, his collaborator on the first series of broadside ballads for Cuala Press, used the same quality of "hardness" to refer to an individual poet's *character*. In a lecture from 1938, Higgins went so far as to apply the notion of "hardness" of character to Yeats himself, describing Yeats's return to the ballad in the early 1930s in textural terms: Yeats "hardened himself, subduing the lavish painting and toning down the rich sounds. He sought to rid himself of elaboration, of redundancy—through various ways: by ballad-writing, for instance."[10]

In the Portofino diary, which was posthumously published by Cuala Press as *Pages from a Diary Written in Nineteen Hundred and Thirty*, much of the detail is inexact, drawn from the recesses of a convalescent's memory. When Yeats describes good poetry as a matter of "inheritance," he illustrates his point by referring to three ballads, the titles of which he slightly garbles: "'As ye came from Walsinghame'—*The Lamentation for Matthew Henderson*, 'For Matthew was a queer man'*—that modern song of the man sailing from Mayo—show hereditary stamina and a great voice."[11] The final poem is identified, through a footnote later added by George Yeats, as F.R. Higgins's "The Ballad of O'Bruadir," and this is the only title to be correctly attributed. In the main text, Yeats appears to conflate "As You Came from the Holy Land," which is anonymous but generally attributed to Sir Walter Raleigh, and "Elegy on Captain Matthew Henderson" by Robert Burns.

The error in the Portofino diary conceals the extent to which the Rapallo poets were turning to Burns as a model for balancing complex forms and a demotic mode. Yeats also misquotes T.W. Henley's introductory essay to *The Complete Poetical Works of Robert Burns*, writing: "A good poet must, as Henley said of Burns be the last of a dynasty, and he must see to it that his court expels the parvenu even though he gather all the riches of the world."[12] What Henley actually said is that unlike Keats, Byron, and Shelley, who were "founders of dynasties," Burns "was the last of a school."[13] Henley's depiction of Burns's ancestry (from "yeoman stock [....] But he had the right tradition"), as well as his description of Burns's reputation as an "amorist at large" appealed to Yeats's sense of his own biography. More to the point, Henley writes that Burns "discovered himself to his public in the very terms—of diction, form, style, sentiment even—with which that public was familiar from of old, and in which it was waiting and longing to be addressed." Henley credits Burns with awakening a national consciousness, and this resonated with Yeats's attempt to put the poet at the forefront of Irish national identity: to revive the Revival in a Free State that was floundering for a unifying idea. But in order for Burns to be positioned ideally, Yeats had to revise Henley's history to establish Burns as the culmination of a dynastic, inherited tradition. In Rapallo—as in Dublin—there could be no "singing school."

From 1930, when the Portofino diary was written, to 1935, when Yeats and Higgins's *Broadside* series was published, Burns repeatedly appears as a touchstone for the Rapallo poets' consideration of the ballad form and the demotic mode, a concept that is foundational to the late modernist turn. The high point of Burns's influence on the Rapallo group appears to be 1933, since that was the year *The Winding Stair and Other Poems* appeared, in which Yeats's "Crazy Jane" sequence experiments with the ballad and the Burns stanza.

Importantly, the change in Yeats's late style was a reworking of his ideas from the 1880s, when, as Wit Pietrzak writes, "Yeats realized that what Ireland needed in order to cast off the bonds of dogmatism was language both simple and evocative, which only [...] old ballad poetry, could offer."[14] In 1888, Yeats had written to Katharine Tynan explaining, "we should not go to old ballads and poems for inspiration but we should search them for new methods of expressing ourselves."[15] Similarly, in an essay for the *Irish Fireside* in 1886, Yeats contrasted Coleridge, Shelley, and Wordsworth (who "write for a clique, and leave after them a school") with "the bardic class—the Homers and Hugos, the Burnses and Scotts—who sing of the universal emotions [....] They do not write for a clique, or leave after them a school, for they sing for all men."[16] *Pages from a Diary Written in Nineteen Hundred and Thirty* restates, almost verbatim, Yeats's early idea that Burns's poetry reflects a spiritual inheritance opposed to a learned tradition. This reassertion indicates Yeats's desire for a second Revival, which he advocates most directly in his prose from the early 1930s.

In addition to marking the publication of *The Winding Stair and Other Poems*, 1933 is the year that Richard Aldington's essay "Robert Burns: the Natural Man" was published as part of a series for the little magazine *Everyman*. There, Aldington argues that Burns restored poetry to "natural speech" after the "vocabulary of poetry [had become] standardized and very nearly meaningless."[17] Aldington differs from Yeats in that he is eager to remove Burns from any nationalistic associations, which Aldington believed caused the popular "attitude towards Burns" to become "impure, a matter of personal or nationalist pride." He continued, "The English cult of Shakespeare, the German cult of Goethe, should warn us how dangerous bardolatry may be to a genuine and unprejudiced appreciation of poetry."[18] Aldington thought that Burns's greatest "lesson was the use of living and not merely literary speech." Although Aldington was in Rapallo only briefly, he corresponded regularly with core figures in the Rapallo group, and their extended conversation about Burns shows how he was one model for the poets' use of demotic speech.

Ezra Pound also advocated Burns as an exemplar. When Basil Bunting wrote to the Mississippi-born aspiring poet, George Marion O'Donnell, in 1934, he urged him:

> Try Burns's admirable and difficult stanza. Or [the medieval French form] ballades [....] nobody is going to get any good out of sonnets, or sapphics, or any other system fixed in advance, if they begin with a scheme, say, four lines long and fill it out to match [....] Pound will tell you whatever is good for you, I have no doubt. He does me, and the rest of us.[19]

Bunting continues, "it's not the sonnet one objects to, but the sins it invites writers to commit against language. Language is speech first and last."

Bunting makes a cameo appearance in Yeats's 1930 diary, where he is identified in a footnote as "A poet whose free verse I have admired."[20] The "free verse" refers to Bunting's first book of poems, *Redimiculum Matellarum*, which was finished in Rapallo and published in Milan in 1930. The volume includes the short poem "Sad Spring" (in the section *Carmina*, Latin for songs or poems), which begins as a ballad in common meter but after the first stanza slowly unwinds into free verse.[21] In his diary, Yeats describes Bunting as rejecting "every kind of unity" and believing that "the ultimate reality [is] anarchy," but he nonetheless praises Bunting's identification of the importance of the rituals of the Church as a means of structuring human life and feeling, and he suggests that Bunting is experimenting with poetic form as a means of creating the same kind of structure.[22]

In 1930, Bunting composed two important ballads, "The Complaint of the Morpethshire Farmer" and "Gin the Goodwife Stint." Neither poem tackles the "difficult Burns stanza," but both are influenced by Burns's use of demotic speech. "Morpethshire Farmer" is a ballad composed in common meter:

> On the up-platform at Morpeth station
> in the market-day throng
> I overheard a Morpethshire farmer
> muttering this song:
>
> Must ye bide, my good stone house,
> to keep a townsman dry?

> To hear the flurry of the grouse
> but not the lowing of the kye?   (Collected Poems, 104)

The first stanza is in the voice of the poet and rhymes abcb; when the voice of the farmer is ventriloquized in the second stanza—there are no quotation marks—the poem moves into perfect rhyme.[23] This technique of moving from imperfect to perfect form is also demonstrated in Yeats's "In Memory of Eva Gore-Booth and Con Markiewicz," which opens *The Winding Stair* (1929 and 1933), although there is no evidence for Bunting's direct borrowing of the technique.[24]

Bunting's other important poem from 1930, "Gin the Goodwife Stint," is a ballad in dimeter (2-2-2-2), reflecting the "goodwife's" economies, and it rhymes abab:

> The ploughland has gone to bent
>   and the pasture to heather;
> gin the goodwife stint,
> she'll keep the house together.
>
> Gin the goodwife stint
> and the bairns hunger
> the Duke can get his rent
> one year longer.   (Collected Poems, 100)

Bunting's use of demotic speech with vernacular accents ("kye" for cow and "gin" for if) intensifies the poem's anti-feudal politics and the "complaint" against forced emigration.

Zukofsky, who was corresponding with Pound, was also thinking about Burns. As he worked on his long poem "A," he became exasperated with Pound's critiques, writing in December 1930: "how I wish again and again that I could still be writing short poems—be excited <u>into</u> song or something as brief and essential <!> i.e. I'd rather be the troubadours (or one of them) than Dante, Burns instead of [Browning....] one of Shakes' songs than any long poem 'built on a plan.'"[25] Bunting, Zukofsky, and Pound continued their conversation about speech as song when they convened in Rapallo in August 1933.

Bunting recalled that one evening, as he, Zukofsky, and Pound sat talking in Bunting's apartment, their discussion turned to the sound of poetry. Zukofsky and he asked Pound to recite "Homage to Sextus Propertius," Pound's loose translation of the Latin poet. The poem had been collected in

Pound's volumes *Lustra* (1915) and *Personae* (1926) and would be published as a freestanding volume with Faber the next year, 1934.[26] Pound's translation had been controversially received, since it departed significantly from the Latin in places, in order, as Thomas Drew-Bear writes, "to present the poetry of Propertius in terms meaningful and alive for the modern reader."[27] For example, Pound translates Propertius's *neruus* (sinew, nerve, or string) as lyre in the line, "Shall be yawned out of my lyre—with such industry." A "literal translation" reads: "I had the / power with sinews such as mine to sing of thy kings, O Alba, / and the deeds of thy kings, a mighty task." Drew-Bear judges Pound's choice of "lyre" to be "definitely closer to Propertius" than the literal "sing [...] whereas Pound's *yawn* is a neat device for retaining both the literal sense of Propertius's verb and a pointed satire on fashionable hacks."[28] The long vowels in "yawned" and "lyre," which are followed by an extended pause, are a masterful example of Pound's comic timing, which can only be appreciated fully if the lines are heard, emphasizing Pound and the other Rapallo poets' conviction that poetry was speech, "first and last."

In the summer of 1933, Pound was completing his *Active Anthology*, which would be published by Faber in October. In his preface, Pound writes about Propertius, Homer, and Catullus as contemporaries rather than predecessors. He begins by quoting from "Tradition and the Individual Talent" before quibbling with Eliot's choice of word: "'Existing monuments form an ideal order among themselves.' It would be healthier to use a zoological term rather than the word monument [....] After all, Homer, Villon, Propertius, speak of the world as I know it."[29] Perhaps inspired by having recently seen Marinetti in Rome, Pound draws a parallel between the poets' work and Marinetti's Futurism, which he describes as "thoroughly simpatico. Writing and orating <u>ut moveat</u>."[30] Moving, living speech is what Pound valued in Bunting's ballads and Zukofsky's "A," and he included "The Complaint of the Morpethshire Farmer" and "Gin the Goodwife Stint" in *Active Anthology*, along with movements six and seven from Zukofsky's long poem-in-progress.

When Pound printed "Morpethshire Farmer" and "Gin the Goodwife," in *Active Anthology* he included footnotes to explain words that would be unfamiliar to the general reader, noting, for example, "kye = cow." The notes contribute to an impression that the words are archaic, and Bunting is reported to have been angry with Pound over the addition of a textual apparatus. However, Bunting's proofs for his section of *Active Anthology*, now in Harvard's Houghton Library, show no emendations. It seems probable that in 1933, Bunting saw his use of the vernacular as a means of displaying living, regional speech in the tradition of Burns, and concerns about archaisms only arose later.

The two movements from Zukofksy's "A" included in *Active Anthology* are also concerned with living speech. The sixth movement begins with the loss of a common language (Hebrew) and a common place of worship (the Temple Mount in Jerusalem): "The Speech no longer spoken and not even a Wall to worship / Tradition's pebbles, the mouth full, / The fugue a music heap, / only be the name's grace music: / Void—fate—fate—fate—fate but unable to write a melody [...]."[31] Zukovsky's anarchic imagery recurs in his depiction of atomized worshipers: "Walk, as arms beat in the circles, past each other: — / Would you persist?" He answers his own question by glossing Spinoza's famous axiom: natura naturans, natura naturata. That is, Spinoza's heretical dualist philosophy of oneness, which asserts that all is God and all is created by God. The poem moves into a dialogue that considers humanity's creation of Fordism; Zukofsky quotes Lenin to critique the capitalistic drive, before the poem's geographical focus shifts eastward to "the roving Red bands of South China [....] Concoctor's of 'hard poetry.'" This reference to Chinese poetry alludes to Pound's work on Fenollosa as well as the essay that was so important to Yeats and Higgins.

Zukofsky's "A" in *Active Anthology* also hints at Yeats: "Dramatic stony lips, centaurs, theatrical rock, / A tower, of course, theatrical rocks and a tower—/ In the best imitation of Sophocles—."[32] Yeats's play *Sophocles' King Oedipus* was published in 1928, and it begins with Oedipus's dilemma of how to overcome his own nature: "Do you know of anything that I can do and have not done? How can I, being the man I am, being King Oedipus, do other than all I know?"[33] Yeats's notes to the play emphasize that he was not writing for "readers and scholars" but for the words "to be sung and spoken. The one thing that I kept in mind was that a word unfitted for living speech, out of its natural order, or unnecessary to our modern technique, would check emotion and tire attention."[34] In Pound's selections from "A" for *Active Anthology*, Zukofsky asks, how is order, which will enable collective feeling and collective movement, to be attained? The seventh movement of the poem returns to the idea of circularity, evoked by the image of wooden horses on a carousel, moving but going nowhere until they are animated by the poet and become horses in-the-flesh, a metaphor for poetry's metamorphosis from the written form back into living speech. In *Pages from a Diary*, Yeats suggests that the poet—"Blind Tiresias" of *Oedipus*—articulates wisdom through the demotic mode: "The use of dialect for the expression of the most subtle emotion—Synge's translation of Petrarch—verse where the syntax is that of common life, are but the complement of a philosophy spoken in the common idiom escaped from isolated method, gone back somehow from professor and pupil to Blind Tiresias."[35]

Condoms and Classics

The Rapallo poets' turn to Burns was for political as well as literary reasons. In Aldington's essay for *Everyman*, he establishes Burns as an opponent of "ignorant and absurd repressions."[36] Burns "vindicate[d] the natural man against the long repression of tyrannical and hypocritical fanatics," and his poem "Holy Willie's Prayer" "never demolished more effectively the pretensions of sanctimonious hypocrisy. It is no wonder that the Holy Willies of the day seized every opportunity of decrying so dangerous a critic." Aldington's essay takes a similar line as Henley's introduction, which proclaimed that Burns "showed that laughter and the joy of life need be no crime."[37] Burns's emphasis on poetry as a celebration of life appealed to the poets of Rapallo, who were mobilizing against the growing threat of literary censorship.

Pound reported to his father in December 1928, "Yeats disgusted with his damn country for copying our putrid postal [censorship] laws" and "W.B.Y. fighting the Irish censor bill, modeled on our own god damnd imbecility."[38] Pound expressed the same sentiment in an angry letter to Desmond Fitzgerald (now Minister for Defense in the Irish Free State): "Because my country is filled with sonzofbitches who have bethrayed their constithooshun with an amendment, and passed a law (Art. 211, Penal code) muddling Dante, postcards and syringes, why the balls shd. Oireland do the same: // Cant you keep condoms and classics in sepharte parts of your lawbook?!!!!!"[39] After receiving no reply, Pound followed up, "ARE you a nation or a dung hill ?"[40] And again, with disturbing clairvoyance:

> I dont know whether any of you people still dream or rave of a united Ireland, but having seen the provisions of the Censorship Bill in the Irish Times, I can assure you that Ulster (which at the moment no one in Europe cares a damn about) would only have to paste up that abortion as a specimen of Free State law, in order to have every intellectual and every literate man in Europe dead FOR Ulster, and dead against her being shoved under any such "legislation."

Fitzgerald, infuriatingly, was not very "worried," since he believed that the "Committee will be enlightened" and "will have an enlightening effect."[41] After all, he suggested provocatively, "You and I are both Censors." Pound rejoined, "On that principle...let us also appoint an "enlightened committee" of five people to decapitate everyone whose face or fyce they dont like."[42]

In retribution, Pound composed the ballad "Song for Informal Gatherings," lampooning the Irish Censorship and Fitzgerald.[43] He sent the poem to James Joyce, who was still smarting from the censorship of *Ulysses*:

> Dear Jhayzus Aloysius Chrysostum [....] Blarney Castle, it come into me mind. Do you know anything, apart from the touchin' ballad about it. I mean when did fat ladies from Schenekdety or Donegal first begin to be he held by their tootsies with their hoopskirts falling over their privates in public to osculate: said stone and for what reason? fecundity? or the obverse? [...].[44]

Joyce replied with the lyrics to the ballad "Groves of Blarney," adding with uncharacteristic prudishness, "There is nothing phallic about the Blarney stone, so far as I know [....] I have never understood why it could not have been kissed from a ladder."[45] Yeats and Higgins would print "The Groves of Blarney" alongside Yeats's own "The Wicked Hawthorn Tree" in their 1935 *Broadside* series, and Pound's interest in the poem may have had something to do with their selection.

When Thomas MacGreevy visited Rapallo at Christmastime in 1928, he and Pound discussed censorship in slightly more measured tones, and on MacGreevy's return to Paris, they continued their conversation. MacGreevy asked Pound for advice on how he might work most effectively to defeat the legislation.[46] Pound replied, "Itz not strictly my business to save Oireland from itself," but he nonetheless offered his opinion, chiefly that MacGreevy participate in the censorship debates "from enlightened Catholic point of view":

> For example, living in remains of civilization one might see a catholic revival, or at least augmentation. ALL the people with any measure of civilization, or wanting any, MIGHT again coalesce against Babbit, against barbarism, as at end of Roman empire.
>
> But every time any intelligent non-catholic develops any such pipe dream, some damn fool in Armagh (usually a bishop's pimp) comes out with a super-Arkansas manifestation of obscurantism.[47]

Pound's suggestion was probably informed (though he would never admit it) by a long letter from Fitzgerald just before Christmas, when Fitzgerald—a devout Catholic—had argued that "enlightened" censorship would increase the reputability of Catholicism in Ireland, since Protestantism had "tried to maintain its alienated existence by preaching that the Catholic Church stands for unenlightenment," and "that prejudice represents the whole Protestant Credo of many people."[48]

Yeats's attempt to engage with the intellectual Catholic perspective came in the form of the essay "The Censorship and St Thomas Aquinas," which had been published in the *Irish Statesman* in September 1928 but had fallen flat. Pound complained to MacGreevy, "The theory indicates that Mr Yeats has heard of Aquinas, but is not very heavy evidence of existence of Thomists in Greek Church." He asked MacGreevy to send "Data re Byzantine Thomists, welcome if you can find any. If you've a copy of R[oger] Bacon's opus Majus I shd be delighted to borrow same."[49] Pound predicted, "The new censorship bill will undoubtedly place Ireland beneath the eternal dunghill, and reduce her to the level of the U.S.A. a land apparently void of human life and pullulating each year more opulently with sons of bitches, and maggots hitherto unknown to ontology."[50]

While Pound quibbled with Yeats's theological argument that the Catholic Church and its predecessors were Thomist at heart—believing, as Yeats summarized in his article, "that the soul is wholly present in the whole body and in all its parts"—Pound missed, or at least neglected to acknowledge, an important implication of Yeats's concept of divinity: that the enlivening of the soul involved the enlivening of the whole body.[51] This idea is central to Yeats's conjoining of dance, spirituality, sexuality, and poetic creation in his sequence of poems written in the persona of Cracked Mary, or Crazy Jane as she was renamed. These poems—published in *Words for Music Perhaps* (1932) and incorporated into *The Winding Stair and Other Poems* (1933)—were integral to Yeats's fight against censorship.

The persona Crazy Jane is drawn from a woman who lived near Lady Gregory in Gort, in south County Galway. Yeats described the real-life character in a letter to Olivia Shakespear as having "an amazing power of audacious speech [....] She is the local satirist and a really terrible one."[52] Of the seven poems in the Crazy Jane sequence, five are variations on the ballad: "Crazy Jane and the Bishop," "Crazy Jane Reproved," "Crazy Jane and Jack the Journeyman," "Crazy Jane Talks with the Bishop," and "Crazy Jane Grown Old Looks at the Dancers." These poems deal with terrestrial concerns, while the two poems that are not ballads ("Crazy Jane on the Day of

Judgment" and "Crazy Jane on God") concern the spiritual plane. This is important since the ballad, in its early manifestation, was "intended as the accompaniment to a dance," so the form—in both dance and song—is inherently linked to the physical body.[53] In *ABC of Reading* (1934), Pound put it another way: "music begins to atrophy when it departs too far from the dance; that poetry begins to atrophy when it gets too far from music: but this must not be taken as implying that all good music is dance music or all poetry lyric."[54]

Three of the Crazy Jane ballads in *Words for Music Perhaps* were written in Rapallo in March 1929: "Crazy Jane and the Bishop," "Crazy Jane Reproved," and "Crazy Jane Grown Old Looks at the Dancers."[55] "Crazy Jane and the Bishop" is a variation on the Burns stanza, which is a sestet that rhymes aaabab and has a complicated 4-4-4-3-4-3 meter. (This form began with the Provençal poets—hence Pound's interest—but was named for Burns because of his extensive use of it.) "Crazy Jane and the Bishop" is a septet rhyming aabcccb, creating a hybrid of a ballad in long meter (four metrical feet per line), a sonnet in subject and length (stanzas of seven lines, dealing with Jane's love of Jack), and a ballade, a medieval French form that is typified by three stanzas and an envoi in which the last line of the first stanza is used as a refrain. The ballade, which Bunting suggested to O'Donnell in Mississippi, was used frequently by Villon, himself the subject of a 1926 opera by Pound and a 1930 poem by Bunting that opened *Redimiculum Matellarum*.[56] The model of Villon stands out in "Crazy Jane and the Bishop," since the final stanza is an envoi, taking leave of the cleric and focusing on Jane's lover—although Jane hurls a final slur in the bishop's direction: "Jack had my virginity / And bids me to the oak, for he / [....] And all find shelter under it, / But should that other come, I spit: / The solid man and the coxcomb."

The earliest existing draft of "Crazy Jane and the Bishop" includes the vernacular word "dreepy" in a line describing the bishop's body ("Slack of jaw & dreepy eyed").[57] The poem begins,

> Bring me to the blasted oak
> That I, midnight upon the stroke,
> (*All find safety in the tomb.*)
> May call down curses on his head
> Because of my dear Jack that's dead.
> Coxcomb was the least he said:
> *The solid man and the coxcomb.* (VP, 507–8)

Yeats had used the seven-line stanza in long meter before, specifically in his poem "Running to Paradise" from *Responsibilities* (1914), where he similarly uses two refrains. Helen Vendler observes of "Running to Paradise" that the first refrain, placed at mid-stanza, is a "personal" refrain, whereas the "collective" refrain appears in the "normal closing position."[58] In "Crazy Jane and the Bishop," Yeats's use of refrain is reversed; the "collective" refrain interrupts Jane, and the disruption implies a commentary on the intrusion of collective, platitudinous religious statement on individual expression.[59] The parenthetical collective refrain in "Crazy Jane and the Bishop" is refuted in "Crazy Jane and Jack the Journeyman," a ballad in common meter, with diction that slows the poem's tempo, reflecting the loneliness of ghosts whose love has gone unconsummated in life. In "Crazy Jane and Jack the Journeyman," Jane articulates in demotic speech the Neo-Platonist idea that divine love is possible between humans; consummation of that love enables communion with "the light" that represents the origin of all things: "A lonely ghost is / That to God shall come; / I—love's skein upon the ground, / My body in the tomb— / Shall leap into the light lost / In my mother's womb."[60]

"Crazy Jane Reproved," the second poem in the sequence, was composed in almost-finished form: two stanzas in long ballad meter that rhyme ababcc:

> I care not what the sailors say:
> All those dreadful thunder-stones,
> All that storm that blots the day
> Can but show that Heaven yawns;
> Great Europa played the fool
> That changed a lover for a bull.
> *Fol de rol, fol de rol.*

Writing to Margot Ruddock in 1934, Yeats described the refrain as extraneous:

> I think when you find words like that in an old ballad, they are meant to be sung to a melody, as [Harry] Partch, the California musician, I told you of sings his "meaningless words." He uses them to break the monotony of monotone. There is no special value in "fol de rol" any meaningless words would do [....] I put "fol de rol" at the end of the stanzas in that poem to make it less didactic, gayer, more clearly a song.[61]

Yeats's qualifying remarks about the seventh line serve to revise the stanzas (as least for Ruddock's reading) into sestets; this has the double-effect of

Yeats presenting the poem to the lover as a sonnet and of emphasizing the inheritance from Burns. His delight in "meaningless words" here also contrasts with the disdain for "polite meaningless words" in "Easter, 1916" published in *Michael Robartes and the Dancer* in a period Yeats, from Rapallo, saw as dominated by "bitterness."[62]

"Crazy Jane Grown Old Looks at the Dancers" is positioned as the seventh and last poem in the published Crazy Jane sequence, disguising its proximity in composition to the first two poems. But its structure belies the connection: seven-line stanzas in long meter with the seventh line functioning as a refrain:

> I found that ivory image there
> Dancing with her chosen youth,
> But when he wound her coal-black hair
> As though to strangle her, no scream
> Or bodily movement did I dare,
> Eyes under eyelids did so gleam;
> *Love is like the lion's tooth.*

This poem was inspired by a dream in Rapallo, which Yeats related in a letter to Olivia Shakespear:

> Last night I saw in a dream strange ragged excited people swaying in a crowd. The most visable were a man & woman who were I think dancing. The man was swinging round his head a weight on the end of a rope or leather thong, & I knew that he did not know whether he would strike her dead or not, & both had their eyes fixed on each other, & both sang their love for one another. I suppose it was Blakes old thought "sexual love is founded upon spiritual hate" [....]
>
> To night we dine with Ezra[63]

"Crazy Jane Grown Old" presents the lovers as evenly matched; when the man attempts to strangle the "ivory image," she draws a knife, and Jane can only look on, leaving them to their fate. In Jane's old age, she reminisces on times when she "Cared not a thraneen for what chanced / So that I had the limbs to try / Such a dance as there was danced—." The irony is that the ballad form allows Jane to participate in the dance with her voice, even if her body is too self-conscious or infirm to attempt it. This theme continues in the poems that follow in *Words for Music Perhaps*, such as "Girl's Song" and "Young Man's Song," in which the lovers mourn the inevitability of age and decrepitude.

In the context of the Irish censorship, as Adrian Paterson has noted, "Writing love poetry was...a political act."⁶⁴ But even then, there were limits. A conspicuous absence in *Words for Music Perhaps* is the first poem that Yeats wrote for the Crazy Jane sequence, "Crazy Jane on the King," which contrasts a "righteous" mythical Irish king with the contemporary English monarch and concludes with the refrain, "May the devil take King George." Part of the inspiration for the poem was Yeats's anger over George V's failure to prevent the execution of the Czar and his family in 1918, causing the end of a dynasty and precipitating revolutionary upheaval. (There were other, more personal animosities, including the controversy over the Hugh Lane pictures.⁶⁵) According to Richard Ellmann, who probably got his information from George Yeats, "Crazy Jane on the King" was not published because Ezra Pound thought that it was a bad idea: Pound reportedly asked George, "Do you really think he ought to publish it? After all the poor old king is ill...."⁶⁶ Was George Yeats, late in life, attempting to show Pound in a positive light? Ellmann's account has been debunked—Yeats withdrew the poem on the advice of George Russell, among others—and in any case, the self-censorship suited Yeats's ambition for the songs to be "all emotion & all impersonal."⁶⁷

Broadside Ballads and the Outward Turn

Pound had praised Yeats's use of the ballad form in the collection *Responsibilities* (1914); when he reviewed the volume for *Poetry*, he lauded Yeats's introduction of "the sound of keening and the skirl of the Irish ballads," which had "driven out the sentimental cadence" of pseudo-Celtic poetry.⁶⁸ The difference between Yeats's use of ballads in his early poetry and the ballads of his late career is their political framing. The early ballads, including those in *Responsibilities* and the even earlier ballad sequence in *Crossways* (1889), are identified as ballads by their name ("The Ballad of Father O'Hart," "The Ballad of Moll Magee," "The Ballad of the Fox Hunter"). These ballads are written in common meter, and they endorse a Protestant Revivalist prioritizing of the natural world, working people, and the good landlord. By contrast, the late ballads don't often identify the form in their name, and they frequently carry an ironic relationship to their subject that reflects the complexity of Yeats's position in Irish society: on one hand, a Nobel Laureate and national poet, and on the other, a political outsider who was at loggerheads with the Catholic, nationalist majority and who was advocating the unique contribution of Irish Protestants to the idea of the state in the past and in the present.

The capacity of the ballad to carry complex irony signals Yeats's impetus for republishing "The Rose Tree" in *Broadsides: A Collection of Old and New Songs*. The poem has a jaunty pace, effected by the lightness of its opening ("O words are lightly spoken") and its sustained use of alliteration. However, the liveliness of the rhyme and rhythm jar against the elegiac theme.[69] The poem was first published in *Michael Robartes and the Dancer* (1921), where it follows "Easter, 1916" and the ballad "Sixteen Dead Men." The political ambiguity of "Easter, 1916" has been explored at length by scholars, but the contradictions in "Sixteen Dead Men" are less recognized, in part because the form of the ballad implies a pro-nationalist sentiment.[70] Yet, the three questions posed in "Sixteen Dead Men" create an opposition between compromise ("give and take"), "logic," and listening to the loitering ghosts. The semantic register grates against the musicality of the verse, and the lively aural impression dominates. Yeats's poems in the *Michael Robartes* sequence become gradually more critical, until "On a Political Prisoner" (about Constance Markievicz) unambiguously asserts Ascendency values as superior to "popular enmity."

If the ironic juxtaposition of form and subject in "The Rose Tree" is not apparent in *Michael Robartes and the Dancer*, it is unmistakable in Yeats and Higgins's May 1935 broadside, which pairs "The Rose Tree" with the traditional Unionist ballad, "The Boyne Water." Yeats and Higgins claim to publish "The Boyne Water" in "the original [...] because of its wildly picturesque description of that Williamite battle which is still celebrated and to-day in less spirited song."[71] By "less spirited," they appear to mean less violent. The first stanza of "The Boyne Water" as recorded in Charles Gavan Duffy's *The Ballad Poetry of Ireland* (1846) concludes, "To fight King James and all his foes, encamped near the Boyne Water, / He little feared, though two to one, their multitudes to scatter."[72] Duffy writes that the verses in his volume are "infinitely more racy and spirited than anything in the song which has strangely superseded them," but Yeats and Higgins enliven the stanza further, replacing the lines in Duffy's edition with "King James he pitched his tents between the lines for to retire / But King William threw his bomb balls and set them all on fire." Yeats and Higgins also recover (or invent) the couplets that are missing from the seventh stanza in Duffy's book, inserting the image of the Catholic army's scorched-earth retreat: "And in the dead time of the night, they set the fields on fire, / And long before the morning light to Dublin they did retire." Ostensibly, "The Rose Tree" and "The Boyne Water" both commemorate a loss by what can be simplistically perceived as the same "side" (nationalist, Catholic Ireland), but by placing "The Rose Tree" first, Yeats and Higgins conclude the May 1935 broadside with the image of uncontrollable Catholic Irish masses: "Although King James and many more were ne're that way inclined" (specifically, murderous), "It was not in their power to stop what the rabble they designed."[73]

Yeats contributed two more ballads to *Broadsides* (1935). "The Hawthorn Tree," which mourns the ruin of Castle Dargan in Sligo—the ancestral home of professional poets in medieval Ireland—is paired with what may be the version of "The Groves of Blarney" that Joyce sent to Pound.[74] Yeats also published "The Soldier takes Pride," which is the third of the "Three Songs to the Same Tune" written for—and rejected by—the Irish Blueshirts.[75] The Blueshirts' "official journal" declared Yeats to be "the greatest living poet writing in English," but the organization's opinion of the marching songs was hedged by qualifying words:

> One of them seems to be a poetical restatement of the central doctrine of Fascism. Another is a light whimsical song which might make a barrack room ballad. The remaining song is one which would not be unsuitable for occasional singing at League of Youth functions, though possibly that is ruled out by the fact that the official rallying song is to the same tune.[76]

Yeats, annoyed by the Blueshirts' rejection, later appended a note to the title "Three Songs to the Same Tune," explaining that the lyrics had been written in a mood of "rancor" against a gangrenous "fanaticism" that "was about to turn our noble history into an ignoble farce."[77] He declared, "For the first time in my life I wanted to write what some crowd in the street might understand and sing," but his efforts had been corrupted through the very process of popularization: "I read my songs to friends, they talked to others, those others talked, and now companies march to the words 'Blueshirt Abu,' and a song that is all about shamrocks and harps [....] I did not write that song."[78] Yeats reclaims authority over his poem by inverting their structures of power: "Anybody may sing them, choosing 'clown' and 'fanatic' for himself." In effect, Yeats's preface forces the singer to ventriloquize a collective voice in which the singer may not be included: "Those fanatics all that we do would undo; / Down the fanatic, down the clown."

The 1935 *Broadsides* use a popular form to reassert elite political power. Conceived for a coterie, featuring hand-colored illustrations, and published in a limited number of 300 copies, Yeats and Higgins invert the eighteenth-century broadside's economics, returning the popular, performed poem to its imagined exclusive origins. Their introduction to the series is titled "Anglo-Irish Ballads," and in their first sentence, Yeats and Higgins locate the beginning of the Irish ballad at "the beginning of the eighteenth century."[79] They claim, "Gaelic civilization had been defeated at the Boyne. Increasing numbers began to speak English words that found no reverberation in their minds; those minds had no sounding-box left, they were all strings." Yeats and Higgins argue that Irish-English words were enlivened by the "Scotch and English" ballads, transmitted "[f]rom the great houses or through wandering labourers." The form was "modified" and "enriched" by the particularly Irish voice: "a reader who knows nothing of Irish music finds that line in 'The Groves of Blarney' unmetrical; a paeon or foot of four syllables, is not permissible in English ballad metre."[80] Yeats and Higgins claim the ballad as a hybrid form and argue that it only exists because of hereditary institutions of power.

The broadsides were published monthly; each paired a contemporary and a "traditional" ballad and included the score (by music editor Arthur Duff) for the tune to which the ballads should be sung. Yeats emphasized in a letter to Hilaire Belloc, "all the music in the Broadsides is for the voice only," an idea that corresponds to Pound's "Homage to Sextus Propertius" in which the lyre is deemed inferior to the voice.[81] Alluding to his own claim to be tone-deaf, Yeats explained to Dorothy Wellesley, "even the poet who thinks himself ignorant of music will sometimes write unconsciously to tunes."[82] Taken literally, Yeats's "unconscious" refers to the developed sensibility that makes lyric poetry, but in the context of W.B. and George Yeats's continued work on *A Vision*, the second version of which would be published two years after the first *Broadside* series, the poet's "unconscious" composition invokes Yeats's ideas about spiritual power, innate knowledge, and inherited skill.

Yeats's introductions, commentaries, and related essays chart the course of his politics as well as his ideas about poetry. The introduction to *Broadsides* imagines that by the end of the eighteenth century, "Dublin street singers had some wealth and much influence; a political ballad had more effect than a speech." Yeats and Higgins suggest that the Irish ballad presents a form that is collective and organic in terms that revisit the Irish Revival's investment in spiritual nationhood:

What change of language did to the hedge-schoolmasters, town civilization does to us all in some measure, imposing upon popular arts a mechanic pattern of sound and shape, upon the arts of the intellectual classes a stark individuality, a bundle of dry sticks.

The fasces, "a bundle of dry sticks," here symbolizes a forced union, opposed to a "natural," living tradition.[83] Yeats's skepticism in the mid-1930s about Italian fascism is indicated in the way he challenges what Paul and Harper describe as "the central fascist figure of speech," a questioning that is echoed in Yeats's essay "Dove or Swan" (dated 1934-6) included in *A Vision* where he asks, "What discords will drive Europe to that artificial unity—only dry or drying sticks can be tied into a bundle—which is the decadence of every civilization?"[84] The *Broadside* series demonstrates the extent of Yeats's investment in the ballad as a form of living speech. Regardless of how democratic the style may seem, Yeats and Higgins's introduction to the series still puts the song in the mouth of one singer, who gives voice to an explicitly "Anglo-Irish" tradition.

Among the poets who survived them, Yeats and Higgins's collaboration on the *Broadside* series was subjected to a great deal of speculation about influence. In an interview about Higgins for the BBC, the poet and broadcaster Donagh MacDonagh said that he thought the partnership "was very bad for Higgins [although] It may have been good for Yeats." He surmised that the difference detectable in Yeats's poetry of the 1930s, its "great richness and kind of folk quality," was taken "deliberately, or unconsciously—I think probably deliberately" from Higgins.[85] However, *Pages from a Diary Written in Nineteen Hundred and Thirty* shows how the 1935 *Broadside* series was part of an extended conversation about the ballad among the poets of Rapallo, ranging from their discussion of Robert Burns to conversations about the political possibilities of demotic speech.

In spring 1939, shortly following Yeats's death, W.H. Auden published "The Public v the Late Mr William Butler Yeats" in the *Partisan Review*. He argued in Yeats's defense that despite the "false or undemocratic ideals" that had preoccupied the late poet, Yeats's diction had continuously evolved "toward what one might call the true democratic style."[86] Auden located the "social virtues of real democracy" in "brotherhood and intelligence," and he described its "linguistic virtues" as "strength and clarity" of expression. The ostensibly democratic "virtues" to which Auden refers denote the directness of voice, ordinary register, and strong cadences that typify Yeats's work from the 1930s, especially the songs of *The Winding Stair and Other Poems* (1933) and the broadside series of 1935 and 1937. Auden goes so far as to say that "the diction of *The Winding Stair* is the diction of a just man."[87] These are the same characteristics that later critics identify as typical of late modernist style. However, Yeats's use of idiomatic speech and demotic form in his ballads from the 1930s show how his late modernist poetics are not at odds with his "undemocratic ideals" but spring from authoritarian political values. The demotic is not the democratic in late Yeats but was born out of conversations with Ezra Pound and the other poets in Rapallo, whose work was concerned with the use of the voice as an instrument, experiments with dialect and vernacular speech, and the refashioning of the ballad lyric to suit their contemporary moment.

These poetic collaborations are a corollary of the concerts and musical projects on which the Rapallo poets embarked with other collaborators, such as Yeats's work with Antheil on the score for *Fighting the Waves* and the concert series that Pound organized with Olga Rudge and Gerhart Münch in which Bunting was involved.[88] Despite the increasingly fraught relationship between the poets of Rapallo, Pound never regretted supporting Bunting and Zukofsky's careers; he wrote to Dorothy Pound in 1934, "find Zuk / in Active An / is still readable / a little at a time / at any rate not simple TOSH," and in 1939, he told Ronald Duncan that Bunting's "two poems on devastation of countryside ARE necessary are PART of the present Anschauung," but since "Bunting is enwroughth with my fascism or whatever," their days of working together were over.[89]

5
Making Living History

"Fascism makes history, it does not write it"[1]

"Young chap called Adrian Stokes has drifted into the village, with a large trunk full of highbrow books (Spengler etc.) which I am swallowing in return for tips on the XV century," Ezra Pound wrote to his parents in January 1927, about three months after Stokes and Pound met on the courts of the English Tennis Club in Rapallo.[2] Stokes left Oxford in 1923 with an ignoble second-class degree; his first stint in Rapallo was dictated by a complicated affair with Osbert Sitwell, but Pound eventually replaced Sitwell as mentor. As in the case of Pound's bigoted comments to Zukofksy, he regularly unleashed cutting remarks about Stokes's sexuality. This chauvinism may have been an attempt to diminish the threat posed by a younger genius; Stokes's theories of Renaissance art—which centered on the Tempio Malatestiano—sculpted Pound's ideas on form, especially *The Quattro Cento* (1930) and *Stones of Rimini* (1934) which made Stokes's name as an art critic.[3] The politics of Stokes's early architectural theories were grounded in fascistic thought, and the Spengler in his suitcase was emblematic of a line that traveled through the Rapallo group.

In 1926, Stokes had published an homage to Oswald Spengler, *Sunrise in the West: A Modern Interpretation of Past and Present*, which looked "to the past for solutions to the problems of the present."[4] The book scrutinized the capacity of art forms to articulate a vision that brought art into relation to "culture, wealth, breeding, and responsibility," ideas that resonate in W.B. and George Yeats's *A Vision* and—less obviously—in Dorothy Pound's ideas about the capacity of aesthetic form to manifest a metaphysical idea.[5] W.B. Yeats's essays for *Dublin Magazine* about the roles of state-sponsored institutions, including museums and schools (in which Gentile's philosophy was also instrumental), and Dorothy Pound's attention to fascist architecture in her letters and drawings indicate the ways that their work was responding to the large-scale cultural projects of the regime.[6]

Pages from a Diary Written in Nineteen Hundred and Thirty shows how WBY's reading of Spengler was shaping his thought as he and George prepared the new iteration of *A Vision*:

> Spengler is right when he says all who preserve tradition will find their opportunity. Tradition is kindred. The abrogation of equality of rights and duties is because duties should depend on rights, rights on duties. If I till and dig my land I should have rights because of that duty done, and if I have much land, that, according to all ancient races, should bring me still more rights. But if I have much or little land and neglect it I should have few rights. This is the theory of Fascism and so far as land is concerned it has the history of the earth to guide it and that is permanent history.[7]

Roy Foster suggests that Yeats's interpretation was "nearer Burke than Mussolini," but the ideas were nonetheless identifiably fascist to reviewers of the 1937 *A Vision*.[8] Stephen Spender refused to credit the idea of a mystical source for *A Vision*, pointing to its textual sources in "Spengler, Stefan George, D'Annunzio, Yeats: is it really so impossible to guess at the 'instructors' who speak behind these mystic veils? It is interesting, too, to speculate whether Fascism may not work out through writers such as these a mystery which fills its present yawning void."[9]

Basil Bunting remarked in a lecture on Pound's *Cantos* that Spengler was pervasive in early twentieth-century thought: "A lot of people in the early part of this century expected to find laws of history like laws of nature—Spengler and Toynbee, for example. But if you are going to get results of the kind they hoped for, you will need more than merely interrogating the dead and churning in the sea of facts."[10] In his speech, Bunting draws an implicit parallel between Spengler's juxtaposition of vastly different historical epochs in *Decline of the West* and the way that Ezra Pound bridges historical and narrative gaps in the Cantos by using images that create strong associative motifs. Despite Bunting's critique of Spengler's prevalence, he saw in the *Cantos* "moments of vision, whether we're talking about the abrupt formation of a new scientific hypothesis or the abrupt contact with God which mystics claim, or merely the insight that comes from a combination of study and natural sympathy."[11] Peter Nicholls theorizes the same gaps—"the tensions between those times and spaces"—as indicative of the way that Pound represents Italy (at least in the first fifty-one Cantos) as both "ideal and 'real' [...] the actual space in which traces of a recoverable history are pursued."[12] Nicholls's interpretation is important because, deliberately or not, Bunting's reading of the *Cantos* has the effect of depoliticizing Pound's metaphysical maneuvers.

Italian fascism conceived of the state as a metaphysical entity whose power was manifested materially in urban town planning projects, archaeological reclamation, and rural development, as well as less tangibly in the visual and performing arts. In the proliferation of art exhibitions and cultural conferences organized by Mussolini's regime, the state refused to prescribe an aesthetic, preferring instead for the spirit of fascism to be articulated across the plastic arts, including in a new style of painting that grew out of a "metaphysical movement."

The metaphysical dimension of the Italian fascist project is evident from its beginnings with D'Annunzio, and "Mussolini's inspirations were D'Annunzio's."[13] Lucy Hughes-Hallett writes of the second duce: "Nietzsche filled him with 'spiritual eroticism.' He had learnt from Sorel. He called himself 'an apostle of violence.'"[14] At the March on Rome, Mussolini declared:

> let us too, pure in spirit and without rancor, raise our thoughts to Rome, one of the world's few cities of the spirit, because at Rome [...] occurred one of the great spiritual wonders that history records [....] Now we aspire to make of Rome the city of our spirit, a city purged, cleansed of all the elements that have corrupted and violated her; we aspire to make of Rome the pulsating heart, the active spirit of the imperial Italy of our dreams.[15]

Giovanni Gentile—whose writing Yeats first encountered in 1925 while visiting the Pounds in Italy—developed with Mussolini the idea that the metaphysical state is a necessary counterpart to its materialism.[16] In 'The Philosophic Basis of Fascism', Gentile argued that fascism

> is eminently anti-intellectual [...] that is, if by intellectualism we mean the divorce of thought from action, of knowledge from life, of brain from heart, of theory from practice. Fascist anti-intellectualism holds in scorn a product peculiarly typical of the educated classes in Italy: the *leterato*—the man who plays with knowledge and with thought without any sense of responsibility for the practical world. It is hostile not so much to culture as to bad culture [....] The Fascist system is not a political system.[17]

Yeats's "Commentary on a Parnellite at Parnell's Funeral" illustrates the appeal of Gentile's scorn for middle-class "intellectualism"; in that essay,

Yeats equates the "cellars" (political activists, especially communists) with the "garrets" (intellectuals divorced from what Gentile describes as the "practical world"). Yeats's incorporation of Gentile into *A Vision* (1937) was worked out in *Pages from a Diary*: "Every nation is the whole world in a mirror and our mirror has twice been very bright and clear [....] Study the educational system of Italy, the creation of the philosopher Gentile, where even religion is studied not in the abstract but in the minds and lives of Italian saints and thinkers, it becomes at once part of Italian history."[18] The passage has specific bearing on another of Yeats's essays, "Introduction to *Fighting the Waves*," in which he sets out his ideas about public education through museums that were sponsored by "Caesar"; in the 1930 diary, Yeats asks, "What idea of the State, what substitute for that of the Toga'd race that rules the world, will serve our immediate purpose here in Ireland?"[19]

The metaphysical explorations of the Rapallo poets have been addressed in the extensive work on Yeats's *A Vision* by Harper and Paul, Neil Mann, and others, while the volleys between Stokes and Pound have been replayed at length in Richard Read's *Art and Its Discontents*. Yet to describe conversations about metaphysics and their relation to early fascist Italy solely in the context of the predominately homosocial relations of Rapallo's male poets is to omit the group's foremost visual artist: Dorothy Pound (Figure 5.1).[20]

Building the Fascist State

Dorothy Pound, "vorticist artist and tolerant English wife," is a shadowy figure in the Rapallo group; even in feminist histories of modernism, she is portrayed as a marginal painter who, by the 1930s, had retreated entirely to a domestic sphere.[21] This is despite the fact, as Moody puts it, "Ezra and Dorothy were often on the move away from Rapallo and from each other."[22] Moreover, the correspondence between the couple during their regular periods apart shows how Dorothy's intellectual interests were important to determining the direction of Ezra's work. When she was back in England caring for her mother, Dorothy was also sorting through her own and Ezra's books and papers in preparation for the move to Italy. In more than one letter, she encouraged Ezra to think about material he had accumulated about Thomas Jefferson, going so far as to urge, "I feel Jefferson deserves yr. notice! but imagine that he will go into Cantos—& be the more pleased."[23] In her advice lay the germs of *Jefferson and/or Mussolini* (1935).[24]

Figure 5.1 Dorothy Pound, circa 1930
Source: With thanks to David Moody.

The Pounds' marriage struck a balance of deep affection and strongly independent minds and bodies.[25] When Yeats was living closely with them in Stone Cottage, he remarked, "I feel quite sure that Ezra & his wife who are obviously devoted, must have fallen in love out of shere surprise & bewilderment they are so unlike each other."[26] Dorothy Pound is "Ezra's wife" in Yeats's letters, and he—like the critics that followed—was dismissive about her art:

> She spends all her daylight hours drawing the most monstrous cubist pictures. I am sure her real test would be to paint with very little brushes, & draw neat outlines with a pencil she took half the morning making sharp enough. She is merely playing up to the revolutionary energy of her husband.[27]

In reminiscences and academic studies, Dorothy's creative autonomy has been subordinated to the role of helpmeet, not least because of the way that she performed the part in public.

In *Etruscan Gate*, Dorothy's only published book (issued a year before Ezra's death), her own work is preceded by a drawing of Ezra by Wyndham Lewis, schmaltzy excerpts from her diaries about the early years of their courtship, mediocre poems that Ezra wrote for or about her, and her declarations of love for him. The editorial note, by Moelwyn Merchant, further diminishes Dorothy's artistic independence and casts her as an amateur: "She early came under the influence of Wyndham Lewis, though never in any formal sense a pupil." This assertion is made despite Dorothy's own account of her relationship with Lewis: "I certainly never had any "lessons" from him [i.e., Lewis] but the movement came just as I needed a shove out of the Victorian... W.L. caught me painting one day—said it was too tight—'do something more free.' The only time he ever criticised me."[28]

Dorothy did not stop working when the Pounds moved to Italy. In fact, quite the opposite happened: her style underwent a substantial change. Leaving behind the Vorticist aesthetics that were concentrated on abstraction, dynamism, and the machine-age, she shifted her attention onto the solidity of the architectural object, which she juxtaposes against the instability of the natural environment. The transformation of her style is indicative of a change across France and Italy, where artists were espousing a Return to Order. In part a reaction against the First World War, the new aesthetic involved a mistrust of the attempts at pure abstraction in movements as diverse as Vorticism, Futurism, and surrealism, and it heralded a return to Classical elements of composition, including Classical figure painting and architectural components.[29] The influences on Dorothy Pound's Return to Order came from several directions: from the Pounds' friendship with Fernand Léger that began during their time in Paris and continued through the thirties, from Italian metaphysical painting that was developed in Paris and led to the Novecento Group that was prominent in the fascist state, and from public conversations about art and architecture that proliferated during the Pounds' early years in Italy.[30]

Dorothy Pound's interest in Roman and Renaissance architecture predates her marriage to Ezra. She saved postcards that her mother, Olivia Shakespear, sent home from her Italian tour in 1902, in which monuments and churches feature. Scrawled notes on the cards give evidence of a more detailed discussion: "This is the church I mentioned in my letter," Olivia jotted on a postcard of the Basilica of St. Paul's Outside the Walls.[31] Olivia's tour provided Dorothy with a knowledge of Italian architecture that informed her advice to Ezra during his early visits to Italy. In 1913, when he was on holiday in Venice, Dorothy urged him to visit the Accademia and the Palazzo Ducale to see specific works by Bellini and Titian. Rebecca Beasley notes that Ezra's replies were almost wholly concerned with poetry and gossip, not art and architecture, although he did send Dorothy "a reminder of the precise meaning of the term 'Quattro cento'": a postcard of the fifteenth-century church of Santa Maria dei Miracoli.[32] Writing to Ezra from Cairo in 1925, Dorothy appraised the city's mosques against an Italian standard: "The minarets are not unpleasantly slender, & as for domes are very squat—the facades enormous! tall & well proportioned. Heaven knows it's not Perugian! But I am agreeably surprised at the 'seriousness' of the buildings."[33] In 1931, she wrote to Ezra from Devon, where she was spending the summer with Olivia Shakespear and the young Omar; she was thinking about the cleanliness of Norman design that was evocative of the quattrocento aesthetic: "Saw lots of beautiful Norman architecture—Its very satisfactory: but save me from points & spires."[34] In the same letter, Dorothy recommended that Ezra visit the "Architecture Show in Milan," referring to the newly relocated Biennial, which had been established in Monza in 1923 and would become La Triennale di Milano, an important venue for debating classical and vernacular designs.[35]

Dorothy Pound's encounters with Italian Futurism were also unmediated by Wyndham Lewis or Ezra. In March 1912, she attended an exhibition of Futurist art in London, where she was accompanied by George Hyde Lees:

> There were two enlightening ones [i.e., paintings] by Severini (I think). One was centripetal force and the other c. fugal. The former, yellows and white, outside, and blues & green inside [*sketch inserted here*]. Centrifugal was a [*sketch here*] of yellow & white in centre & blues and green solidly surrounding it. Georgie & me—we decided! My receptive yellow outside—her ferment inside, being calmed by the ring of blue & green![36]

In the same letter she writes about identifying in the work of the Futurist Giacomo Balla a "restlessness" that she thought was distracting; the stability exemplified by the Return to Order had exceedingly more appeal.

Since Dorothy Pound's death, her painting has rarely been exhibited. In 2011, the Tate included her in "The Vorticists: Manifesto for a Modern World," and in 1996 David A. Lewis curated "The Introspective Eye: Dorothy Shakespear's Modernist Vision" at Hamilton College, where the

Ruth and Elmer Wellin Museum of Art has very recently catalogued and provided an approximate dating for its extensive holdings of Dorothy Pound's work.[37] In David Lewis's catalogue, he notes that Dorothy Pound's painting expresses "something akin to that quality of monumentality one sees in the paintings of Piero della Francesca (1416–1492), whose work was just being 'discovered' around the time she worked in this manner."[38] This "discovery" hints at the art writing by Giorgio De Chirico and Carlo Carrà, the founders of *pittur metafisica* (metaphysical painting), a short-lived collaboration between the pair when they were living in Paris in 1917.

Metaphysical painting—which was developed outside of Italy—became integral to public debates about architecture's relationship to the visual arts, and these conversations were significant in the development of aesthetic fascism as the Italian regime was consolidated. For example, in *Il Mare* in 1933, Monotti proclaimed "a new art is dawning, Fascist art. An interpretation of our times [....] from De Chirico to [Corrado] Cagli and [Franco] Gentilini, it is the only one that managed to understand the reinvigorated tradition of Rome and to express that complex spiritual turmoil that is not only present in Italy, but rather throughout the whole world, and goes by the name of Fascism."[39]

The nature and roles of Italian "fascist art" were contested in lectures, periodicals, and exhibitions from the mid-1920s right through to the mid-1930s, hotly debated but never with the intent of formalization. As Giovanni Gentile summarized, "Fascism prefers not to waste time constructing abstract theories about itself."[40] In the magazine *Valori Plastici*, which was published in Rome in French and Italian editions, Giorgio De Chirico argued for a "return to order"; Carlo Carrà gave a more substantive explanation of how this return related to the fascist state: "Here in Italy more than anywhere else the love for well-ordered surfaces and balanced substantiality—which is classicism in action—[is] naturally felt."[41] Carrà argued that it was necessary for artists to "arrive at 'a form of refreshed and tranquil synthetic art.'"[42] The new metaphysical art would evoke the past through solid forms, not the "cold and misty lands of the gnomes and witches." Architectural historian D. Medina Lasansky explains how this was articulated in De Chirico's work: "Buildings and piazzas are reduced to their basic forms, exposed, isolated, and monumentalized in a manner reminiscent of the 'liberation' trends of early Roman renewal projects, the streamlined modernism of contemporary architects [...] as well as Renaissance urban ideals."[43] Lasansky describes how the state embarked on a process of "editing" public space, in order to create a link between contemporary civic identity and an historical past.[44] This "editing" focused on Renaissance structures that were themselves renovations of Classical constructions. While De Chirico and Carrà's architectural aesthetics were used to support ideas about the organization of public space and Italian fascism's attempt to evoke and revive a Roman past, De Chirico and Carrà were not "fascist artists." The regime was openly resistant to the idea of a singular "fascist art"; when the Novecento Group was launched in 1923 at the Pesaro Gallery in Milan, Mussolini was among the speakers at the preview, and he made it clear that he was not endorsing one particular movement: "Far be it from me to encourage something that appears to resemble the art of the State."[45] His noncommittal remarks reflect ongoing debates in *Critica Fascista*, the principal outlet for discussing how Italian fascism should be practiced. Giuseppe Bottai, the journal's editor, argued that aesthetics could not be imposed on artists; as Marilisa Casturà summarizes, it was believed that "only the younger generations, educated under the regime, would create a fascist art."[46] The National Fascist Party (PNF) principally delineated aesthetics through a set of negative guidelines rather than positive recommendations; for example, Bottai labeled "'psychoanalytic, fragmentary, syncopated' works as 'rebellions against the great Italian artistic tradition.'"[47] The artists who were most often singled out for praise, such as De Chirico and Carrà, fused "tradition" with an avant-garde style.

Architecture was a key component in the Return to Order and in aesthetic fascism; in *Critica Fascista*, the art critic Mario Tinti argued that there should be a "hierarchy among plastic arts, where architecture was considered the true expression of fascism because it combined all other art forms, and could regulate their styles and functions, making production homogenous in the realization of public commissions."[48] Ideas about what this new architecture would look like were centered on an opposition between Rationalism (functionalism, as it developed from Le Corbusier) and traditionalism (e.g. Classicism), with favor generally falling on the side of traditionalism. Ardengo Soffici, writing in *Critica Fascista*, accused Rationalists of "lacking imagination and plastic understanding, real culture, natural simplicity and national instinct."[49]

The words "plastic" and "plasticity" appear frequently in discussions among the political right in Italy and surface at important moments in the writing of the Rapallo poets.[50] At the Novecento Group's 1929 exhibition in Milan, its second major show, Mussolini "praised the 'decisiveness and precision of line, clarity and richness of colour, the solid plasticity of objects and human figures'" in the paintings.[51] "Solid plasticity" seems like an oxymoron, but Mussolini was referring to the capacity of the solid architectural object—specifically, Roman and Renaissance structures—to evoke an idea of Italy that was not fixed in the past or the present but was nonetheless firm, tangible, and anti-mystical. In *Jefferson and/or Mussolini*, Pound argued, "We know what the artist does, we are, or at any rate the author is, fairly familiar with a good deal of plastic and verbal manifestation. // Transpose such sense of plasticity or transpose your criteria to ten years of fascism in Italy. And to the artifix," that is, Mussolini himself.[52]

The similarity of Giorgio De Chirico's Novecento work to Dorothy Pound's painting has been noted in passing, but the politics of the aesthetic have not been discussed as they relate to Dorothy Pound's endorsement of the Italian fascist project.[53] The watercolours and drawings that she published in *Etruscan Gate* show the changes that she made to her painting after leaving Paris. In Rapallo, her work—including her drawings for *A Draft of XXX Cantos*—moved away from the rigid lines and sharp angles that had characterized her Vorticist style for a decade.[54] In her painting from the late 1920s and into the 1930s she distinguishes between fixed architectural forms and a fluid, amorphous natural environment. For example, in "Villa Adriana" the solid arches, walls, and paving stones are set against a nebulous landscape. (Ezra was less impressed with the site, describing the Adriana as "a pseudo-palace or Giudecca—gorgeous views but rather imitation antico."[55]) Dorothy's depiction of the twelfth-century House of the Knights of Rhodes juxtaposes the clean, light walls and arches of the Renaissance building against the dark, modern temporary structure below. Her caption, "After excavations while making Mussolini's road to the Forum," points explicitly to the regime's extensive urban planning projects, which interested Ezra and which he writes about in *Jefferson and/or Mussolini*.[56]

One of the most important paintings in *Etruscan Gate* is the eponymous watercolor that depicts the Augustan Arch in Perugia: one of eight city gates that led into the ancient city, only two of which survived into the modern period. The gate was constructed in the third century BC, restored by Augustus in 40 BC and again at the end of the quattrocento, when a loggia—or gallery supported by columns and arches—was added to the upper left of the main arch. The scale and quality of the ruins in Perugia helped inspire the fascist regime's establishment in the city of a *università per stranieri*, or "university for foreigners" in 1921, which had the aim of "advertising the excellence of Italian culture."[57] The Pounds visited Perugia in April 1922 (and again in May), on their tour of places for Ezra's parents to retire.[58]

MAKING LIVING HISTORY   115

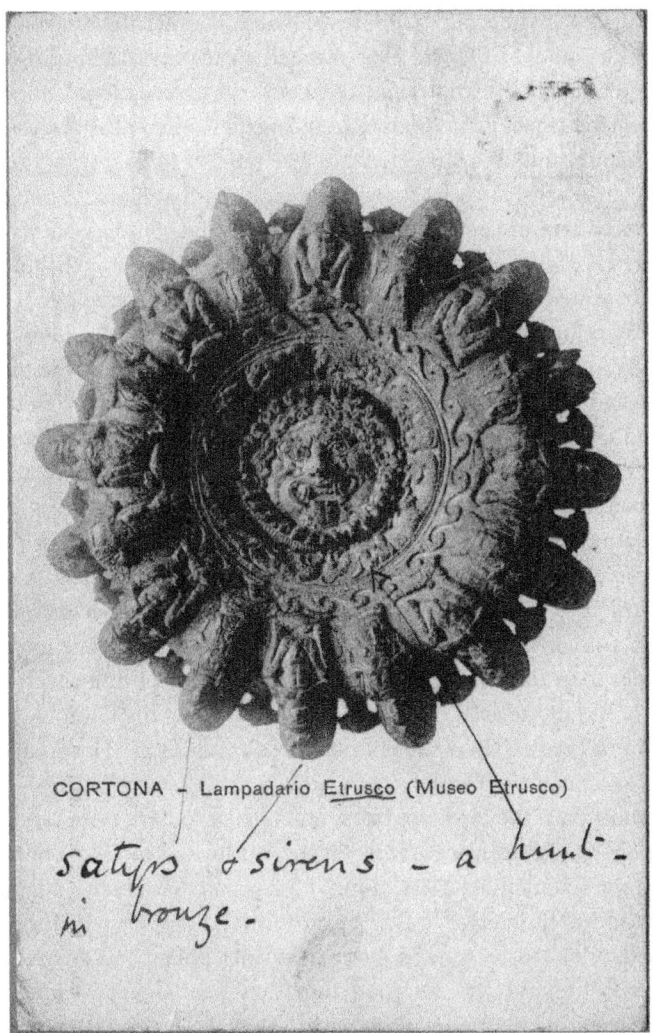

Figure 5.2 Postcard from the Etruscan Museum, Cortona
Source: Pound Family Postcards, Omar S. Pound Archives, Hamilton College, Clinton, NY.

From Cortona, Dorothy sent her mother a postcard of a bronze Etruscan sconce (Figure 5.2): "anything in Frazer about Etruscan symbols? Have been to an Etruscan family vault—deeply interested! Gorgeous picture gall. [in] Perugia."[59]

Postcards, a phenomenon of bourgeois tourism in the late nineteenth and early twentieth centuries, had particular importance in interwar Italy, when the country was suffering from the global economic depression and the sharp devaluation of the lira that resulted in a stark decline in tourism. Mussolini focused on improving the country's international standing by hosting international exhibitions, like the Volta Conferences discussed later in this chapter, and the regime tried to lure tourists to Italy with glossy promotional materials, such as those produced for Rapallo.[60] While historic sites featured on early postcards, such as those Olivia Shakespear sent to her daughter, the fascist regime gave renewed attention to the way that these sites were represented in an attempt to propagate the state's ideology. Lasansky notes how postcards in the 1920s and 1930s established "monuments not only as sites untouched by modernity but also as places where the interested tourist could still visit the medieval and Renaissance past."[61] The Pounds embraced this idea with their tours to research the Malatesta cantos in the early 1920s and in their excursions after they settled in Rapallo, which shaped both Ezra and Dorothy Pound's representations of Italy's living history.

The Pounds were specifically interested in the regime's urban planning projects in South Tuscany and Umbria. They collected postcards on their tour of the area in 1928 that document the aesthetics that focused their attention, similar to the way that W.B. and George Yeats's collection of postcards from their tour of Sicily with the Pounds in 1924 influenced the discussion of Byzantine aesthetics in *A Vision*.[62] Among the Pounds' extensive collection of images, there are six postcards from Ascoli Piceno, five from Perugia, and one from Gubbio ("not v much to see," according to Dorothy). For the most part, the cards are blank and appear to have been kept as aides de memoir. One card from Ascoli Piceno, addressed to Olivia Shakespear and postmarked October 1928, notes: "Gorgeous drive here—a large town full of beautiful buildings."[63] The "beautiful buildings" included the gate to the Palazzo Bonaparte, framed by quattrocento pillars and an arch, which the Pounds thought was so good that they sent one postcard of it to Shakespear and kept one for themselves. They were also fascinated by the thirteenth-century Basilica of Saint Francis of Assisi, and they purchased postcards of the side gate with the quattrocento façade and the interior colonnade, landmarks that reappear seven years later in one of Ezra Pound's most notorious treatises.

In *Jefferson and/or Mussolini*, Ezra Pound writes about the aesthetics of the regime as they are captured in Dorothy Pound's art:

From Sicily up to Ascoli [...] the pure lines of the Romanesque are dug out, the old ineradicable Italian skill shows in the anonymous craftsmen

Figure 5.3 Postcard from Ascoli Piceno, denoting the Roman-era "twin gates"
Source: Pound Family Postcards, Omar S. Pound Archives, Hamilton College, Clinton, NY.

[....] It is a reconquest of ancient skill, such as I saw the head artisan using in Teramo or in Ascoli Piceno up in the mountains over there by the Adriatic "where nobody goes."[64]

At Ascoli, the Pounds bought a postcard of a panorama of the bridge and new road leading to the city from the countryside to the north, and another of the Porta Gemina, a gate dating from the Roman period that shows clear signs of fascist-era "rediscovery" in the cement pillars buttressing one of the ends (Figure 5.3).[65] It seems probable that Ezra Pound referred back to these images when he writes, "here a column, there an entire cloister—or a school of practical art, rising again and making new plinths, capitols, and ornamental pieces, with perfection equal to the ancient, when they are missing the originals."[66]

When they were in Teramo, about twenty miles south of Ascoli Piceno, the Pounds bought a postcard of a Roman gate that had been remodeled in the quattrocento, was occupied by present-day citizens, and was undergoing fascist "rediscovery," denoted by the wooden buttresses that indicated a renovation in process; the abbreviation "Mon. Naz." (Monumento Nazionale) is superimposed at the top of the image (Figure 5.4).[67] These postcards

Figure 5.4 Postcard from Teramo, showing the fascist-era "recovery" of the city's monuments
Source: Pound Family Postcards, Omar S. Pound Archives, Hamilton College, Clinton, NY.

document the change captured by Antonio Maraini, writing for *L'Illustrazione Italiana*:

> In the Foro Mussolini, the Arco di Bolzano, the Casa Madre dei Mutilati, the Palazzo delle Corporazioni, stadiums, Fascist Party branch offices, stations, schools, and innumerable public buildings in Rome and other cities of Italy [...] even in the new agricultural centres of the grained Aries in Littorio and Sabaudia, it is here, in this magnificent sprouting of palaces, squares, streets open to life, study and the traffic of the nation, that a Fascist art has principally been developed.⁶⁸

The direct connection between the Pound family's postcards and Dorothy Pound's drawings is indicated by a card from the southern Tuscan town of Pitigliano, depicting the city walls and the arches of a Roman aqueduct. On the back is a drawing in Dorothy's hand of arches and walls illuminating the letter P (Figure 5.5).⁶⁹

The sketch resembles an attempt at one of the alphabet designs for the Hours Press edition of *A Draft of XXX Cantos* and is a strong indication that Dorothy Pound's interest in the fascist revival of the Roman past was instrumental in shaping—perhaps even motivating—Ezra's interest in

MAKING LIVING HISTORY 119

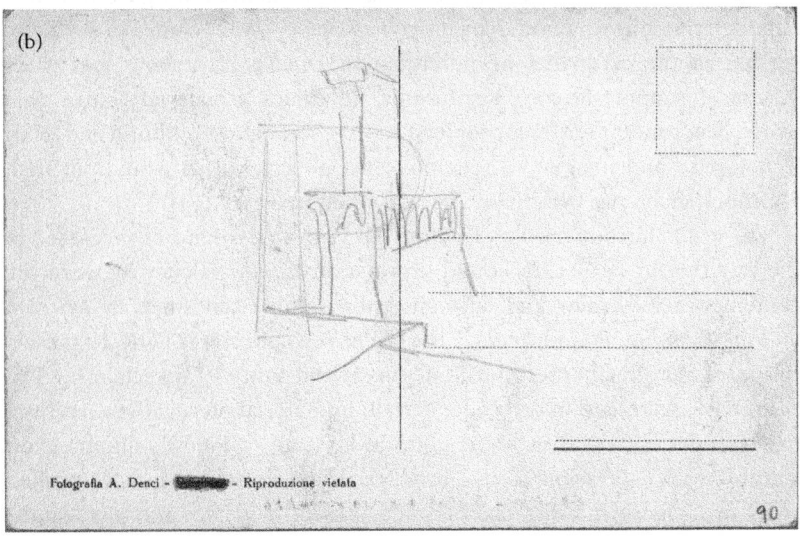

Figure 5.5 Postcard from Pitigliano, (a) with the name of the town scratched out on both sides, and (b) Dorothy's sketch of the "P" and aqueduct design
Source: Pound Family Postcards, Omar S. Pound Archives, Hamilton College, Clinton, NY.

architectural forms. The success of the limited edition of *A Draft of XXX Cantos* inspired the Pounds to embark on an expanded Cantos project featuring architectural elements, but those plans were cut short by the onset of the Second World War.[70] The importance of recognizing the link between the shift in Dorothy Pound's aesthetic and the wider context of interwar Italy isn't a matter of simplistically underscoring her fascism: it's to understand how the change in her aesthetics indicates a late modernist turn in her work, and it's to see how this turn is intricately related to conversations among the Rapallo poets about art and architectural forms.

Writing for Caesar's Eyes

W.B. Yeats's letter following Mussolini's March on Rome, in which he praised Italy as a bastion of order that could be a model for post-revolutionary Ireland, and his speech at the Tailteann banquet two years later when he quoted Mussolini as a "great popular leader" are two remarkable instances of him referring to Italian fascism directly and with a positive tone. Both occasions were in the context of a private audience. In his public writing, he was far more circumspect, wary of endorsing any contemporary government—although his "Introduction to *Fighting the Waves*" (1932) comes close. In the version of the essay that he published in *Dublin Magazine*, Yeats lauds "Caesar's" support of state institutions, advocates a material culture that would be a conduit for Irish people to access their nation's cultural and intellectual past, and imagines a state educational system that would put Irish philosophers on par with their Classical counterparts.[71]

The 1932 "Introduction to *Fighting the Waves*" is a kind of precursor to the way that in 1935 Ezra Pound draws a direct equivalency between the contemporary dictator and an eighteenth-century statesman in *Jefferson and/or Mussolini*. Pound writes, "The fascist revolution was FOR the preservation of certain liberties and FOR the maintenance of a certain level of culture [....] a refusal to surrender certain immaterial prerogatives, a refusal to surrender a great slice of the cultural heritage."[72] Pound's emphasis on culture as an expression of an "immaterial prerogative" may have pushed Yeats to increase the distance between present-day Italy and eighteenth-century Ireland in his own writing. When Yeats redrafted his "Introduction to *Fighting the Waves*" for publication in the collection *Wheels and Butterflies* in 1934, his references to Italy all but disappear, and he omits the idea that material culture is the manifestation of an immaterial ideal. But in the 1932 introduction, historical time is collapsed, and the present is in dialogue with a living past.[73]

Yeats's 1924 Tailteann speech is the bedrock for understanding his projection of the new Italy as a political and cultural model for Ireland, even though Yeats's interest quickly moved away from party-political Italian fascism emblemized by Mussolini to aesthetic (and philosophical) fascism in its principal articulation by Giovanni Gentile.[74] The Tailteann Games were an occasion with broad ideological significance; as Mike Cronin has shown, the Games were an attempt "by the government to create a feeling of consensus in the Irish population and to encourage an identification with the new state." Moreover,

> the staging of an art competition within Aonach Tailteann represents an attempt by the state to present an image of itself for domestic and international consumption that embraced positive aspects of the Irish tradition for creativity, rather than the negative and destructive imagery of war and death.[75]

The attempt with Tailteann to "paper over the ideological cracks" was not unique; the Free State's method of using large-scale cultural projects to perform and to unify national consciousness is paralleled in what has been described as the "cult of display" in early fascist Italy.[76] The Italian state sponsored international art exhibitions and hosted international conferences on art and theater in order to perform the idea of a unified nation and to propagate the image of a mature state that cultivated its rich past, as Ruth Ben-Ghiat argues, to "convince foreign elites that fascism cared about culture."[77]

Yeats's praise of Mussolini in 1924 demonstrates his attraction to the "new Italy," at least insofar as it was being publicized, and this affinity continues up to at least 1932. In the 1925 version of *A Vision*, Italian thinkers are a model for modern Ireland, but by the 1937 book, his vision of Italy is drastically tempered.[78] In August 1937, Yeats included in a letter to Dorothy Wellesley his draft of a lyric that explicitly severs his own thought from contemporary politics: "Though I have bid you turn / From the cavern of the mind; / (There is more to bite upon / In the sunlight and the wind); // I did not say attend / To Moscow or to Rome / Turn from drudgery / Call the Muses home."[79]

Yeats did attend to Rome, at least once in a quasi-political capacity, when in early October 1934, he—accompanied by George, in the essential role of translator—was a delegate to the Volta Conference on theater.[80] While there, they may have also attended the Exhibition on the Fascist Revolution, which ran for two years from 28 October 1932 to 28 October 1934 and attracted nearly three million spectators.[81] A copy of the English-language exhibition catalogue rests in the Yeats Library; there is no record of its acquisition nor any correspondence mentioning the book in the extant W.B. Yeats letters, which suggests that W.B. or George Yeats procured it for themselves.[82]

The Exhibition of the Fascist Revolution exemplifies how the proclaimed capaciousness of the fascist state's aesthetics—articulated by Mussolini, Gentile, Bottai and others in the mid-1920s—was, by the mid-1930s, more fixed, more recognizably propagandistic and totalitarian. As the regime was consolidated, as Ben-Ghiat notes, "exhibitions took on a central importance as agents of indoctrination and mass mobilization."[83] Nominally, artists were still committed to the concept of "plasticity," but by 1934 the ideological referents were more clearly discernible. Marla Stone describes the professed aims of the artists included in the Exhibition of the Fascist Revolution:

> The artists believed in the malleability of artifacts and the possibility of using modernist art forms [...] to make the objects speak a number of messages [....] An interest in stretching the boundaries between "art" and "objects" allowed the artists' varied styles to blend and produce a coherent whole. The blurring of the distinction between "art" and "artifacts" gave the show its spiritualized character and its shape as a total experience.[84]

Ezra Pound visited the exhibition in December 1932, just two months after it opened. He commented briefly in a letter to Olga Rudge that it was an impressive example of "senso storico" or historical sensibility.[85] Ezra wrote to Dorothy, "Xposition of Xenio rather impressive. Not Art-show, but a history show to inskrukt."[86]

W.B. and George Yeats's impression—*if* they attended in person—seems irrecoverable. Despite the paucity of evidence regarding their views on the Exhibition, it *is* possible to reconstruct W.B. Yeats's participation in the Volta Conference and its effect on his ideas about theater, particularly the notion of heroic drama and its connection to a national culture. Yeats's thinly veiled comments at Volta about the Italian state may allude to his impression of the Exhibition of the Fascist Revolution; at the least, he comments on other manifestations of totalitarian aesthetics that were contradicting the purported "plasticity" of early Italian fascism.

Prior to the Volta Conference on theater, schisms arose over questions about the Conference's objectives, especially its privileging of dramatic theater over other types of performance. A letter, possibly by Marinetti, addressed to Arturo Marpicati, the Secretary of the PNF, cautioned against the polemical aim of the conference as it was initially formulated and recommended that the participants were selected with a view to their open-mindedness about theater. Marpicati in turn wrote to Mussolini, expressing the view that a polemical conference would be injurious to the aims of the Conference.[87] Ultimately, the Volta Conference on theater proclaimed—superficially, at least—the same openness that characterized the state's attitude to the visual arts, reflecting Bottai's idea that "the first reason for the relationship between art and the State is the vibrant and active participation of the artist in the State, the inescapable need, for the spiritual economy of the nation, for good artistic production."[88]

Ezra Pound may have been involved in bringing Yeats to Rome. In a letter to Homer Pound on March 21, 1928, Ezra wrote that he had received a letter from "Sem Benelli's onforchoonate sekertary who hopes to import the Celtic Drammer into Italy. deeply grateful for my assistance."[89] As founder of the Irish National Theatre, Yeats was a figurehead for state-sponsored theater in Europe, so he was an obvious choice of delegate, with or without Pound's involvement.

The Volta Conference on dramatic theater was held October 8–14, 1934, a date proclaimed in the conference's program as Year XII of the fascist regime.[90] The conference was sponsored by the Royal Italian Academy, whose president was Marconi, the pioneer of radio transmission, and it was presided over by Pirandello, who had been awarded the Nobel Prize earlier the same year and was in the midst of a sustained campaign for his own state-subsidized theater. Marinetti served as the conference's secretary.[91] The lavishly published program for the conference, preserved in the Yeats Library, outlines five aims: to put theater in dialogue with other art forms and media (specifically cinema, opera, and radio); to consider innovations in the architecture and scale of theater (both "theater of the masses" and little theatres); to explore new possibilities for stage design; to consider the role of performance in the moral life of the people; and to consider the idea of a State Theater—including the history of their organization throughout Europe, the need for state theaters in the present-day, the content of state theaters' programs, and the possibility for exchanges between state theaters.[92] Major figures in European drama were present; alongside Yeats were his long-term collaborator Edward Gordon Craig, and Ashley Dukes, whom Yeats hoped would be instrumental in producing a program of his plays for the Group Theatre in London that same autumn.[93]

In the midst of the Volta Conference, Yeats wrote to the dancer Margot Ruddock about the proceedings. The previous day, Walter Gropius, the first director of the Bauhaus School, had "described his latest invention," a pliable mechanical stage. Gordon Craig—hailed by Yeats as "the great man of the conference, all the young actors & producers gather round him"—mocked Gropius's new technology, saying, according to Yeats, "A producer who works for that theatre must know all that so & so knows [....] & when he knows all that his art will be dead; and when art is dead the nation is dead. I want men of 25 in the theatre."[94] Yeats animatedly described Alexander Tairoff, the founder of the Kamerny Theatre in Moscow, rising in agreement with Gordon Craig, while Marinetti violently disagreed: "his hands went round & round in mid air as though he were turning a wheel, & faster & faster as his passion climaxed [....] everybody shouted, while the helpless chairman Dukes rang his bell. So on for another hour."[95]

In Yeats's letter to Ruddock, the exchange is depicted as a comic interlude in a conference attended by larger-than-life personalities. But the disagreement epitomizes questions at the heart of Volta: what was theater's relationship to emergent technologies? How was theater to remain a living art? These questions were intrinsically political: Gordon Craig articulated and the debate exhibited the delegates' consensus that what happened in the theater set the course for the nation.[96] Tairoff's defense of Craig is important, since in Moscow, Tairoff had creatively negotiated the stalemate between psychological realism and "objective spectacle" that beset Russian theater in the 1920s.[97] Tairoff sought to synthesize "emotion and form" by developing a flexible performance space in which the width, depth, and height of the stage could be adapted according to the "emotional and rhythmic effect sought in each scene of each play."[98] These innovations were in concert with Gordon Craig's use of light, color, and screens—a method of stage design with which Yeats was still enthralled.

The aims of the Volta Conference illuminate an important aspect of Italian fascism's informal co-option of the theater, which was less prescriptive than the German National Socialist or Soviet Russian ideas that a "political public" could be created by the theater.[99] At the conference in Rome, practitioners focused on the adoption of existing theatrical practices rather than the formulation of a new dramatic theory that could disseminate the ideals of the Italian fascist state. Mussolini's view of theater was of a form that could be politically instrumental; as Bonsaver writes, the dictator was "the supreme arbiter of what was going to appear on Italian stages."[100]

Among the dramatists that Mussolini most admired were Gabriele D'Annunzio and George Bernard Shaw: "I am a great admirer of Shaw," Emil Ludwig reports the dictator saying, "but sometimes find his freakishness annoying [...] Pirandello writes Fascist plays without meaning to do so! He shows that the world is what we wish to make it, that it is our creation."[101] W.B. Yeats also admired Pirandello and dismissed Shaw—and for similar reasons. In August 1930, Yeats had written to Wyndham Lewis: "Your work, like that of Pirandello, who alone of living dramatists has unexhausted, important material, portrays the transition from individualism to universal plasticity, though your theme is not, like his, plasticity itself."[102] Yeats's interpretation of Pirandello's "plasticity" (his drama's availability to political meaning without being restricted to it) is probably informed by descriptions of Pirandello by a director on the Abbey Theatre's board, Walter Starkie, who was a scholar of Italian, don of Trinity College, and a proponent of European fascism.[103]

In Starkie's 1926 biography of Pirandello, he writes that it is unsurprising that Pirandello turned to drama, "in order that his ideas might find plastic representation [....] the plots are not so much mere *tranches de vie*, or tales of blood and passion, as the plastic interpretation of some profound thought."[104] Starkie adds, "The plays of our author, with their power of stimulating active reflection, are the very antithesis to the passive art."[105] Starkie's admiration for Pirandello's "active" theater chimes with his essays in the *Irish Statesman* the same year, in which he explains how Italian fascism has been "misunderstood in foreign countries" and how it articulates a "sane, idealistic patriotism" in which "the dictator" is welcomed by the Italian people because he "is able to appeal to their sense of the heroic."[106] Starkie's advocacy for a malleable, heroic theater resurfaces in his review of the Abbey Theatre's production of Yeats's *Oedipus at Colonus* (1927), which he admired as "graceful and pliant [....] through the paths of folk drama and folk poetry [.... Yeats calls] up before us the image of the Athenian national soul."[107] Starkie believed that the Abbey's performance instigated a collective response: "the audience...were profoundly moved [and] sat in solemn silence as though listening to the performance of some great ritual."[108] Shortly after Volta, in early December 1934, the Abbey staged Pirandello; Yeats told Margot Collis that the production of *Six Characters in Search of an Author* would be a test of the director of the second company's future at the Abbey.[109]

At the Volta Conference, Yeats's speech invested his plays with political meaning. Echoing Starkie's estimation of Pirandello, Yeats proclaimed that his own drama was "active" and that it had the potential to reunite a divided people who were without a unifying heroic personality. Similar to his Tailteann speech nearly a decade earlier, Yeats referred to the Parnellite split. Throughout his writing life, Parnell served as Yeats's touchstone for the heroic, and at Volta the references to Parnell carried additional weight, standing as a cipher for his critique of the recent Irish "revolution."[110] Yeats asked his audience: "Had Parnell been betrayed? Who had betrayed him? Families were divided, son against father, brother against brother." He continued, "In the midst of that disillusionment, of that bitterness, the Irish imaginative movement began."[111] Just as the Irish Revival could be imagined as being born out of the Parnellite split, so too Yeats's attempt at a second Revival—indicated in his essays and speeches, and the resurgence of his own work in Rapallo—were enlivened by the "bitterness" of the Irish Civil War.

Yeats regaled his audience with the story of the riots over the *Playboy of the Western World*: "Picturesque, poetical, fantastical, a masterpiece of style and music, it roused the populace to fury."[112] He implied that the Irish National Theatre's history was a long struggle against a "populace" or "mob" that had been miseducated by party politics and who lacked a heroic leader. Yeats described his squabble with the Abbey's company over Lady Gregory's play, *The Rising of the Moon*: "The players would not perform it because they said it was an unpatriotic act to admit that a policeman was capable of patriotism. One well known leader of the mob wrote to me, 'How can the Dublin mob be expected to fight the police if it looks upon them as capable of patriotism?'"[113] Yeats concluded, "Every political party had the same desire to substitute for life, which never does the same thing twice, a bundle of reliable principles and assertions."[114]

This last line is an echo of Yeats's long essay "Synge and the Ireland of His Time," which was published by Cuala Press as a little book in 1911. Just as he returned to the Irish Civil War in his Volta speech, Yeats reached back even further: to the riots over *The Playboy of the Western World*, and Dublin's rejection of the man that Yeats believed embodied Ireland's greatest genius. In his poem "On Those That Hated *The Playboy of the Western World*," he made Synge an incarnation of Don Juan, signifying sexual prowess and intellectual power.[115] Where his earlier declaration dismissed the "reliable principles" of the Irish nationalist movement as impotent, his disparagement of the "bundle of reliable principles" at Volta indicates his rejection of the totalizing iconography of the Italian fascist state as it was manifested under Mussolini and as it was articulated in Pound's increasingly totalitarian writing.

While Yeats dissented from party-political fascism, his ideas about theater are in alignment with Mary Ann Frese Witt's formulation of "aesthetic fascism" in Italy, which she describes as "On one level [...] part of the early modernist belief that innovation in art could lead to revolutionary change in politics [....] On another, it is a product of the aesthetic nature of certain political experiences such as the merging of self with a crowd representing national identity—the totalizing work of art representing the totalitarian state made famous by Walter Benjamin."[116] Starkie's description of *Oedipus at Colonus* gestures to his reception of Yeats's drama as a totalizing work of art. Yeats's own interest in totalizing theater is illustrated in his discussion of *The King of the Great Clock Tower*, a play that he was revising during the Volta Conference. (It would be renamed *A Full Moon in March* and would be a contender for Yeats's intended program for the Group Theatre in London.) In a letter to Edmund Dulac in December 1934—about six weeks after Volta—Yeats described *The King of the Great Clock Tower* as "theatrically coherent, spiritually incoherent." He told Dulac that his revision was driven by the need to "work out" a "blood symbolism" that had "laid hold upon" him, an impulse that Yeats believed came from "beyond the will."[117]

Conversations in Rome about forms of performance and their availability to political meaning were incorporated into Yeats's attempt to define a new kind of drama, which he described in his 1934 "Introduction to *Fighting the Waves*" as arriving at a "concrete universal," an Hegelian concept that has precise bearing on Yeats's right-wing politics.[118] When Yeats told Lennox Robinson that the idea of George Antheil as composer for the play's score was a matter of "divination," he also said that Antheil's music captured "the rhythm of the sea," which symbolized "that concrete universal which all philosophy is seeking."[119] As a complement to the metaphysical music, Yeats used Irish mythology surrounding the hero Cuchulainn as a means of giving his drama concrete expression. In the 1934 version of "Introduction to *Fighting the Waves*," Yeats imagined that he could create a dramatic form that would be mythical in its remove from "character and circumstance" and would be given "concrete" expression through a heroic figure.

Since his *Four Plays for Dancers*, Yeats had been exploring through his collaborations the possibilities of moving from a "literary" to a more physical theater that would retain the openness that he thought characterized the best drama. The political aspects of his early uses of physical expression are exemplified in his introduction to Pound and Fenollosa's *Certain Noble Plays of Japan* (1916) and its relation to Yeats's play *The Dreaming of the Bones* (1919). For Yeats, dance embedded the contingency (what Starkie, Yeats, Mussolini and others called "plasticity") that made drama resistant to a particular political meaning and ensured its universality. By the same token, Yeats grounded his plays in specific political meaning through the publication of paratexts—his introductions and commentaries—that interpret his play texts but also work as freestanding essays.[120] These prose pieces take forms as various as polemical treatise (as in his essays for *Dublin Magazine*) and esoterica intended for a particular intellectual elite, as in the small books that were published in very limited runs by Cuala Press.

Yeats's two remarkably different introductions to *Fighting the Waves* provide coordinates for his changing attitude to Italian fascism. Importantly, the play text of *Fighting the Waves*, which is a reworking of an earlier play *The Only Jealousy of Emer*, does not change after 1929. The play begins with Cuchulainn lying on what may be his death bed; his ghost is separate from him—played by another actor—and is visible onstage. His wife Emer and his mistress Eithne Inguba keep vigil. While Cuchulainn is in limbo, the women wage a spiritual battle to restore his life: Emer renounces her love for him in exchange for the return of his soul to his body, then Eithne Inguba calls to him; he awakens and shelters in Eithne Inguba's arms, and she claims to have saved him. The play's resolution is ironic: the warrior Cuchulainn is reunited with his lover, but he remains tied to the carnal instead of being elevated to a spiritual plane. This lack of spiritual fulfillment is clearer in the play's epilogue, which contains a thrice-occurring refrain intimating the failure of Cuchulainn to attain ultimate heroic transcendence: "O bitter reward / Of many a tragic tomb! / And we though astonished are dumb / And give but a sigh and a word, / A passing word."[121] The death of Cuchulainn—which marks the warrior's metamorphosis from the historical hero to the mythological hero—is delayed, and the heroic tragedy ends in disappointment.

Although the play text does not change after 1929, interpretations of the action of *Fighting the Waves* change in relation to the frames that Yeats provides in introductions that were published in *Dublin Magazine* (1932) and his book *Wheels and Butterflies* (1934). The differences in the two versions illustrate how the slipperiness that allows Yeats's drama to maintain its aesthetic quality also enables its function to express aesthetic fascism. Only the first paragraph of the introductions is identical, and the *Dublin Magazine* text significantly opens *Fighting the Waves* onto its Irish and Italian political contexts. In *Dublin Magazine*, Yeats's vision for his drama is framed as actively counter-revolutionary:

> We might, if the Irish Government at the establishment of the Free State had done something no revolution of strong farmers, clerks and lawyers

would permit, have founded a school that could have substituted, as only a literature without satirical or realistic prepossessions could, positive desires for the negative passion of a national movement beaten down into party politics, compelled for a century to attack everything, to suspect everybody. Only a Caesar could do what I want, but now that the Cellars and Garrets have taken to some kind of half pious communism they may produce one. I write for Caesar's eyes.[122]

In this essay, Yeats develops the idea of cellars and garrets that he raised in his 1931 *Dublin Magazine* "Commentary" where political workers ("cellars") and impoverished intellectuals ("garrets") are grouped together.

The unlikely union is facilitated by Yeats's interpretation of Hegel; in the "Genealogical Tree of Revolution" that accompanies Yeats's "A Race Philosophy," he writes that Hegel had resolved the antimonies, enabling "a diametrically opposed yet related series of propositions, centring on the materialist/idealist polarity.... Fascism, which had once seemed the antithesis of communism, now looked more like its mirror image."[123] (Ezra Pound resolves the antinomies simplistically: "Nowadays two are the men who knew how to 'move' to the highest degree, who had the mastery of language which produces action: Il Duce and Lenin."[124]) Claire Nally has argued, "For Yeats, both political regimes [communism and fascism] represent the suppression of individual freedom and thus are to be rejected."[125] However, Yeats did not immediately reject fascist movements: both the "Commentary on a Parnellite at Parnell's Funeral" and the 1932 "Introduction to *Fighting the Waves*" engage with Yeats's support for the Irish Blueshirts; he writes in the 1932 Introduction, "I know half a dozen men any one of whom may be Caesar—or Cataline." The Blueshirts' vacillation between authoritarianism and what Mike Cronin describes as an "allegiance" to "liberal democracy" contributed to Yeats's frustration with the Irish fascist movement.[126]

Yeats's arguments in favor of authoritarianism stem from his reading in Rapallo, and are partly rooted in his interpretation of Swift, particularly the 1701 essay "Discourse on the contests and dissentions between the nobles and commons of Athens and Rome."[127] Against the background of Yeats's long, intensive reading Swift, his specific use of the figure of Caesar in the 1932 "Introduction to *Fighting the Waves*" draws from his reading and discussion of Spengler with the Rapallo group. In *Decline of the West*, Spengler characterizes Caesar as "a pure man of fact gifted with immense understanding."[128] He formulates "the time of Caesar" as "the birth [of] the great religions of Salvation," and as a consequence "the Culture rose to bright day, and what followed continuously throughout one or two centuries was an intensity of religious experience, both unsurpassable and at long last unbearable."[129] In a long section on "Caesarism" in the chapter on "State and History," Spengler explicates the wholly anti-democratic nature of his terminology: "By the term 'Caesarism' I mean that kind of government which, irrespective of any constitutional formulation that it may have, is in its inward self a return to thorough formlessness." Spengler's "formlessness" is a manifestation of the concept of "plasticity" that is broadly advocated in Italian fascist aesthetics and is used very particularly as a virtue when Mussolini and Starkie refer to the work of Pirandello and Yeats.

Spengler believed that "Caesar-men," capable individual leaders, were "the very elementals of Becoming": the necessary "powers of the blood, unbroken bodily forces, [that] resume their ancient lordship."[130] When Yeats writes to Edmund Dulac that *The King of the Great Clock Tower* is made necessary due to a "blood symbolism" that comes from "beyond the will," he approximates a connection between himself and these "Caesar-men." Spengler argues very clearly that the "will" of Caesar is not individualistic in the "Napoleonic sense" but draws from the "root-feeling of the Roman soul": as Yeats put it, from "beyond the will."[131]

In the 1932 "Introduction to *Fighting the Waves*," Yeats imagines that the new Caesar—for whom he claims to write—will define and direct a national culture through public institutions:

> let Caesar talk to the Curator of the Museum; first doubling the Museum's inadequate grant [....] let Caesar command our Irish schools and colleges to teach Berkeley, side by side with more modern philosophy, or side by side with Aquinas as though he were Gaelic, and Kant or Aquinas Greek, and so save us from that popular science that is the opium of the suburbs.[132]

Yeats's references to museum culture draw from his campaign for a Municipal Gallery for the Hugh Lane pictures, when his national and artistic ambitions for Dublin were pitted against the city's financiers, principally William Martin Murphy. A belief in the importance of museums to Ireland's national life was shared among Yeats's political contemporaries; Count Plunkett, then director of the National Museum of Ireland, had commented in 1912 that "a Museum is more than a system; it is part of the national life, it is an expression of the national life and of the higher qualities of the people to whom it belongs."[133]

In Yeats's 1932 "Introduction to *Fighting the Waves*," his long campaign for national cultural institutions is conjoined with his intense interest in Berkeley's philosophy of immaterialism. In this essay, Yeats collapses the distance between the material object and the idea of the object in the mind of its perceiver, echoing Berkeley's concept that ideas were the only reality.[134] Berkeley and Swift come together in Yeats's play *The Words upon the Window-Pane* (written and performed in 1930; published in 1934), when the spiritualist medium Mrs. Henderson channels a dialogue between Swift and Vanessa in which Swift articulates the capacity of thought to bring about reality: "When I rebuilt Rome in your mind it was as though I walked its Streets." Similarly, in Yeats's 1931 introduction to Hone and Rossi's *Bishop Berkeley: His Life, Writings, and Philosophy*, he argues that the editors' treatment "makes Berkeley stand forth as a very real and solid...figure."[135] Hone and Rossi emphasize "Berkeley's return to philosophizing at a time when Berkeley's interests were more and more becoming 'practical morality, architecture and scientific curiosities, politics, economic conditions, the Bermuda enthusiasm.'"[136]

Hone and Rossi's emphasis on Berkeley's material concerns may have influenced Yeats's focus in the 1932 "Introduction to *Fighting the Waves*" for *Dublin Magazine*, where the material culture of eighteenth-century Ireland—the furnished rooms through which Yeats imagines visitors walking; the mundane objects and costumes of eighteenth-century Irish society—communicates a spiritual idea of the eighteenth century and brings it to life in the present. As much as Yeats draws from Berkeley, here he is also adapting Spengler's idea of Caesar. In the chapter on "Philosophy of Politics" in *Decline of the West*, Spengler concedes, "Caesar grasped the fact that on the soil of a democracy constitutional rights signify nothing without money and everything with it."[137] Spengler thought that materialism was necessary, but it was only a precursor to what he imagined as a "final battle between Democracy and Caesarism, between the leading forces of dictatorial money-economics and the *purely political* will-to-order of the Caesars."[138]

The connection between material culture and the idea of Caesar was being realized in the Italian fascist regime's urban planning projects, such as the building of the via dell'Imperio and the restoration of the imperial fora in Rome, which connected the seat of Mussolini's government at the Palazzo Venezia and the Roman Empire's "most visible monument."[139] Pound admired the project and its archaeological overseer, Corrado Ricci, whose excavations stood as a metaphor for Pound's idea of clearing away the "rubbish" as part of a continual process of cultural renewal.[140] In *Jefferson and/or*

Mussolini, Pound compared Mussolini as visionary architect to Brancusi, signifying—as Catherine Paul has argued—Pound's belief in Mussolini's "modernist vision" that stripped the excess away in order to reveal a selected "cultural heritage."[141]

Yeats thought that Pound's political treatises, which often segued into "money economics," were the line in the sand that differentiated him from the potential "Caesar-men." In 1934, the two poets had a spectacular disagreement over Yeats's new play, *The King of the Great Clock Tower*: a falling out that was the nadir of W.B. and George's visits to Rapallo. Tensions had been building for more than a year. When Homer and Isabel Pound took over the apartment, there were skirmishes about money that "the WBs" owed. Dorothy mediated because Ezra was too annoyed to get anything done: "DAMN the WBs / why don't they send their bleating RENT?!?!?! [....] Whether Yeats defection is the cause of [the agent] Piag. / being written again, I cant tell. At any rate YTZs ought to be smacked."[142] In fact, George had paid up, sending the rent directly to Homer who had neglected to pass it on to the agent.[143] At the end of June 1934, Ezra could only say, "dined with the Wm/B's last eve. Oh hell!!"[144]

Yeats's absence from Rapallo seems at least to have eased Pound's relations with Beerbohm: "Max, with perfect precision telephoned that it wd / be with gt / pleasure that he wd / see the YEAT // I told him it was now safe to xpress them senti mengs."[145] (Hauptman made his exit about the same time: "Gerhart finally left town / in [oh well, questionably whether rage, despair, anyhow ESCAPE]").[146] Pound and Yeats's history of friendly disagreement is proof that the poets knew how to differ without it ruining their relationship. But the clash between Yeats and Pound in 1934 was more than a conflict of personality. It may have been a quarrel with political implications: the influence of Spengler's Caesarism on *The King of the Great Clock Tower*, which Yeats was working on in Rapallo that June.[147]

In August 1934, Yeats wrote to Olivia Shakespear, enclosing a review of the play: "show to Ezra Pound that I may confound him. He may have been right to condemn it as poetry but he condemned it as drama."[148] In truth, Pound had been more scathing. The previous June in Rapallo, when Yeats shared the play with Pound, his response provoked such a passionate reaction that Yeats was compelled to write a defense in one of his Rapallo notebooks:

> He condemned it "Nobody language." At first I took his condemnation as a confirmation of my fear that I am now too old. I have ~~hardly~~ written

little verse for three years. But "nobody language" is something I can remedy. I never write in verse, but first in prose to get structure.[149]

In Cave's study of the manuscript materials for *The King of the Great Clock Tower*, he shows how Pound's critique prompted an immediate redrafting: Yeats developed his types into full characters, transforming the King into O'Rourke of Breffny and creating connections between O'Rourke's ancestry and Dervorgilla, who was important to his earlier Noh play *The Dreaming of the Bones*, itself very much a product of Stone Cottage. The revision had the effect of tying *The King of the Great Clock Tower* to the poets' history as collaborators, but—as Cave notes—the changes didn't stick; the revised text could possibly "rouse expectations that Yeats was writing to a political agenda; this would seriously jeopardize the communicating of his metaphysical theme about the slain but risen god."[150] But in the context of Yeats's modeling of his ideas after Spengler, the danger seems less that Yeats was concerned about a specific "political agenda" and more that he was worried that naming his characters and limiting his play to a particular set of mythologies would restrict the play's plasticity. In Spengler's terminology, *The King of the Great Clock Tower* would no longer embody aesthetic "formlessness."[151]

In the Cuala Press edition of *The King of the Great Clock Tower*, Yeats denounces a thinly anonymized Pound in terms that render Pound absurd but that also, more codedly, pitch Pound's contemporaneity against Yeats's timeless intellectual pedigree:

> I asked him to dine, tried to get his attention [....] he would not speak of art or literature, or of anything related to them. I had however been talking to his latest disciple [almost certainly Adrian Stokes] and knew that his opinions had not changed: Phidias had corrupted sculpture we had nothing of true Greece but certain *Nike* dug up out of the foundations of the Parthenon, and that corruption ran through all our art; Shakespeare and Dante had corrupted literature [....] [He] would talk of nothing but politics.[152]

In addition to portraying Pound as having a general disregard for tradition, Yeats depicts Pound as devoted to a single leader: he quotes Pound on "Mussolini and that hysterical imitator of his Hitler." By the time Yeats relays Pound's condemnation—which Yeats reduced to a single word "Putrid" at the end of the essay—the reader has already been persuaded that

Yeats's deep tradition is superior to Pound's frivolity and transience. Many readers after the Second World War would agree with Yeats all the more.

Conversations about Spengler in Rapallo reverberate in the "Introduction to *Fighting the Waves*" that was published in *Wheels and Butterflies* in 1934, with amorphous aesthetic-fascist ideas replacing the explicitly Italian line. In the *Wheels and Butterflies* version of the essay, Yeats criticizes contemporary European politics and privileges the kind of formlessness that Spengler associates with cultural purity:

> by the end of the nineteenth century, the principal characters in the most famous books were the passive analysts of events, or had been brutalised into the likeness of mechanical objects. But Europe is changing its philosophy. Some four years ago the Russian Government silenced the mechanists because social dialectic is impossible if matter is trundled about by some limited force. Certain typical books—*Ulysses*, Mrs. Virginia Woolf's *Waves*, Mr. Ezra Pound's *Draft of XXX Cantos*—suggest a philosophy like that of the Samkara school of ancient India, mental and physical objects alike material, a deluge of experience breaking over us and within us, melting limits whether of line or tint; man no hard bright mirror dawdling by the dry sticks of a hedge, but a swimmer, or rather the waves themselves [...].

Where the 1932 Introduction is focused on material artifacts as conduits for a spiritual past—ideas inherent to Italian fascism and expressed most directly in the Exhibition of the Fascist Revolution—the 1934 Introduction praises the way that the spiritual is communicated materially through great writing that is without limits. The changes that Yeats made to "Introduction to *Fighting the Waves*" reflect the development of *A Vision* (1937), where he asks, "What discords will drive Europe to that artificial unity—only dry or drying sticks can be tied into a bundle—which is the decadence of every civilisation?"[153]

In 1934, Yeats seems to believe that any kind of materialism is politically dangerous, perhaps taking Spengler's idea of the ultimate battle to its conclusion. Yeats describes,

> the greatest, perhaps the most dangerous, revolution in thought Europe has seen since the Renaissance, a revolution that may, perhaps, establish the scientific complement of certain philosophies that in all ancient countries sustained heroic art. We may meet again, not the old simple

celebration of life tuned to the highest pitch, neither Homer nor the Greek dramatists, something more deliberate than that, more systematised, more external, more self-conscious, as must be at a second coming [...].

They might after considering the demand of the black, brown, green, and blue shirts, "Power to the most disciplined," ask themselves whether D'Annunzio and his terrible drill at Fiume may not prove as symbolic as Shelley, whose art and life became so completely identified with romantic contemplation that young men in their late teens, when I was at that age, identified him with poetry itself.

In this later version of the essay, Yeats rejects the conflation of the poet and the historical individual, and he reconsiders what the heroic means in terms of *Fighting the Waves* (1929) and its 1932 Introduction. Where the 1932 essay describes at length the importance of state institutions and a state-sanctioned material culture—"We know nothing of the past if we do not know where men lived, what they handled and wore"—the 1934 Introduction dismisses the idea that the individual might stand for a material and spiritual whole: "The heroic act, as it descends through tradition, is an act done because a man is himself, because, being himself, he can ask nothing of other men but room amid remembered tragedies; a sacrifice of himself to himself, almost, so little may he bargain, of the moment to the moment."

The idea of "plasticity" that was integral to aesthetic fascism in Italy and that was so important to Yeats's late concept of theater is what enables his work to survive any one political meaning. The openness of the play texts obscures their aesthetic fascism, which can only be understood by considering each play text in relation to its framing devices. Yeats's introductions and commentaries have fixed temporal and political coordinates that change the meaning of the plays' action. In the decade between Yeats's praise of Mussolini in 1924 and his critique of fascism's "bundle of dry sticks" in 1934, the crosscurrents of exchange are deep and muddy, but they ultimately show that Italy was important to Yeats as more than a place of convalescence. Fascist ideas circulating through Rapallo and, later, Rome, were vital to the reinvigoration of his writing in the last phase of his career.

Figure 6.1 Ezra Pound on the rooftop of his apartment, overlooking Rapallo
Source: Photo by James Angleton; with thanks to David Moody.

6
Accounting for Rapallo

In Nancy Cunard's memoir, *These Were the Hours*, she recalls first meeting Richard Aldington "in Rome, in October 1928, after a party at Ezra Pound's apartment [….] I remember we had a delightful afternoon in Rome, or rather in the strikingly beautiful Roman countryside."[1] Cunard's stress on the words Rome and Roman—the location is repeated three times in the space of four sentences—insists that her encounter with Aldington, a classical scholar, occurred in a culturally rich and historically acceptable setting that is easily isolated from the weighty connotations of 1920s Italy.

Yet Cunard made regular trips to see Ezra Pound in Rapallo (Figure 6.1), and Rapallo was where Aldington and Brigit Patmore visited the Pounds in February 1929. Cunard's insistence on Rome may be a matter of misremembering, since she also errs in the dating of Richard Aldington's *The Eaten Heart*.[2] Even so, her emphasis on Rome and her repression of Rapallo is indicative of a strong tendency in literary history to situate Pound in metropolitan modernist networks and to imply—if not outright assert—that his move to Italy in 1924 was the beginning of a rapid decline into literary irrelevance, political extremism, and/or mental instability.[3] Cunard concludes her account of meeting Aldington by quickly reinserting Pound into the frame and then immediately removing him again: "We suddenly both thought of Ezra. Had he recovered from the previous evening? We would investigate at once. Calling at his place we found him, prone, with Dorothy hovering nearby. Ezra chatted, but he had soon to be left alone."[4]

The outbreak and aftermath of the Second World War meant that Pound's political allegiances became undeniable, and writers who had been in Rapallo felt compelled to account for their proximity to him and their presence in Italy during Mussolini's regime. Although H.D. was never in Rapallo, the place exerted strong psychic pressure on her past with Pound.[5] In her apologia, *End to Torment: A Memoir of Ezra Pound* (the title speaks more of her coming to terms with herself than with Ezra) she writes about visiting a Venetian church with Pound, shortly following her marriage to Aldington: "Years afterwards, I went again and I carried the votive card of

Santa Maria that the sacristan had given me, in my handbag, with another (St. Mark's) token picture, during the [World] War II years in London. Ezra was in Rapallo, as we all know."[6] Speaking on behalf of Pound's friends, she writes, "I can not say that any of us are satisfied with the equation, Fascist-party-line-by-short-wave-to-America + Poet = *Senilität*. There is, as I myself felt [...] the hint of a *crime passionnel*, for which [...] 'no jury' as the phrase has it, 'will convict.'"[7]

H.D. was compelled to write *End to Torment* after reading the essay "A Weekend with Ezra Pound" about the young scholar David Rattray's visit to St. Elizabeths, which was published in *The Nation* in 1957.[8] Aldington sent H.D. the article; she returned it, asked for it again, and offered to return it a second time, but Aldington told her to keep it, adding, "It is such a welcome change to have [Pound] reported as a human being, and not as journalist's abstraction or political 'cause.'"[9] By the mid-1950s, Aldington's feelings about Pound had mellowed, but in his more immediate writing, he holds Pound in deep contempt. In a lecture on Eliot and Pound that Aldington delivered in the United States in 1939, he recounted the dinner party in Rapallo when Yeats asked, "How do you account for Ezra?" Aldington elaborated, "only the other day I was telling this little anecdote to a young friend who asked: 'You mean to say neither of you knew the answer?' 'Yes.' 'Why, it's perfectly simple. In real life Pound is himself—in his best poems he's always someone else.'"[10]

In Aldington's own accounting for Ezra, *Life for Life's Sake* (1941), published in the midst of the Second World War, he denied culpability for time spent in Italy and described Pound as "a Rapallo troglodyte, suffering from the mental indigestion following on a feast of fascism plus the too-too solid hokum of Social Credit. *Que diable allait-il faire dans cette galère*."[11] The quote from Moliere—*What the devil was he doing with that crowd?*—applies, just as aptly, to Aldington himself. Born nearly a decade before "the Auden generation," Aldington takes pains to distance himself from the writers of the thirties:

> In my judgment the 1920s formed a brilliant but anarchic period fully deserving both in a bad and good sense its favourite adjective, "amusing." The ideals and differences of artists were largely aesthetic only. In reaction, the 1930s gave themselves up to political fanaticisms, and were consequently duller and less sincere—they all quacked what the big doctrinaire duck trumpeted. Moreover, the decade became more and more clouded with menaces and fears, so that many artists were tempted beyond the

boundaries of their legitimate activities; and in some countries were forced over them.[12]

In W.H. Auden and John Garrett's anthology *The Poet's Tongue* (1935), they are careful to explain that poetry as action is not didacticism: "Poetry is not concerned with telling people what to do, but [...] perhaps making the necessity for action more urgent and its nature more clear, but only leading us to the point where it is possible for us to make a rational and moral choice."[13] For Aldington, the idea of poetry as action was too similar to Pound's vision of the poet as political advisor. In *Life for Life's Sake*, he goes so far as to describe Imagism—of which he was a prime instigator—as a totalitarian takeover:

> I don't claim to be the Fuehrer of the Imagists [....] The fame or otherwise of Ducedom must go to Ezra, who invented the "movement" [....] Whenever Ezra has launched a new movement—and he has made such a hobby of it that I always expect to find one day that Pound and Mussolini are really one and the same person—he has never had any difficulty about finding members. He just called on his friends.[14]

Aldington uses the excuse of age to exonerate himself: "I was five years younger than the next youngest member of the group, and when the first Imagist poems appeared I was all of twenty."[15]

Dismissing as youthful folly the considerable body of work he had written before the First World War, Aldington presents the war as a coming-of-age rite and implies that the avoidance of conscription had stunted Pound's poetic growth. (This was not far off Pound's own worry that his lack of experience of war hampered his ability to write effectively about it.[16]) In language evocative of H.D.'s psychoanalytic register, Aldington chastises Pound as "one of the problem children of modern poetry." He cites Ford Madox Ford, who despite being twelve years older than Pound had enlisted and nearly died at the Somme: "Hueffer used to say that Ezra is so ignorant of the English language that it is impossible to understand him."[17] Aldington similarly accuses Yeats of an inability to comprehend how the First World War had changed poetry; he wrote to Thomas MacGreevy in 1931,

> We helped to carry the world on our bayonets at twenty, and we are entitled to a certain respect in consequence. We passed beyond life and death, beyond good and evil, and a man like W.B. should be able to tell the

difference [....] It is not a question of our gifts but of experience; we are men, while they are eternally adolescent. Discuss the same unto W.B., firmly, when you next see him.[18]

Pound's failure to enlist in the First World War still rankled as late as 1959, after Aldington (according to H.D.) had arrived at a more charitable view of Ezra. That year, Aldington wrote to MacGreevy about the newly published *Casebook on Ezra Pound*, which compiled "evidence" for and against Pound's indictment for treason: "I think he was too crazy to realise what he was saying [in the broadcasts from Rome], but one of them is a distinct appeal (or order) to the US troops in Africa to stop fighting! 'Pétan was defending Verdun while Blum was defending a bidet,' says he [the quote is from the *Pisan Cantos*]. Well, and what was Ezra doing in 1914–18? Dodging the draft!"[19]

Gertrude Stein's invention of "the Lost Generation" created the terms by which Aldington and MacGreevy could define their comradeship as poets and their differences to their peer, Pound, and predecessor, Yeats.[20] Their affinity shows that literary generations are not dependent on strict chronology—the proximity of birthdays and death dates—but are created by writers who sense a commonality in experience and expression.[21] (Hemingway, reflecting on a statue of Michel Ney, who had made a "fiasco [...] of Waterloo," wrote memorably, "I thought that all generations were lost by something and always had been and always would be."[22]) In Aldington's and MacGreevy's memoirs, they both focus extensively on Yeats as a poet of the *fin de siècle*, not a "modern" who was their contemporary. Aldington comes close to caricature in his depiction of a bumbling, esoteric, naïve elder who had the "curious trait" of "misplaced intellectual loyalty":

> Every influence, however distant, which had come into his poetical life had to be cherished and somehow reconciled with all the later influences and Yeats's own continuous developement [*sic*]. He seemed unable to take the more rational position of admitting frankly that such people had once been valuable to him, but that while he was grateful to them he had gone on to something new. This persisted even in Yeats's later years when he made that remarkable recovery and wrote some of the most beautiful lyrics of our time.[23]

For Aldington, Yeats's eccentricity and achievement excuses his irrationality. Letters between Aldington and MacGreevy puzzled over Yeats's strange devotion to Pound, and Aldington gossiped, "Yes, the W.B.—Olivia amour seems certain, and is widely known. Indeed, I have to expend some energy in contradicting professors who are asserting that Dorothy is Yeats's daughter, which of course would explain his otherwise inexplicable entanglement with Ezra [....] As to the W.B. Ezra link—as you know, D. and George were cousins and lived almost as sisters, which surely is enough to explain the Ezra situation?"[24]

The title of MacGreevy's 1966 essay "W.B. Yeats: A Generation Later" alludes to the way that a new generation was created by Yeats's death in January 1939. What first appear to be idiosyncratic points of focus for MacGreevy's argument on closer examination are revealed as attempts to justify Yeats's politics in the 1920s and 1930s, after the Second World War made the aesthetics of violence untenable. For example, MacGreevy chose to write about *The King of the Great Clock Tower*, over which Yeats and Pound disagreed, and he stresses the play's similarity to Oscar Wilde's symbolist play *Salome*. In Yeats's published notes to *The King of the Great Clock Tower*, he acknowledges the proximity of his subject to *Salome* but emphasizes that in Wilde's play, "the dance is before the head is cut off."[25] Yeats deliberately diminishes *fin de siècle* associations and calls attention to his own play's use of music, dance, and costume as characteristic of the Noh, disguising too the resonances with Spengler that are evident in Yeats's private correspondence about the play.[26] In "W.B. Yeats: A Generation Later," MacGreevy writes that of all Yeats's plays, he prefers *The Unicorn from the Stars* (1907); in the notes to *The Unicorn from the Stars*, which MacGreevy doesn't cite, Yeats specifies that the play "had to be done without hurry or violence."[27] It seems that MacGreevy's choice of text is calculated to exculpate Yeats from association with a violent, fascistic aesthetic: "That play [*Unicorn*] was written in 1908 twenty-five years before Adolf Hitler came to power in 1933, but when I saw it played in London in 1940 it seemed to me so cogent to the European situation of the day that (apart needless to say from the beauty of the treatment) it might have been commissioned from some Allied literary propagandist."[28]

The punitive treaties imposed after the First World War delineated the political fault lines of the Second, and the roots of some of the most harrowing events of the 1930s and 1940s can be traced back to the cultural nationalism that pervaded late nineteenth-century Europe. Even so, due to a seductive narrative of Irish oppression and liberation, the lumping in of Ireland with other "small nations" during and after the First World War, and problematic Irish neutrality during the Second World War, the Irish Revival has not come under the same scrutiny that has been applied to other western and central European cultural nationalisms. So, in 1966—the centenary of the Easter Rising—MacGreevy could write assuredly, without making himself or his subject vulnerable to aspersions, that Yeats "accepted the idea that a distinctive cultural heritage implies distinctive nationhood."[29]

MacGreevy still had to account for Yeats's belief in an intellectual aristocracy that was preserved by the Irish Protestant landed class, and drafts of "W.B. Yeats: A Generation Later" show him struggling to construct an adequate defense.[30] He decided to tackle Yeats's 1924 Tailteann speech head-on:

> In his lecture, W.B. put forward these two [i.e., Swift and Burke], and George Berkeley with them, as reactionary (which to him, in his political innocence, meant merely orderly) counterblasts to the revolutionaries. Politically, W.B. was as innocent as most laymen. About 1923 or 1924 he told me he believed that Mussolini represented the rise of the individual man as against what he considered the anti-human party machine. I was most distrustful about "Il Duce" but I did not know enough then to answer that Mussolini was believed to be in the hands of an economically, and therefore politically, powerful group of men in Italy. W.B. did know enough abstract history, to know that it is axiomatic that revolution has to be followed by reaction. The Irish ascendency as a whole had tended to be selfishly reactionary [....] W.B. would insist on trying now to provide the ascendency with a group of philosophic avatars, Swift and Berkeley and Burke, who were reactionary but not selfish.[31]

It is tempting to give MacGreevy the benefit of the doubt about whether Yeats knew the meaning of "reactionary"; however, in a letter to Lady Gregory in 1913 Yeats had deployed the term with biting accuracy: "I hear that Prof Trench is a candidate for Dowden's place. I hope he does not get it as a protestant bigot is the last thing desirable in TCD & his ideas of teaching seem to me reactionary."[32] (Yeats also used "reactionary" to great effect against Shaw.[33])

W.B. Yeats's death in the January before the Second World War erupted in September eased MacGreevy's claim of "political innocence," but there remains the problem of Yeats's most extreme pronouncements—not only the 1924 Tailteann speech and *Irish Times* interview but also the 1935 "Commentary on a Parnellite at Parnell's Funeral." MacGreevy turns Yeats's strident support of constructive authoritarianism in that essay into an unsolved proposition: "The question was whether, in the new order of things created in Ireland by the Treaty, ascendancy people as a whole could be persuaded to play a constructive part. That could help towards the ultimate realisation of the unified and cultured Ireland of W.B.'s dreams."[34] Couching Yeats's arguments as ineffective, MacGreevy claims they are also innocuous: "There is little evidence to show what influence his famous lecture has had on the ascendancy."[35]

In 1932, Richard Aldington and Thomas MacGreevy had corresponded about the impending danger in Europe. That June, Aldington warned of "a general collapse somewhere between July and late September" and advised that MacGreevy and "Sam [Beckett] would be wise to get back to Ireland this summer. Every government will have to try to ration its nationals, but it won't be pleasant to be in a foreign country, especially if there are moratoriums flying about."[36] Near the end of September, Aldington wrote again, suggesting that MacGreevy had been (and perhaps still was) naïve about the danger:

> Italy is so spoiled and one gets so weary of Fascist brag and interference. They've killed the old Italy—one more sweet benediction of that blessed war. And you will have seen that Germany has failed as a democracy and has gone reactionary. They've begun by a purity campaign, which always means preparation for War [....] War was nearer than you perhaps realise. I saw what was happening in Italy, and we were prepared to leave at an hour's notice. Those Italians in power now are shits, real shits, and a most disturbing force in Europe.[37]

Aldington's advice may have been the deciding factor in MacGreevy's taking leave of Paris for home—first going back to his native Tarbert in County Kerry, then to Dublin for the whole of 1933, before moving to London where he stayed long enough to help remove paintings from the National Gallery during the Blitz.

In 1955, MacGreevy was awarded the Order of Merit of the Italian Republic by President Luigi Einaudi; the same year, Italy and Ireland joined the United Nations. MacGreevy was shocked when, a mere three years later, Ireland's long-standing Taoiseach, Eamon de Valera, proposed to replace the electoral system of proportional representation with the single non-transferable vote (the British "first past the post" system). MacGreevy responded angrily with the essay "Strong and Able Government Versus

Good Government" in which he poured out his wrath on Irish politics and Italian recent history: "The Irish people also have a shrewd idea of what the influences were that made Eamon de Valera commit Ireland so gratuitously to the recognition of the Italian Black and Tannery in Abyssinia [....] The influences to which De Valera has submitted in the case of the Abyssinian scandal are now being brought to bear on him with a view to the repression of minorities at home."[38] MacGreevy suggests that a blend of populism and Catholic nationalism was to blame; he continued, "'Strong and able' government means the tyranny of authority imposed by unproductive capital from above, not derived from the productive life of the masses below. Ask the representatives of any of the progressive minorities who survive from the days of relative liberty in Germany or Italy. They know."[39]

Apologia and Amnesia

Unlike Aldington and MacGreevy, who visited Rapallo relatively early in Pound's fascist involvements, Louis Zukofsky did not visit Rapallo until 1933, and he maintained a close relationship with Pound up to at least 1939 (Figure 6.2). In Steve Shoemaker's essay, "Between Contact and Exile," he describes Pound and Zukofsky as "two men, of two different generations and two different ethnic backgrounds, who referred to each other as 'Sonny' and 'Papa' in their correspondence, [and] were caught in a conflict that was at once private and public, intimate and historical."[40] Shoemaker argues that Zukofsky sublimated an "ethnic identity" to fall in line with Pound's totalitarian dictate, while Zukofsky also "forged an aesthetics and an ethos, of survival." Undoubtedly, Zukofsky felt that he had to submit to the editorial control of his patron. What is less clear is the degree to which he suppressed an "ethnic identity," given his statement in 1931 to Carl Rakosi, the son of German Jewish parents that had immigrated to Wisconsin, "a Jewish ethics—I ain't got it myself—it's purely a family affair."[41]

In August 1945, two months after Pound was sent to the Disciplinary Training Camp outside Pisa, Zukofsky proposed that he and Basil Bunting make a public statement on Pound's behalf. He also suggested that Bunting's diplomatic connections might be worked in Pound's favor. Bunting replied, "I have worried about Ezra. But there is nothing I can do. Your name and mine would carry no weight anyway, and if they would, what excuse could we find him that any portion of the public would understand?"[42] Bunting saw clearly where Pound had gone astray—"Bitterness with his own public,

Figure 6.2 Postcard picturing Rapallo
Source: Zukofsky Collection, Harry Ransom Center, The University of Texas at Austin.

astute flattery from 'the great,'"—but Bunting thought "it would take a whole volume to make it plain even to sensitive folk."[43]

As Zukofsky sought the words that might give some accounting, he was paralyzed by the horror of *what* he would have to account for. Confronted with an ethical crisis, he wondered if he might find an answer in Spinoza, whose philosophy he had debated with Pound in the 1930s.[44] Bunting consoled, betraying his own racist language,

> Spinozism is the essence of good Judaism, I imagine. But he [Spinoza] was not an Orthodox Jew, nor, in the ordinary sense, a Jew by religion at all: which is what I meant.
>
> And I can't & don't blame you for standing on principle & not writing Ezra. You will remember I asserted that principle in that way myself, before the War. But I am a kind of Christian. Ezra is no longer a danger to things I hold to be the essence of Christianity, such as the fact that Jews & Christians are all sons of one father (with Niggers & Hindus as well).[45] All he is now, is an old man in distress, who seems to look to me and Eliot for a kind of help no one else can quite give him.[46]

The incident "before the war" that Bunting mentions took place in 1938, when he had defended Zukofsky because Zukofsky would not defend himself.

Bunting saw a letter that Pound wrote to Zukofsky in which he blamed the Rothschild family—not the Nazis—for the persecution of Jewish people. It was the last straw. Bunting wrote angrily to Pound:

> I cant take it. I wish I were not as much indebted to you as I am [....] Every anti-semitism, anti-niggerism, anti-moorism, that I can recall in history was base, had its foundations in the meanest kind of envy and greed. It makes me sick to see you covering yourself with that filth [....] Either you know men to be men, and not something less, or your make yourself an enemy of mankind at large.
>
> To spue out anti-semitic bile in a letter to Louis, as I yesterday accidentally discovered you to be doing,—to Louis who has shown his devotion to you over many years, and who even now insists that you are to be forgiven because after all you are Ezra—to write such a letter is not a mere lapse of taste: it is uncommonly close to what has got to be called the behavior of the skunk [....]
>
> I suppose if you devote yourself long enough to licking the arses of blackguards you stand a good chance of becoming a blackguard yourself. Anyway, it is hard to see how you are going to stop the rot of your mind and heart without a pretty thoroughgoing repudiation of what you have spent a lot of work on. You ought to have the courage for that: but I confess I don't expect to see it.[47]

Despite Bunting's confrontation, Zukofsky remained deferential to Pound, claiming not to have been offended by the letter about the Rothschilds. He told Pound it had "offended Basil because he feels I'm a very Jewish Jew, which I don't feel [....] It was none of his business to take it upon himself etc, but I admire him for having done it, whatever reservations I may have as to the usefulness of his action."[48] Bunting's letter was the most emphatic of a long correspondence with Pound about politics, going back to at least 1934.[49] Because Bunting felt he had engaged ethically with Pound, and because he had enlisted in the Second World War explicitly to "stop Hitler and his appalling career," after the war and during Pound's internment and hospitalization, he could respond compassionately.

By withholding "blame" and respecting Zukofsky's decision not to write to Pound, Bunting offered a kind of absolution from the guilt of inaction that plagued Zukofsky. Bunting freed Zukofsky to write *about* Pound, if not *to* him. Zukofsky made his first public account for Pound in a short piece for Charles Norman's book, *A Case of Ezra Pound* (1948); even then, he began with a confession: "I should prefer to say nothing now. But a preference for silence might be misinterpreted by even the closest friends."[50] The essay is adapted from a letter that Zukofsky wrote to Norman, which was revised by William Carlos Williams.[51] Williams's deletions temper Zukofsky's statement, eliminating his railing against "the stupid" who could not understand the "truth" of Pound's essay "Medievalism" and Zukofsky's complaint that the United States citizens who "effectively supported the cause Pound foolishly broadcast have not been brought to justice."

Charles Norman's biography *Ezra Pound* (1960) was born out of the 1948 *Case of Ezra Pound*, in which he professes "strict impartiality" but which makes an argument *for* rather than about Pound.[52] Norman claims, for example, that in Rapallo, Pound "lived in renowned seclusion, a poet and scholar out of touch with the world, hugging to his bosom medieval manuscripts and modern economic theories over which he cogitated."[53] He states matter-of-factly, "It was during the regime of Benito Mussolini."[54] Norman's framing of Pound's life in Rapallo compounded Zukofsky's ethical dilemma and also created an image problem for Zukofsky as a writer who was Jewish. Norman explains that the postscript to Pound's *ABC of Economics* was dated "Feb. 12, anno XI dll' era Fascista—that is, February 12, which is Lincoln's Birthday, in the 11th year of the fascist era, which was 1933."

If it were not enough that Norman implicated Zukofksy in visiting a known fascist in 1933, Norman writes that when Pound visited the United States in 1939, he "brought his enthusiasm for fascism, his theories on economics, and his anti-Semitism. He was not a welcome visitor; friends of a lifetime shut their doors on him in disgust; the most charitable view was that he was a sick man."[55] But Zukofsky had not shut his door; he had welcomed Pound in, and—according to Zukofsky—they had simply agreed to disagree: "When he was here [i.e., New York] in 1939, I told him that I did not doubt his integrity had decided his political action, but I pointed to his head, indicating something had gone wrong [....] Whatever you don't know, Ezra, you ought to know *voices*. This exchange of frankness was accepted tacitly by both of us as a dissociation of values above personal bickering."[56]

Zukofsky's justification for remaining proximal to Pound was that he "never felt the least trace of anti-Semitism in [Pound's] presence [....] If we had occasion to use the words 'Jew' and 'Goy' they were no more or less ethnological in their sense than 'Chinese' and 'Italian.'"[57] In Mark Scroggins's biography of Zukofsky, *The Poem of a Life*, he gives Zukofsky's "disingenuous" claim a loophole: "Zukofsky had only met Pound twice in the course of their twenty-year relationship."[58] Contributing to Norman's *Case of Ezra Pound* helped Zukofsky construct a narrative of his relationship with Pound that made it possible for him to continue his career as a poet:

> [Pound] may be condemned or forgiven. Biographers of the future may find his character as charming a subject as that of Aaron Burr. It will matter very little against his finest work overshadowed in his lifetime by the hell of Belsen which he overlooked.[59]

Zukofsky's withholding of judgment (unlike the long contribution by William Carlos Williams excoriating Pound) reflects Spinoza's advocacy of forgiveness: a wrongdoer should be presented before a judge but should not be judged by citizens individually.[60]

Norman aimed to present "the two sides of Pound—the poet and the Axis propagandist." But Spinoza had rejected this kind of thinking as contradictory, and Zukofsky also found it hard to tolerate. Since Zukofsky was not able to bring himself to write to Pound directly, Bunting reported to him on Pound's condition in St. Elizabeths. By 1953, nearly a decade into his confinement, Pound's delusions had intensified into something that Bunting called "Hebraiophobia":

> The Jew imported by the neoplatonists is God's enemy, and this notional Jew contaminating the notional Greek gets mixed up with the real Jews about the place, who of course include truculent Zionists, vulgar profiteers, ridiculous philistines etc.[61]

Out of mercy for both of his friends, Bunting turned Pound's slurs that endorsed genocide into a commentary on the abyss of Pound's mental illness. The mediation helped Zukofsky come to terms with his own past inaction and his living inheritance. When Zukofsky published his statement for the *Case of Ezra Pound* in his collection of essays, *Prepositions* (1967), he gave it the title "Work/Sundown," words from Pound's "Canto 49," ensuring—in his own way—that Pound's poetry would not be "overshadowed."[62]

Through their correspondence, Bunting kept Zukofsky apprised of England's preparations for war and also raised questions about any easy delineation of political fault lines that equated Nazism as anti-Semitic and the Allies as democratic. In May 1939, Bunting wrote, "There are trenches all over the place—school playgrounds, parks, every vacant lot: useless trenches, gas-traps and half-full of water. People are beginning to throw dead dogs into them." The only good thing to report was that "Wyndham Lewis has written a book to prove that the Jews should not be persecuted: that's one up on Ezra, who, I hear, has sailed for the States."[63] Bunting was skeptical about Stalin's capacity to stop Hitler, not least because

> the propaganda of the Mosely Fascists & the Communists [in England] is now identical [....] They are very active, covering walls with anti-Semite chalkings; trying to hamper evacuation of schoolchildren [from mainland Europe] because "when their brats are bombed, it will bring the Jewish bankers to their knees" etc. How any Jew can sympathise with what has become an almost more violent anti-Semite party than the Nazi's themselves, beats me.[64]

In a letter from 1940, Bunting remarked on the persecution of Jews in England: the "Home Office's vindictive Anti-Semitism" was proven by the arrest of 64,000 Jews, some of whom "had fought in Flanders." He lamented, "If there had been in the world, as far as I know, any country still free of racial persecution, I think I would have repudiated England. But where they don't persecute Jews they persecute Negroes—it is a stinking horrible world."[65]

Marion Bunting, long divorced from Basil, was too afraid—for her ex-husband's reputation or for her own—to admit that the Ezra Pound they had known was any sort of fascist at all:

> I can say with certainty [...] that Pound was hostile to Mussolini & scornful of him at the time when we left Italy for Tenerife in September, 1933.

Mussolini had refused to allow Hemingway to come into Italy & this was one count against him. We felt we were likely to be spied upon there & while conversing in public places we never mentioned Mussolini's name—used a substitute. The only praise I heard of him was that he had forbidden Italians to shoot small birds. His law against profanity was considered absurd since both Basil & Ezra enjoyed the lusty fertility of the Italian's swearing.[66]

After Basil and Marion left for Tenerife, they kept in touch with the Pounds; Marion sent a postcard to Ezra's parents in April of 1935 with news of their "good house which we rent completely furnished," the "tropical garden" where they grew their own vegetables, and the joy that the children took in swimming at the beach, adding, "Basil finds it hard to work in this climate but hopes to do something now we have [the] house" (Figure 6.3).[67]

It is surprising to see signs of affection between the Buntings and the Pounds as late as 1935, since in the years immediately following Pound's death in 1972, Basil also took strides to put distance between himself and Ezra, attempting to fulfil his own "wish," declared to Pound in 1938, "I were not as much indebted to you as I am."[68] The publication of *Briggflatts* in 1966 was met with critical acclaim, and Bunting's *Collected Poems* (1970)

Figure 6.3 Basil and Marion Bunting in Rapallo
Source: Bunting Collection, Durham University. Reproduced by permission of Durham University Library and Collections Library and the Estate of Basil Bunting.

garnered wider public interest in his work. In the *Collected Poems*, Bunting acknowledges Pound and Zukofsky's influence, but renewed attention to Pound's fascism on his death in 1972 made the association difficult.[69] Speaking with Jonathan Williams and Tom Meyer that year, Bunting refused to acknowledge his literary inheritance from Pound. Williams asked where Bunting learned his technique of "condensation": "Is it Pound?" Bunting admitted that Pound had "plainly stated" the concept "before the First World War," but

> I came from a totally different direction and following a different road; never having heard of Pound or Eliot or anybody of that sort, I came to pretty much the same conclusions that they had reached, about 1918 or so.[70]

Bunting ignores the importance of "Dichten" (condensing) to his work with Pound on *Il Mare*, and he recasts the half decade that he spent in Rapallo talking and working with Pound as a period of independence: "on the whole it was a very pleasant time. I got a good deal of poetry written, I enjoyed conversation, enjoyed sailing my boat, enjoyed the sunshine [....] Pound was there then and various other people. Yeats was there. I saw a good deal of Yeats. But of few others. I don't enjoy literary society or literary conversation."[71] Other critics followed Bunting's lead in minimizing his association with Rapallo, while ignoring his admonition "I have always found Memory to be a cunning and persistent liar."[72] In *Bunting: The Making of His Verse*, Peter Makin depicts interwar Italy as pre-modern and safely apolitical: "Rapallo was then a different world. To be an American in Paris in the 1950s might mean very little; now it means even less. Rapallo too had a small world of resident foreigners, but it also had a yet unchanged Italy."[73]

In a broadcast for BBC Radio 3 in 1975, Bunting inverted the power dynamic of his relationship with Pound in Rapallo.[74] The interviewer, Eric Mottram, asked Bunting if he recalled any of Pound's advice about reading poetry aloud: "No," Bunting replied, "but I can remember our saying something to Pound—Louis Zukofsky and myself [....] He changed his way of reading after that."[75] Mottram pressed, "Why do you think Pound changed his way of reading from that to a way you approved of?"

BUNTING: Well, because Zukofsky and myself told him it was wrong.
MOTTRAM: And he set himself to change, did he?
BUNTING: He didn't say a word, but afterwards the way of reading did change.[76]

Bunting stressed his authority the next time Mottram mentioned Pound. Bunting insisted that Pound's "individual voice" didn't affect his work; rather,

> one sees the processes a man uses, whether he's a living man or a dead one, and one then attempts to make use of them oneself. They are useful tools. Now Pound has provided a box of tools, as abundant for this generation as those that Spenser provided for the Elizabethans, and a man who is not influenced by Pound, in the sense of trying to use at least some of those tools, is simply not living in his own century.[77]

Bunting was so eager to maintain a critical distance that he refused William Cookson, the editor of the literary magazine *Agenda*, permission to reprint the laudatory essay on Pound that Bunting had written for the *New English Weekly* in 1932: "No no no no no no. The article you have exhumed from the New English Weekly is altogether too jejune for any purpose worth considering this lifetime later. Leave it to be dug up, if it ever is dug up again, by the pedants who will gnaw any carrion when I'm dead."[78]

Bunting's attempts to control his intellectual and poetic lineage did not lesson his mercy for Pound as a fellow human being; in 1972, he felt the same as when he wrote so openly to Zukofsky nearly forty years before. He told Jonathan Williams and Tom Meyer that Pound "got himself into a hell of a mess":

> I don't think I could say much about it. I've been in messes myself. Pound had his own notions of politics and economics and all this and he really believed, foolish as it seems, that Franklin Roosevelt had upset the Constitution of the United States and the United States was united no longer. I was extremely sorry at the way the Americans treated him [....] when Pound was treated the way he was, in England the feeling was one of shock. P.G. Wodehouse did more in the way of helping the enemy. I mean, he was a much more popular writer than Pound, so his effect was probably greater. He was arrested and let go almost at once. That's all. We were really shocked. Pound may have had grievous intentions. Goodness knows, I don't think so, but he may have had. He certainly was silly. But his effect must have been absolutely nil.[79]

Bunting refused to give Pound credit for introducing him to Yeats: "It was at Rapallo that I met him. I dined or lunched or supped or underwent some similar formal presentation in the flat he had taken at the top of a big modern block overlooking the bay. I remember nothing about it."[80]

When Bunting was invited to the Yeats Summer School in 1973, he gave a reading of Yeats's "Byzantium" that was so profound, "Even the Midwestern children dragged there by their academic parents deserted the television set in the pub below to hear his resonant chanting."[81] His lecture for the occasion was mostly anecdotal, but it took a serious turn when he told his audience, "The young are apt to say that Yeats was an old square, or even a fascist beast. Such criticism may be irrelevant to poetry—I think it is—but it is as well to get it out of the way as possible. There were plenty of other fascist beasts about in the thirties, and among the poets, Yeats's close friend Ezra Pound is the most obvious. Eliot is another, the more insidious for being disguised as an English gentleman."[82]

Bunting argued that the biography of a poet was irrelevant to the poetry, but his vacillations about Pound's influence show a weakness in this resolve. His lecture in Sligo touches on the concept of aesthetic fascism, which proved difficult for him to sever from the individual's life:

> What these poets and many other writers really had in common was a love of order. With order in society it matters little whether you are rich or poor [...] you can plan your life's work within known limits, not felt as limits because they are as unavoidable as the limits imposed by our physique or the duration of human life. Whether an orderly society ever really existed or could exist is beside the point [....] Yeats went further than the rest when he called for ceremony, manners as elaborate as those he imagined in the Byzantine court. All such fancies assume tacitly that the regulations and ceremonies are made by extremely wise and perfectly unselfish rulers, not by Stalin or Hitler or even Mussolini [....] Yeats's love of order is something he shared with Dante and Shakespeare and probably far more than half of the world's great poets.[83]

Yeats's limited political action enabled Bunting's tempering of his political affinities: "if Yeats's political thought hardly differed at bottom from what was current all around him [...] politics and religion were not his business except in the sense in which they are everyone's business."[84]

The Totalitarian Man and the Women of Rapallo

Virginia Woolf's 1938 treatise *Three Guineas* proposes that the Totalitarian "Man [....] called in German and Italian Führer or Duce; in our own language, Tyrant or Dictator" is the product of the inequality of the sexes and the dissociation of the ethics of literature from the ethics of other spheres of life. Woolf argues, "the public and private worlds are inseparably connected"; if men "forget the private figure, or if we [women] in the intensity of our private emotions forget the public world," then "such will be our ruin."[85] But if the public and private are regarded as "one world, one life," and men and women work in partnership, the "evil" can be defeated. She reasons that this can only be achieved with a respect for women's difference: "we can best help you to prevent war not by repeating your words and following your methods but by finding new words and creating new methods."[86]

The different ways that Brigit Patmore, Dorothy Pound, Marion Bunting, and George Yeats spent and accounted for their time in Rapallo demonstrates Woolf's argument about the inseparability of private and public spheres. Dorothy Pound's sympathies for the fascist regime were not explicitly addressed in her art but are encoded in the aesthetics of her architectural drawings and watercolors. Long before the publication of *Etruscan Gate*, she actively established her reputation as subservient wife rather than take credit for her work as an independent artist or even as Ezra's collaborator. In 1955, when the Pound scholar Douglas Hammond asked Dorothy if she would meet him, she replied that she had

> led a hell of a life these last sixteen years, first the bloody war, and these nine years here [in Washington D.C.] [....] She thought ["Americans" were] "rather stupid" when it came to understanding Italy, the war, and Mr Pound's activities. She said that her one purpose right now is to keep "Ezra happy and reasonably well" so that he may complete the cantos on which he is presently working.[87]

Samuel Hynes, who visited Pound in St. Elizabeths around the same time, described Dorothy as "a prim-looking woman, like a schoolteacher or a housekeeper. Her gray hair was drawn neatly back in a bun, and her face was colorless, expressionless. She sat quietly, her hands folded in her lap and her feet tucked under her chair, as though this afternoon watch on the lawn were a protective duty."[88]

Hynes's impression is similar to H.D.'s in *End to Torment*, where she portrays Dorothy Pound's "heroic fortitude, though I do not visualize her as Penelope in this special instance, but rather as that 'mortal once / Who now is a sea-god'": Leucothia, who saves Odysseus's life and is invoked in Pound's Canto 93.[89] H.D. also exalts, "Dorothy is the *Bona Dea* of classical definition."⁹⁰ This may be closer to Dorothy's own ambitions for herself: the Roman woman, protector of the state and the people. While Dorothy was happy to be seen as Ezra's savior, a Leucothia who rescued him from the depths, for critics to constrain her life in this way is to misrepresent the way that Dorothy found her "own methods" to engage with public life, although these methods were put into the service of constructing rather than tearing down the Totalitarian Man.

Brigit Patmore's disapproval of Dorothy's wifely devotion slips through in her memory of dancing with Ezra, whom she describes as moving "with extremely odd steps [....] [It was] easier to waltz with a robot." But Dorothy, "sweet, faithful Dorothy said innocently: 'Ezra has a wonderful sense of rhythm.' Yes indeed."⁹¹ Even in Patmore's private, unpublished journals, she seems reluctant to give her outright opinion of Ezra and Rapallo. In an undated notebook, she reflects on how her gender affected her capacity to write:

> I resist my own desire to expression in every way; I do useless things— clean a couch, tidy a drawer, think out letters and messages even darn stockings, a loathsome depressing job rather than bring out my thoughts imaginations & life-reactions. Is it a childish distrust & suspicion, & dislike, fear of ridicule or is it female secretiveness—the life inside sufficient—also because I have always been reduced to silence through living with people who were not interested in my interests?⁹²

Patmore's relationship with Aldington was symptomatic of what she perceived as a lack of respect and support. His constant need for her approval of his work meant that she was always reading his writing, leaving no time to focus on her own.⁹³ When their liaison ended, Patmore re-entered life as a writer and began to process, in a very public forum, what she had experienced in Italy.

In 1930, Patmore wrote an essay for the British women's weekly, *The Sphere*, which offered political commentary that was often thinly veiled by "feminine" concerns.⁹⁴ Patmore's article takes the guise of a piece on European travel, but it also speaks to her complicated private life with Aldington, her impressions of the poets of Rapallo, and her ideas about the fascist regime, a subtext indicated by her provocative title "A traveller's lament on THINGS one is NEVER TOLD." She describes Italy as

> one of these plaguey spots on the map for me; first, because to be British and not know Italy is not to know your own father, and yet never to hear

the end of that paragon of parents; and secondly, because *everybody's* been there. This last reason is a nasty, envious one, but it's difficult to be a prisoner against your will and noble all the time.[95]

Privately, Patmore confessed that only two people "could influence [Ezra] intellectually, & they, Ford Hueffer & Wyndham Lewis, were not in Italy." While "Yeats was someone he honoured & I think, loved," Pound "looked for no guidance from him: indeed I doubt if he would accept direction from anyone, his confidence & courage & self-will were enough."[96]

In Patmore's account in *The Sphere*, she makes it clear that she is not sympathetic to the Italian fascist regime or its aesthetics:

> I was confused by the innumerable Roman remains. Remains is a dreary word—suggests crumbs from a feast, left-overs—it rhymes with drains. Unattractive. And broken columns, forums, Roman roads (always going straight where they wanted, drat them!), Julius Caesar (a feeling that there's some uncollected tax owing to him still!), busts of men awfully like the nicest elderly men I knew, but without their stiff collars.

For Patmore, Roman ruins did not signify a latent, spiritual state awaiting resurrection; her Italy is haunted by the specter of an unsatisfied dictator, waiting for the settlement of old debts. There was nothing pleasing to Patmore in the straight lines and hard edges that Dorothy Pound found so compelling.

Amidst Italy's "confusing history," "violent men," and "fulminating popes," Patmore caught glimpses of everyday life that she relished, such as "the creature—crone, old man, or small boy—who rings a tea bell wildly outside Sicilian churches while mass is being celebrated."[97] The reader senses that these moments of unrestrained expression were occasions of great relief. Patmore also mentions the "lovely frescoes by Simon di Corbetta," of whom "not a highbrow has hinted." Similar to Woolf's selection of photographs in *Three Guineas*, Corbetta appears as a matter of personal preference, but the reference is also an act of resistance: Corbetta's fourteenth-century frescoes exemplify the medieval history that the fascist regime discarded in order to herald the revival of the Roman past.[98]

George Yeats was an extensive collaborator in her husband's work, and after W.B.'s death she was an attentive editor and a vigilant administrator of his literary estate. In *Becoming George*, Anne Saddlemyer draws a parallel between Dorothy's life in the 1950s and George's in the 1930s, "when she too was trying to keep her husband's poetry alive."⁹⁹ Saddlemyer asserts that it was not until Jack Yeats's death in 1957 that "'our rock George' was freed at last from attendance on Willy's generation."¹⁰⁰ Saddlemyer's biography goes to great lengths to show how George Yeats was instrumental in W.B.'s creativity, but to imply that George was never fully herself during the marriage is to neglect the ways that the couple's collaborations spoke to their shared political and philosophical views and the ways that these ideas relate to aesthetic concerns. Margaret Mills Harper's *Wisdom of Two*, about the making of *A Vision*, illustrates the multiple and important ways that George was a progenitor of the books' aesthetics.¹⁰¹ Although the 1937 iteration of *A Vision* shows a disillusionment with the idea of the Italian fascist state ("only dry or drying sticks can be tied into a bundle"¹⁰²), as Paul Corner demonstrates in his work on "Collaboration, Complicity, and Evasion," this kind of disillusionment was common in the late 1930s, when "even confirmed fascists were reduced to complaining about the 'little Mussolinis' who, strutting in their 'Napoleonic uniforms', dominated many Italian provinces."¹⁰³ While Yeats's writing from the mid-1930s illustrates his disagreement with the Italian incarnation of fascism, this does not indicate a rejection of the fascist ideal or aesthetic fascism as artistic practice.

Most of the other poets of Rapallo regarded W.B. and George Yeats's mysticism as absurd. Aldington wrote to MacGreevy in 1958,

> I kept up correspondence with Ezra in that dreadful captivity (the C. of E. instructs us to succour captives) and he offended me by writing that "of course Yeats was a gargoyle". I re-read him [WBY] down here in this damp little hamlet smelling of cows and cabbages, and he seems more than ever a great and noble spirit. I can't follow him into that Vision book—remember? How right you were at Rapallo when you made me see that he and George looked like witches. They did. But that makes no difference to the great and soaring spirit he was. "It was the bananas that levitated, and not the lady."¹⁰⁴

But Basil Bunting identified a sinister aspect to the Yeatses' spiritualism: he detected in their use of magic a mechanism for exerting "power": Yeats "thought of himself as one of a governing class, with obligations, but with privileges too [....] Yeats felt he had a right to power that he did not share with the greater part of mankind. If you have none of the real power of armies and police and huge fortunes, magic is an unsatisfactory, but often irresistible way of pretending to yourself that you have an equivalent."¹⁰⁵

Bunting only considers W.B. in his letter—presumably relegating George to domestic irrelevance—but she was the medium for (and, most critics agree, the inventor of) the spirits who communicated the philosophy. Scholars have acknowledged the timely revelation of George's mediumship, coming into fruition just as W.B. was struck by post-wedding cold feet. If George's spiritualism was a means of obtaining or retaining power in her domestic life, then it is equally true that her ideas enforce the assertion of power in the public sphere.

In his remembrance of George Yeats, "Hours with the Domestic Sybil," Donald Pearce writes, "As I think back about George, it is surprisingly Ezra Pound, of all the people making up her husband's literary circle, whom she most resembled. They had the same down-to-earth, no-nonsense directness [...] each, moreover, preserved a kind of private inner mysticism."[106] Pearce relates George's admiration for Pound's "gifts," "his art," and "his endless sense of fun and wonderful irrepressibility," and her somewhat odd comparison of Pound and D'Annunzio; she told Pearce, "If you put your hand on Gabriel D'Annunzio's hair—he had a great shock of silver hair—and pressed down, it would stay flat. But if you pressed down on Ezra's hair—poof!—it would spring right up again!" This observation was followed by a "hearty, slightly wheezy laugh, head tipped back, eyes twinkling, but engaging me fixedly, as if an important confidence had just been imparted. As, of course, it had." Pearce presumes George wanted him "to realize and enjoy that side of Ezra," not pursuing—or at least not disclosing—the occasion of the encounter with D'Annunzio or its implications.

During the Second World War, George Yeats "listened secretly to Pound's broadcasts from Italy to America that began in January 1941"; Saddlemyer concludes, "no matter what he said, the sound of Ezra's voice brought a lost world somewhat closer."[107] Daphne Bush's recollection of George's listening to the broadcasts makes it clear that George understood fully the illicit nature of Pound's ideas and her own act of listening in: Bush was "shocked" when after dinner one evening, George suggested "in a humorous, half-conspiratorial sort of way 'Let's listen to Ezra.'"[108] After the Second World War, George was concerned about what had happened to Ezra, as were so many of his friends who agreed or disagreed with his opinions. She enlisted the young scholar Richard Ellmann to investigate and was relieved to hear that Pound was in the United States, having escaped "the custody of un-intelligent military officials who think poets are punk."[109] But when George heard about his confinement in St. Elizabeth's, she "raged" to David Clark, "It's like caging a tiger" to lock up someone "so completely alive, so bursting with splendid energy."[110] Ten years on, George asked Paul de Man (who would be posthumously outed, in 1988, as a Nazi collaborator) to visit Pound in hospital and to send her news of his condition.[111] Pound wrote to George in 1947 asking for news of other people that could distract him from his surroundings and, after his release from St. Elizabeths, he corresponded with her from Italy. In 1965, after Pound attended T.S. Eliot's memorial service in London, he went to see George in Dublin. The record of their meeting is as sparse as the silence that surrounds George's politics; Ellman describes them as two friends, sitting beside one another, unspeaking.[112]

The silences and obfuscations—deliberate and unintentional—about Rapallo that were propagated by the poets themselves and by the generations of scholarship that followed have only recently begun to be broken: in detailed biographies including Foster's *W.B. Yeats*, Moody's *Ezra Pound*, and Burton's *Life of Basil Bunting*, alongside Paul and Harper's extensive studies of W.B. and George Yeats's *A Vision* that situate those books in their historical and philosophical contexts. *The Poets of Rapallo* builds on this scholarship to show the extent of the network that reached out from the small, unassuming town on the Ligurian coast. The creative work that occurred in Rapallo and that was undertaken afterward in response to private conversations and public events there demonstrates late modernism's outward turn; their experiments with everyday speech and demotic forms were sometimes—but not always—democratic. The poets of Rapallo have in common a change in literary style that was an attempt to create publicly engaged works of art that would not stand apart from the world, as high modernism had done, but would actively shape it.

Notes

Front Matter

1. Thomas S. Davis, *The Extinct Scene: Late Modernism and Everyday Life* (New York: Columbia University Press, 2016), 11.
2. Davis, *Extinct Scene*, 11, 14.
3. Tyrus Miller, *Late Modernism: Politics, Fiction, and the Arts between the World Wars* (Berkeley: University of California Press, 1999). For late modernist scholarship's focus on anti-fascist writers and liberal and leftists politics since Miller's book, see Davis, *Extinct Scene*; Robert Genter, *Late Modernism: Art, Culture, and Politics in Cold War America* (Philadelphia: University of Pennsylvania Press, 2010); Benjamin Kohlmann, *Committed Styles: Modernism, Politics, and Left-Wing Literature in the 1930s* (Oxford: Oxford University Press, 2014); Marina MacKay, *Modernism and World War Two* (Cambridge: Cambridge University Press, 2007); Ashley Maher, "'Swastika Arms of Passage Leading to Nothing' Late Modernism and the 'New' Britain," *ELH* 80.1 (Spring 2013), 251–85; Michael Murphy, "Neoclassicism, Late Modernism, and W.H. Auden's 'New Year Letter,'" *Cambridge Quarterly* 33.2 (2004), 101–18; Maroula Joannou, "'Our Time': Sylvia Townsend Warner, Virginia Woolf and the 1940s," *Literature Compass* 11.12 (DecDecember 2014), 732–44; for pioneering research on late modernism's connections to anarchist sensibilities, see James Gifford, "Place, Personalism, Anarchism, and Fantasy: Recasting Late Modernism," *Literature Compass* 12.7 (July 2015), 322–32. Although Alan Gillis does not identify it as such, his reading of Yeats's nihilism in his thirties poetry broaches late modernist terrain: "In one sense, nihilism [in the sixth movement of Yeats's 'Vacillation' from *The Winding Stair*] is legitimized by the expansion into history and myth"; Alan Gillis, *Irish Poetry of the 1930s* (Oxford: Oxford University Press, 2005), 147.
4. See McCormack's discussion of Yeats's refusal to write a letter in support of the release of the German journalist and Nobel Laureate Carl von Ossietzky from a labor camp.
5. Peter Brooke, "The Troubled Mirror," Dublin Review of Books, https://www.drb.ie/essays/the-troubled-mirror (accessed Oct. 31, 2019).
6. Donald Torchiana, *W.B. Yeats and Georgian Ireland* (Washington, D.C.: Catholic University of America Press, 1992 [1966]), 156, 158.
7. Torchiana, *Yeats and Georgian Ireland*, xiii–xiv.
8. Reed Way Dasenbrock, rev. Elizabeth Cullingford, *Yeats, Ireland and Fascism*, *MLN* 97.5 (Dec. 1982), 1262–5.

9. See Seamus Deane, *Celtic Revivals: Essays in Modern Irish Literature, 1880–1980* (London: Faber, 1985).
10. David Lloyd, "The Poetics of Politics: Yeats and the Founding of the State," *Qui Parle* 3.2 (1989), 76–114.
11. Lloyd, "The Poetics of Politics," 84.
12. Lloyd, "The Poetics of Politics," 102.
13. For "aesthetic fascism," see my discussion of Mary Ann Frese Witt's study *The Search for Modern Tragedy: Aesthetic Fascism in Italy and France* elsewhere in this book.
14. Conor Cruise O'Brien's essay "Passion and Cunning" makes the case for Yeats's authoritarianism as fascism while regarding the poetry as other to the politics; see *Passion and Cunning and Other Essays* (London: Faber, 2015).
15. Davis, *Extinct Scene*, 6.

Chapter 1

1. W.B. Yeats to Lady Gregory (Feb. 7, 1928), *CL InteLex* Acc #5073.
2. Ann Saddlemyer, *Becoming George: The Life of Mrs. W.B. Yeats* (Oxford: Oxford University Press, 2002), 392; for a discussion of WBY's illness, their journey south, and their first season in Rapallo, see R.F. Foster, *W.B. Yeats: A Life* (Oxford: Oxford University Press, 2001), ii, 352–65.
3. See Hartwig Fischer and Sean Rainbird, *Wassily Kandinksy: The Path to Abstraction* (London: Tate, 2006).
4. Foster, *Yeats*, ii, 356.
5. Margaret Mills Harper and Catherine E. Paul, *A Vision: The Revised 1937 Edition* (New York: Scribner, 2015), 3 (hereafter *AVB*).
6. Foster, *Yeats*, ii, 356.
7. Michael North, "The Dialect in/of Modernism: Pound and Eliot's Racial Masquerade," *American Literary History* 4.1 (Spring 1992), 56–76.
8. Samuel Hynes, "Meeting E.P.," *The New Yorker* (June 12, 2006), 74–100.
9. Paul notes that Pound probably knew about Yeats's poetry "since his days at Hamilton College, and in 1907 he called Yeats 'The celtic Eagle' who 'set a whole land singing.'" See Catherine E. Paul, "A Vision of Ezra Pound," in Neil Mann, Matthew Gibson, and Claire Nally, eds., *W.B. Yeats's "A Vision": Explications and Contexts* (Liverpool: Liverpool University Press, 2012), 252–68, 252.
10. Lucy McDiarmid, *Poets and the Peacock Dinner: The Literary History of a Meal* (Oxford: Oxford University Press, 2014), 24–5.
11. Dorothy Shakespear Pound, *Etruscan Gate: A Notebook with Drawings and Watercolours*, ed. Moelwyn Merchant (Exeter: Rougemont Press, 1971), 1.
12. Pound to a Friend (Nov. 27, 1910), from Bornstein, *Ezra Pound Among the Poets* (1985), quoted by John Kelly, to whom I'm grateful for his lecture

"Yeats and Pound: Expats in England" (June 19, 2019), Notre Dame Irish Seminar, Oxford University.
13. WBY to Mabel Beardsley [Jan. 7, 1915], *CL InteLex* Acc #2574. Misspellings here and in subsequent correspondence are WBY'S own.
14. WBY to Olivia Shakespear (Nov. 23, 1928), *CL InteLex* Acc #5191.
15. Anne Conover, *Olga Rudge and Ezra Pound*: "What thou lovest well—" (London: Yale University Press, 2001), 55.
16. Conover, *Olga Rudge and Ezra Pound*, 56. For a marvelous depiction of H.D., see Francesca Wade, *Square Haunting: Five Women, Freedom and London between the Wars* (London: Faber, 2020).
17. See James Longenbach, *Stone Cottage: Pound, Yeats, and Modernism* (Oxford: Oxford University Press, 1988).
18. WBY to Lady Gregory, *CL InteLex* Acc #2540.
19. I owe the *mot juste* regarding George and Dorothy's social class to Roy Foster.
20. McDiarmid notes that "the first congress" between EP and Iseult Gonne was probably "in Yeats's rooms in Woburn Buildings," *Poets and the Peacock Dinner*, 102. Longenbach's *Stone Cottage* shows how the three winters in Ashdown Forest were foundational to major turns in both Yeats and Pound's work: "Stone Cottage was a seedbed for *The Cantos* and for Yeats's later esoterica, but it was also a breeding ground for some of the unfortunate excesses of [Pound's 1935 treatise] *Jefferson and |or Mussolini* and *On the Boiler*"; *Stone Cottage*, xi–xii. The dangerous element of their relationship lay in what Longenbach describes as Yeats and Pound's sense of "the secret society of modernism."
21. See W.B. Yeats's introduction to Pound's *Certain Noble Plays of Japan* (Dublin: Cuala Press, 1916).
22. For a discussion of their purchase of the tower and their move to Coole Park, see "Poet's Tower" in A. Norman Jeffares, *The Circus Animals: Essays on W.B. Yeats* (London: MacMillan, 1970), 29–46.
23. The essay first appeared in *The Irish Statesman* (1919), was reprinted in the Boston magazine *The Living Age* (1920), and was collected in George Yeats's edition *Explorations* (London: Macmillan, 1960).
24. For WBY's early friendship with Constance Markievicz (neé Gore-Booth), see my *Revolutionary Lives: Constance and Casimir Markievicz* (Princeton: Princeton University Press, 2016).
25. EP to Homer Pound (Dec. 21, 1924) and Isobel Pound (Dec. 28 [1924]), in Mary de Rachewiltz, *Ezra Pound to His Parents: Letters 1895–1929* (Oxford: Oxford University Press, 2010), 550–1.
26. Saddlemyer, *Becoming George*, 340; Pound wrote to his father, "Yeats & Mrs. Due in Siracuse about Jan. 6" (Dec. 21, 1924), de Rachewiltz, *Pound to His Parents*, 549.
27. EP to Homer Pound (Jan. 23 [1925]), de Rachewiltz, *Pound to His Parents*, 552.

28. For WBY and EP trying out the acoustics, see A. David Moody, *Ezra Pound: Poet* (Oxford: Oxford University Press, 2010), ii, 64–5; for George's photographs, see Saddlemyer, *Becoming George*, 340.
29. *Baedeker's Southern Italy and Sicily*, 298–9 in Yeats Library, National Library of Ireland (hereafter NLI); there are also marks next to the descriptions of the small church, San Cataldo, located off the Piazza Bellini and containing Saracenic arches, three Byzantine domes, and a frieze with Arabic inscriptions. The name of La Martorana, the larger church, is also marked, along with the description of nuns of Aloyisia Martona to whom the church was presented in 1433.
30. For an extensive discussion of the source texts, see Catherine E. Paul and Margaret Mills Harper, eds., W.B. Yeats, *A Vision (1925)*, in *Collected Works of W.B. Yeats 13* (New York: Scribner, 2008) (hereafter *AVA*).
31. Russell Elliott Murphy, "'Old Rocky Face,' look forth': W.B. Yeats, the Christ Pantokrator, and the Soul's History (The Photographic Record)," in *Yeats: An Annual of Critical and Textural Studies* XIV (1996), ed. Richard Finneran, 69–117, 71.
32. Murphy, "Rocky Face," *passim*; Murphy lists the photographs and focuses specifically on the image of Christ Pantokrator (Christ Sustainer of the World), who is always depicted holding a sacred book that represents the four Gospels.
33. EP to Homer Pound (Jan. 28, 1925), de Rachewiltz, *Pound to His Parents*, 553.
34. EP to Homer Pound (Jan. 23, [1925]), 552; also see Moody, *Pound*, ii, 65.
35. Ronald Bush, *The Genesis of Ezra Pound's Cantos* (Princeton: Princeton University Press, 1976), 183.
36. EP to William Bird (Apr. 1, 1924), in D.D. Paige, ed., *The Letters of Ezra Pound 1907–1941* (London: Faber, 1950), 258.
37. Ninety copies were printed; five of these were printed on Imperial Japan paper and autographed by Pound; fifteen were printed on Whatman paper, and seventy copies were printed on Roma Paper with the special watermark; NLI YL 1616. Michael Kindellan writes, "in Pound's mind deluxe editions address two distinct audiences: cognoscenti, to be supplied with copies in 'plain red capitals'; and those who might nevertheless still buy the expensive editions outright"; see "Ownership and Interpretation: On Ezra Pound's Deluxe First Editions," in *Reconnecting Aestheticism and Modernism: Continuities, Revisions, Speculations*, eds. Bénédicte Coste, Catherine Delyfer, and Christine Reynier (London: Routledge, 2017), 187–202, 189.
38. Lewis to Yeats (Nov. 18, 1928) in Richard J. Finneran, George Mills Harper, and William M. Murphy, eds., *Letters to W.B. Yeats* (London: Macmillan, 1977), ii, 488.
39. Ann Saddlemyer, "Friendship with George and W.B. Yeats," in Susan Schreibman, ed., *The Life and Work of Thomas MacGreevy: A Critical Reappraisal* (London: Bloomsbury, 2013), 212–26, 217.

40. Saddlemyer notes that she signed her letters to Robinson and MacGreevy "Georgie": "she need not always project the strong 'George' image that WBY required"; see "Friendship," in Susan Schreibman, ed., *The Life and Work of Thomas MacGreevy: A Critical Reappraisal* (London: Bloomsbury, 2013), 218.
41. Thomas MacGreevy to WBY (Feb. 6, 1928), Trinity College Dublin (hereafter TCD).
42. WBY to H.J.C. Grierson (Feb. [14?], [1925]), *CL InteLex* Acc #4698.
43. Saddlemyer describes Ezra and Dorothy as arriving at a "convenient *modus vivendi* of dignified silence"; *Becoming George*, 394.
44. Rainey writes that this "famous project [...] was partly an attempt to normalize, to regularize, the workings of an otherwise capricious institution, patronage." See Lawrence Rainey, *Institutions of Modernism: Literary Elites and Public Culture* (New Haven: Yale University Press, 1998), 108.
45. Ernest Hemingway, *A Moveable Feast* (London: Vintage, 2000 [1964]), 181.
46. Richard Aldington to EP (Mar. 18, 1922), Lilly Library, Indiana University (hereafter Lilly).
47. George Antheil to EP (n.d. [early July 1923]), Lilly.
48. Basil Bunting to EP (n.d. [Oct. 6, 1923]), Lilly.
49. Moody, *Pound*, ii, 41–52.
50. Moody, *Pound*, ii, 47.
51. Moody, *Pound*, ii, 52.
52. DP to EP (n.d. [Aug. 2, 1924]) and EP to DP (Aug. 4, 1924), Lilly.
53. Ezra Pound to Isabel Pound (Aug. 11, [1926]), de Rachewiltz, *Pound to His Parents*, 602.
54. Ernest Hemingway to Howell G. Jenkins (Feb. 2, 1925) in Sandra Spanier et al., eds., *The Letters of Ernest Hemingway, Volume 2 1923–1925* (Cambridge: Cambridge University Press, 2013); Hemingway to Ezra Pound (Nov. 8, [1925]) in *Letters of Hemingway*, ii, 411; ([c. Nov. 6, 1926] and [c. Nov. 14, 1926]) in Rena Sanderson et al., eds., *The Letters of Ernest Hemingway: Volume 3 1926–1929* (Cambridge: Cambridge University Press, 2015), 133, 142.
55. Ernest Hemingway to EP ([c. Nov. 20, 1926]), in Sanderson et al., Letters of Hemingway, iii, 160; Mrs. Butler refers to Alice Carter Butler, who had written a "flattering profile" of Mussolini for the *Chicago Tribune* in spring 1923; see *CL Hemingway*, iii, 161 n.3. When planning a trip to see Pound in Italy in 1923, Hemingway joked, "Can I [...] preserve my incognito among your fascist pals? or are they liable to give Hadley castor oil?" For this letter and a discussion of Hemingway's articles critiquing Mussolini, see Spanier et al., Letters of Hemingway, ii, 5–7.
56. Monotti, "Acqua Acestosa," *Il Mare*, 188. Trans. Bruna.
57. See EP to Homer Pound (Jan. 29, 1925), in de Rachewiltz, *Pound to His ParentsL*, 553–4.
58. Moody, *Pound*, ii, 55.

59. Ezra Pound to Homer Loomis Pound (Oct. 15, 1924) quoted in Moody, *Pound*, ii, 64.
60. Paige, Letters of Ezra Pound, 261.
61. Brigid Peppin, "Women that a Movement Forgot," *Tate Etc.* 22 (Summer 2011), https://www.tate.org.uk/context-comment/articles/women-movement-forgot.
62. Moody gives details of correspondence between Ezra and Dorothy from 1938 about the Church's position on the Italian regime's attitude to Jews; Dorothy probes, "Is the Pope opposing racial purity?" Moody, *Pound*, ii, 259.
63. Frederic Wertham, "The Road to Rapallo: A Psychiatric Study," *American Journal of Psychotherapy* 3.4, 585–600, 592.
64. Paige, *Letters of Ezra Pound*, 260.
65. Paige, *Letters of Ezra Pound*, 260.
66. EP to Isabel Pound (Oct. 30, 1924), de Rachewiltz, *Pound to His Parents*, 546. The American Robert McAlmon was editor of the little magazine *Contact*; he was friends with Pound and James Joyce in Paris and in 1921 married Bryher (the penname of Annie Winifred Ellerman) who was lover and patron of H.D. as well as an accomplished writer in her own right.
67. Harper and Paul, *AVB*, xxxii.
68. Brigit Patmore, *My Friends When Young: The Memoirs of Brigit Patmore*, ed. Derek Patmore (London: Heinemann, 1968), 109.
69. For a discussion of Tailteann's cultural scope, see Mike Cronin, "The State on Display: The 1924 Tailteann Art Competition," *New Hibernia Review* 9.3 (Autumn 2005), 50–71, doi: 10.1353/nhr.2005.0050; see also Kevin Hora, *Propaganda and Nation Building: Selling the Irish Free State* (London: Routledge, 2016).
70. Foster, *Yeats*, ii, 265.
71. Foster, *Yeats*, ii, 266.
72. Stanley Weintraub, "GBS and the despots," *TLS* (August 22, 2011), https://www.the-tls.co.uk/articles/public/george-bernard-shaw-and-the-despots/.
73. "From Democracy to Authority: Paul Claudel and Mussolini—a New School of Thought," *Irish Times* (Feb. 16, 1924), 9.
74. *CL InteLex* Acc #4020; see also Paul Scott Stanfield, "The Irish Free State and the European Crisis," in David Holdeman and Ben Levitas, eds., *W.B. Yeats In Context* (Cambridge: Cambridge University Press, 2010), 57–68, 58.
75. Thomas MacGreevy, "W.B. Yeats: a Generation Later," TCD MS 8000/6 (12).
76. Peter Allt and Russell K. Alspach, *The Variorum Edition of the Poems of W.B. Yeats* (London: Macmillan, 1966), 834–35 (hereafter *VP*).
77. Paul and Harper, *AVA*, xliv.
78. For the idealism of the 1925 text and its revision for the 1937 edition, see Paul and Harper, *AVA*, xliv–xlv.
79. *CL InteLex* Acc #4582.

80. Lucy Hughes-Hallett, *The Pike: Gabriele D'Annunzio: Poet, Seducer and Preacher of War* (London: Fourth Estate, 2013), *passim*.
81. Rebecca Beasley, *Ezra Pound and the Visual Culture of Modernism* (Cambridge: Cambridge University Press, 2007), 155, 197–8.
82. On Jan. 31, 1904, WBY wrote, "at present…I do not like to say that I do not like D'Annunzio's plays.…I do see most lovely passages in his work, but it will take me perhaps a long time to understand him as an artist that has influenced the whole of Europe," in John Kelly and Ronald Schuchard, eds., *The Collected Letters of W.B. Yeats. Volume 3: 1901–1904* (Oxford: Oxford University Press, 1994), 269 n.3.
83. Foster, *Yeats*, ii, 265.
84. For the wave of strikes, socialist protests, clashes with police, and subsequent attacks on socialists by Fascist squads, see Christopher Duggan, *The Force of Destiny: A History of Italy since 1796* (London: Penguin, 2008), 421–5.
85. Stanfield, "Free State," 58; Foster *Yeats*, ii, 266; Claire Nally, "The Political Occult: Revisiting Fascism, Yeats and 'A Vision,'" in Neill Mann, Matthew Gibson, and Claire Nally, *W.B. Yeats's "A Vision": Explications and Contexts* (Liverpool: Liverpool University Press, 2012), 331, doi: 10.5949/liverpool/9780983533924.003.0014 and W.B. Yeats, "From Democracy to Authority," in John P. Frayne and Colton Johnson, eds., *Uncollected Prose by W. B. Yeats*, Vol. 2: *Reviews, Articles, and Other Miscellaneous Prose, 1897–1939* (London: Macmillan, 1975), 435.
86. Nally, "Political Occult," 338.
87. *VP*, 832–3.
88. Ezra Pound, *Jefferson and/or Mussolini: L'idea Statale: Fascism As I Have Seen It* (London: Stanley Nott, 1935), 14.
89. Pound, *Jefferson and/or Mussolini*, 17. Unlike WBY, Pound did not endorse governance according to heredity; he points out that Adams believed in hereditary government while Jefferson, having no sons, did not; Pound goes on to assert that Adams was the only president to have produced a "line of descendants who have steadily and without a break felt their responsibility and persistently participated in American government throughout its 160 years"; *Jefferson and/or Mussolini*, 19.
90. The communicators put Pound at Phase 12 in Yeats's System; his personality was characterized by "intellectual ugliness" and "violence," although this was also "the phase of the hero, of the man who overcomes himself, who spends his life in oscillation between the violent assertion of some commonplace pose, and a dogmatism which means nothing, apart from the circumstance that created it"; see Paul, "A Vision of Ezra Pound," 254–5.
91. *CL InteLex* Acc #4567.
92. DP to EP (n.d. [July 29, 1924]), Lilly.

93. "W.B.Y. tells me that you are coming over here for the Tailteann Games and that you habitually have trouble about your passport. I enclose notes which may assist you if any hitch arises about your passport. I am looking forward to seeing you"; Desmond Fitzgerald to EP (July 11, 1924) in Mary Fitzgerald, "Pound and Irish Politics," *Paideuma* 12.2 (Fall/Winter 1983), 377–418, 383. Pound and Fitzgerald had first dined together (along with other members of the Irish Provisional Government) in Paris during the International Irish Race Congress; see Moody, *Pound*, ii, 33. Ezra wrote to Dorothy, "I have writ W.B. that I cant arrive in Oireland by Aug. 1;" EP to DP (July 31, 1924), Lilly.
94. Elizabeth Delehanty, "A Day with Ezra Pound," *New Yorker* (Apr. 13, 1940), 92.
95. E. Fuller Torrey, *The Roots of Treason: Ezra Pound and the Secret of St. Elizabeths* (San Diego: Harcourt Brace Jovanovich, 1984), 123, citing Pound's 1933 article "The Master of Rapallo Speaks."
96. EP to Aldington (Nov. 10, [1927]), Harry Ransom Humanities Research Center, University of Texas (hereafter HRHRC) 5.4.
97. EP to Isabel Pound ([before Jan. 21, 1927]) and (Nov. 11, 1927), de Rachewiltz, *Pound to His Parents*, 618, 639.
98. WBY to Gregory (Nov. 27, [1928]), *CL InteLex* Acc #5194.
99. EP to Aldington (May ?16, [1924]), HRHRC.
100. EP to Aldington (n.d. [?May 1924]), HRHRC.
101. EP to Zukofsky (Aug. 12 1928) in Barry Ahearn, ed., *Pound/Zukofsky: Selected Letters of Ezra Pound and Louis Zukofsky* (New York: New Directions, 1987), 13.
102. Pound to Zukofsky (Aug. 12, 1928), Ahearn, *Pound/Zukofsky*, 13.
103. EP to LZ ("2 Nov or 3 or whenever the hell it is" [1931]) sending $10 for the purchase of *The Education of Henry Adams* and Walter McDaniel's *Roman Private Life and its Survivals*; any other books could be purchased with what is left. EP to LZ (Feb. 6, [1931]) asks for Adams's "Discourses on Davila" and John Quincy Adams's diary and published papers. EP to LZ (n.d. [Oct. 5, 1931]) asks for a copy of "autobiography of Martin VanBuren or mebbe it's a 'diary.'" EP to LZ (Feb. 20, [1931]) jokes, "prpaps when I finish with T.J. thur won" be leff nothing but th HAM bone. Haaaaaaaaaam bone"; HRHRC. Zukofsky sent Pound Worthington Chauncy Ford's *A Cycle of Adams Letters 1861–1865*, noting, "Mebbe the family's attempt at diplomacy and action will interest you"; Pound replied, "Glad to have em as dilettante readin but they don't bear on what I want," which was Adams's *History of the United States During the Administrations of Jefferson and Madison* (1930); see Ahearn, *Pound/Zukofsky*, 37.
104. Ahearn, *Pound/Zukofsky*, 35 and 35 n.202.
105. EP to Zukofsky (Oct. 4, 1931) and EP to Zukofsky (Apr. 5, [1933]), HRHRC.
106. Zukofsky to Carl Rakosi (Jan. 7, 1931), HRHRC. In 1935, in the pages of *New Masses*, a young Norman MacLeod accused Zukofsky of being an "Adulator of Herr Ezra Pound," but another contributor, H.R. Hays, maintained: "As a communist sympathizer, Mr. Zukofsky has no interest in Zion except to expose it."

Zukofsky responded with his own letter to the editor, defending himself against "nazism" by writing: "'The Jews are a fact. Mr. Zukofsky has not emphasized the phenomenon' says Mr MacLeod. I have emphasized the fact thoroughly in *Poem Beginning 'The,'* first printed in *Exile, No 3,* 1928, and reprinted in *Active Anthology,* London, 1933. I have also given the proletarian position on this fact in the fourth, fifth and sixth movements of *A,* which appeared in *An 'Objectivists' Anthology* in 1932 [....] I would rather not attribute Mr Macleod's error to tactics subversive of the Communist position, but to not having read me." H.R. Hays to *New Masses* (Mar. 15, 1935) and Zukofsky to *New Masses* (Apr. 6, 1935), HRHRC.

107. EP to Zukofsky (Apr. 3, 1931), HRHRC.
108. EP to Zukofsky (June 8, [1933]), HRHRC.
109. EP to Zukofsky (Apr. 24, [1933]), HRHRC.
110. William Carlos Williams to Zukofsky (May 6, 1933) and (June 25, 1933), HRHRC.
111. Bunting to Zukofsky (n.d. [1935]), HRHRC.
112. Bunting to Zukofsky (n.d.), HRHRC.
113. Bunting to Zukofsky (n.d. [Aug. 1933]), HRHRC.
114. Bunting to Zukofsky (Aug. 8, 1933), HRHRC.
115. Quoted in Foster, *Yeats,* ii, 357.
116. Torrey, *Roots* of *Treason,* 126.
117. Foster, *Yeats,* ii, 357.
118. Quoted in Foster, *Yeats,* ii, 359.
119. Foster, *Yeats,* ii, 360.
120. Patmore, *My Friends When Young,* 110.
121. WBY to Susan Mary Yeats, *CL InteLex* Acc #5195.
122. Foster, *Yeats,* ii, 380.
123. Foster, *Yeats,* ii, 373; WBY to EP (Aug. 26, 1928), *CL InteLex* Acc #5147.
124. Foster, *Yeats,* ii, 378; WBY to Olivia Shakespear (Aug. 12, 1928), *CL InteLex* Acc #5142.
125. WBY to Gregory ([Feb. 28, 1928]), *CL InteLex* Acc #5081.
126. WBY to Olivia Shakespear (Feb. 23, [1928]), *CL InteLex* Acc #5079.
127. Thomas S. Davis describes the "outward turn" of Late Modernism as "the form of attention [late modernism] gives to the temporalities, spaces, surface appearances, textures, and rhythms of everyday life—and the disorder in the world-system that pushed the locus of global power from Britain to America"; *The Extinct Scene: Late Modernism and Everyday Life* (Columbia: Columbia University Press, 2016), 2. While *The Poets of Rapallo* contests Davis's positioning of late modernism as left-leaning, it reinforces his claim that "late modernism's encounter with everyday life is not primarily aesthetic or ethical; it is simultaneously aesthetic *and* political"; see *Extinct Scene,* 6.
128. Foster, *Yeats,* ii, 381.

Chapter 2

1. Patmore, *My Friends When Young*, 116–17; this appears to have been the first, but not the only visit between Aldington and Yeats; Pound remarks in a letter to his father on Jan. 10, 1929, "Yesterday mostly spent [...] in convarsation with W.B.Y. and R.A. or vice-versa"; de Rachewiltz, *Pound to His Parents*, 680.
2. Review, *This Impassioned Onlooker* in *Spectator* (January 15, 1927), 24. Patmore is also the model for D.H. Lawrence's character, Clariss Browning, in D.H. Lawrence's *Aaron's Rod* (1922).
3. Patmore 3.7, HRHRC.
4. Patmore, *My Friends When Young*, 105.
5. Patmore, *My Friends When Young*, 105.
6. Victoria Whelpton, *Richard Aldington: Poet, Soldier and Lover 1911–1929* (Cambridge: Lutterworth, 2013), 28.
7. Aldington recalls being asked by an English society woman in London whether he "admired Coventry Patmore," to which Aldington replied, "cheerfully, 'not a bit' "; see *Life for Life's Sake: A Book of Reminiscences* (New York: Viking, 1941), 132.
8. Whelpton, *Richard Aldington*, 27.
9. Whelpton, *Richard Aldington*, 28.
10. In *Life for Life's Sake*, Aldington recalls his tutelage under a Mr. Grey, who taught him Italian as a boy and urged him to go to Italy once he had finished university: " 'If you want to go to Italy badly enough, you'll get there somehow.' I didn't believe him, but he was right," 52.
11. Whelpton, *Richard Aldington*, 66.
12. Whelpton, *Richard Aldington*, 68.
13. H.D., *End to Torment: A Memoir of Ezra Pound*, ed. Norman Holmes Pearson and Michael King (New York: New Directions, 1979), 5.
14. Norman T. Gates locates the beginning of Patmore and Aldington's long affair as beginning at Port-Cros, where Aldington and Yorke were entertaining D.H. and Frieda Lawrence; see Richard Aldington: An Autobiography in Letters (University Park: Pennsylvania State University Press, 1992), 89.
15. Patmore, HRHRC.
16. Whelpton, *Richard Aldington*, 306.
17. Richard Aldington to Babette [Plechner] (Jan. 23, 1928), HRHRC.
18. Patmore, HRHRC.
19. Patmore, *My Friends When Young*, 111. Adrian Paterson observes that in an early draft of "Three Things," "a man fetched his 'deepest thought' from the blind/Ignorant mind of a woman, as if half-recalling the genesis of *A Vision* [....] such unfeminist metaphysical speculations drop away from the finished version, leaving its attention purely on the physical. The female voice Yeats personifies is determined to recall only pleasure." Adrian Paterson, "Words for

Music Perhaps," in *Essays on Music and Language in Modernist Literature*, ed. Katherine O'Callaghan (London: Routledge, 2018), 140–58, 144.
20. Pound adds a footnote, "*ch*, Neo-Celtic for *t*." *ABC of Reading* (New York: New Directions, 1934), 197–8.
21. Foster, *Yeats*, ii, 380.
22. Patmore, "W.B. Yeats: Some Memories of Him," HRHRC.
23. Aldington compared the reception of *Death of a Hero* to *All Quiet on the Western Front*: "the intense opposition of the minor highbrows has caused a lot of people to think that it's a failure and not worth reading. They've done the same thing to Remarque, the blighters." Aldington to MacGreevy (May 25, 1931), TCD.
24. Patmore, undated notebook, HRHRC.
25. Gates, *Aldington*, 99.
26. Whelpton, *Richard Aldington*, 314–15.
27. Richard Aldington, *Death of a Hero* (London: Penguin, 2013 [1929]), xxi–xxii.
28. Thomas MacGreevy, *Richard Aldington: An Englishman* (London: Chatto & Windus, 1931), 8; for a discussion of Graves's satire, see Paul Fussell, *The Great War and Modern Memory*, int. Jay Winter (Oxford: Oxford University Press, 2013), 220–39.
29. Aldington, *Death of a Hero*, 23. Whelpton observes similarly about the poems, "what distinguishes Aldington's poetry of the aftermath from that of Blunden, Sassoon or Read is the absence of any nostalgia for the war;" *Richard Aldington*, 262.
30. Aldington, *Death of a Hero*, 22–3.
31. Aldington, *Death of a Hero*, 23, 327.
32. Aldington, *Death of a Hero*, 101.
33. Aldington, *Death of a Hero*, 166.
34. Antheil to EP ([?May 1924), Lilly.
35. Aldington, *Death of a Hero*, 293–4.
36. Aldington, *Death of a Hero*, 293.
37. Aldington, *Death of a Hero*, 294.
38. Aldington, *Death of a Hero*, xxii.
39. Aldington, *Death of a Hero*, 314–15.
40. Aldington, *Death of a Hero*, 335.
41. Aldington, *Death of a Hero*, 343.
42. Aldington, *Life for Life's Sake*, 218.
43. Aldington, *Life for Life's Sake*, 218.
44. Aldington to Patmore (n.d. [1929]), HRHRC.
45. Aldington, *Life for Life's Sake*, 336.
46. Patmore, *My Friends When Young*, 113 and Patmore 3.7, HRHRC.
47. WBY was reading Swift in December 1928 and tested his theory in conversation with Josephine McNeill (married to the newly appointed Governor-General of

Ireland, James McNeill) on the McNeill's visit to Rapallo: "we dislike the present Royalties because of the impression Swift made on the Nation, when his enemies the whigs brought their ancestors from Germany"; WBY to Lady Gregory (Dec. 28, [1928]), *CL InteLex* Acc #5206. In 1930, WBY would read Alice Drayton Greenwood's biography, *Horace Walpole's World: A Sketch of Whig Society under George III*, in preparation for his play on Swift; see Foster, *Yeats*, ii, 396.

48. Peter Cunningham, ed., *Horace Walpole's Letters*, vol. 1 (London: Richard Bentley, 1857), 61; the letter is Walpole to Richard West, Esq (Oct. 3, 1740).
49. MacGreevy, *Richard Aldington*, 38–41.
50. Aldington, *A Fool i' the Forest*, epigraph, n.p. When the poem was reviewed for the *New Republic* by Glenn Hughes, author of a sympathetic study of the Imagist poets, Hughes identified a remnant of Robert Frost rather than Walt Whitman in *Fool*. See Glenn Hughes, rev. *A Fool i' the Forest*, *New Republic* (1 July 1925), 160–1. Hughes was editor of the University of Washington series that published Aldington's *D.H. Lawrence: An Indiscretion* (1927) and Pound's *Ta Hio* (1929).
51. Aldington, *A Fool i' the Forest*, n.p.
52. Thanks to Meg Harper for first suggesting that Whitman's vers libre was at the heart of WBY's objection to Whitman, in conversation at the "Yeats and Late Modernism" roundtable discussion, Modernist Studies Association, Boston, 2015.
53. Aldington, *A Fool i' the Forest*, 17.
54. The omission of Dante is typical of English war poets: in *The Great War and Modern Memory*, Paul Fussell writes, "Because Dante has never really been domesticated in Protestant England, when an English sensibility looks for traditional images of waste and horror and loss and fear; it turns not to the *Inferno* but to *Pilgrim's Progress*"; in fact, Aldington turns to neither. See Fussell, *Great War*, 150–1.
55. Aldington, *A Fool i' the Forest*, 28.
56. Aldington, *Fool i' the Forest*, 29.
57. MacGreevy, *Richard Aldington*, 24.
58. Ezra Pound, *Selected Poems*, intro. T.S. Eliot (London: Faber, 1959), xx.
59. Pound, *Selected Poems*, xi.
60. Pound, *Selected Poems*, xi.
61. Pound, *Selected Poems*, viii. Eliot describes his own verse as "nearer to the original meaning of *vers libre* than is any of the other types" since it was informed by his "study of Laforgue together with the later Elizabethan drama; and I do not know anyone who started from exactly that point." Basil Bunting disagreed with Eliot and thought that Pound's "Homage to Sextus Propertius" "takes over" from Whitman's musical experimentation with poetic rhythm; see Jonathan Williams and Tom Meyer, "A Conversation with Basil Bunting [1976]," *Poetry*

Information 19 (Autumn 1978), 38; the next year, 1979, Bunting made it clear that "Pound would not have liked me *at that date* [i.e., 1932, in Bunting's essay on Pound for the *New English Weekly*] to draw attention to the relationship with Whitman," quoted in Richard Burton, *A Strong Song Tows Us: The Life of Basil Bunting* (Oxford: Infinite Ideas, 2013), 219. In a letter to Massimo Bacigalupo, Bunting identified Whitman's "Sea Drift" as "where Ezra caught the hint" of "Homage to Sextus Propertius." See Bunting to Bacigalupo (Mar. 20, 1985), Bunting MS 385/1–2, Durham University Archives & Special Collections (hereafter Durham).

62. Pound, *Selected Poems*, viii–ix. Eliot identifies the earliest influences evident in the volume as those of Browning and Yeats; ix; Peter Quartermain argues to the contrary: "a progression can be discerned from Whitman through Pound to [Basil] Bunting," and he bases this reading on the poets' musicality; see "'To Make Glad the Heart of Man': Bunting, Pound and Whitman" in Carroll Terrell, ed. *Basil Bunting: Man and Poet* (Orono, ME: National Poetry Foundation, 1981), 145–59, 151.

63. Ursula Bridge, ed. *W.B. Yeats and T. Sturge Moore: Their Correspondence, 1901–1937* (New York: Oxford University Press, 1953), 128.

64. NLI, Yeats Library, 28.

65. Raphael Ingelbien, "Metres and the Pound: Taking the Measure of British Modernism," *European Review* 19.2, 285–97, 288.

66. Ingelbien, "Metres and the Pound", 289.

67. *A Packet for Ezra Pound*, 5; *AVB* 7, quoted in Paul, "A Vision of Ezra Pound," 262.

68. Ezra Pound, "What I feel about Walt Whitman" (1909) in William Cookson, ed., *Selected Prose 1909–1965* (London: Faber, 1978), 115–16. In *ABC of Reading* (1934), Pound qualified his earlier remarks: "From an examination of Walt made twelve years ago the present writer carried away the impression that there are thirty well-written pages of Whitman; he is now unable to find them. Whitman's faults are superficial, he does convey an image of his time, he has written histoire morale, as Montaigne wrote the history of his epoch. You can learn more of nineteenth-century American from Whitman than from any of the writers who either refrained from perceiving, or limited their record to what they had been taught to consider suitable literary expression [....] If you insist, however, on dissecting his language you will probably find that it is wrong NOT because he broke all of what were considered in his day 'the rules' but because he is spasmodically confirming to this, that or the other [...] using a bit of literary language, and putting his adjectives where, in the spoken tongue, they are not;" *ABC of Reading* (New York: New Directions, 2010 [1934]), 192.

69. Ezra Pound, *The Spirit of Romance: An Attempt to Define Somewhat the Charm of the Pre-Renaissance Literature of Latin Europe* (London: Dent, 1910), 178. In Harriet Monroe and John Untermeyer's anthologies, Whitman—along with

Sandburg, Frost, Lindsay, Robinson, and Master—were selected "as the dominant poets of the period"; see John G. Nichols, "Editor, Anthologist," in Ira B. Nadel, ed., *Pound in Context* (Cambridge: Cambridge University Press, 2010), 65–74, 66. Pound's challenge to these anthologies is discussed below.
70. Pound, *The Spirit of Romance*, 179.
71. EP to Zukofsky, in Ahearn, *Pound/Zukofsky*, 4.
72. Zukofsky to EP, in Ahearn, *Pound/Zukofsky*, 5; Pound, *Exile* 3 (1928), 13. Zukofsky compared Tagore's "impact in English" to "Whitman [who] offering us senses and the people's common sense as against the illusions of categories of Western epistemology"; Zukofsky to N. Chatterji (Aug. 18, 1965), HRHRC. For the "rediscovery" of Whitman by mid-century American poets, see Christopher Beach, *ABC of Influence: Ezra Pound and the Remaking of American Poetic Tradition* (Berkeley: University of California Press, 1992), 67–84.
73. Aldington, *Life for Life's Sake*, 119–20. Basil Bunting also had a strong interest in Whitman, but for avowedly different reasons; in an interview from 1978, he recalls reading Whitman "about the time of the beginnings of the [F]irst World War. Whitman was in very poor repute everywhere [....] But I came across a copy of *Leaves of Grass* pushed behind other books in the school library [...] and became very enthusiastic about it." He says his attraction was Whitman's musicality, his "cadences, produced something which is in a way parallel to what was being done by his contemporaries in music, particularly Liszt." See Eric Mottram, "Conversation with Basil Bunting on the Occasion of His 75th Birthday," *Poetry Information* 19 (Autumn 1978), 3–10, 6.
74. Aldington, *Life for Life's Sake*, 331.
75. EP to Homer Pound (Jan. 20, [1929]), de Rachewiltz, *Pound to His Parents*, 679.
76. Pound, *The Spirit of Romance*, 55.
77. See Roxana Preda, ed. *The Cantos Project*, Canto 4, note 9: http://thecantosproject.ed.ac.uk/index.php/a-draft-of-xvi-cantos-overview/canto-iv/companion-to-canto-iv.
78. Preda, *The Cantos Project*.
79. Ezra Pound, Canto IV, *XVI Cantos of Ezra Pound* (Paris: Three Mountains, 1925), 13; Pound includes Canto IV in his selections for *Active Anthology* (1933), 238–39.
80. Aldington revisits the legend in *A Dream of the Luxembourg* (London: Chatto & Windus, 1930); Ford Madox Ford touched briefly on the legend of the eaten heart in his book *Provence: From Minstrels to the Machine* (1935), and Aldington knew Ford's book, mentioning its general importance in *Life for Life's Sake*, 158.
81. Richard Aldington, trans. *Tales from the Decameron* (London: G.P. Putnam, 1930), 288.
82. Aldington, *Decameron*, 291 and *The Eaten Heart* (Paris: Hours Press, 1929), n.p. ("the legend of the Eaten Heart").
83. Aldington, *Eaten Heart*, n.p.

84. In *AVA*, Yeats describes Pound's generation as artists "who either eliminate from metaphor the poet's phantasy and substitute a strangeness discovered by historical or contemporary research or who break up the logical processes of thought by flooding them with associated ideas or words that seem to drift into the mind by chance"; see Paul, "A Vision of Ezra Pound," 255. The propensity for associative imagery and the concomitant lack of control are the characteristics of the "shell-shocked Walt Whitmans" that Yeats disparaged.
85. The allusion conflates (possibly through misspelling) Joyce's Leopold Bloom with Léon Blum, who entered French politics after the Dreyfuss Affair (1894) and joined the French Socialist party leadership soon after the First World War erupted.
86. Aldington, *Eaten Heart*, 10.
87. Aldington, *Eaten Heart*, 10.
88. Aldington, *Eaten Heart*, 11.
89. Aldington, *Eaten Heart*, 12.
90. Aldington, *Eaten Heart*, 15.
91. Aldington, *Eaten Heart*, 13.
92. Aldington, *Eaten Heart*, 14.
93. Roger Boase, *The Origin and Meaning of Courtly Love: A Critical Study of European Scholarship* (Manchester: Manchester University Press, 1977), 83; Aldington writes, "our bodies are we, and the 'soul' is a metaphor / To express the unknown in ourselves, / As 'God' is the unknown in the universe [....] / And only through the known, exterior body / Do we reach the mysterious unknown within"; *Eaten Heart*, 5–6.
94. Aldington, *Eaten Heart*, 1–2.
95. Boase, *Origin and Meaning of Courtly* Love, 81–3.
96. Saddlemyer, *Becoming George*, 641.
97. Peter Ure, "A Source of Yeats's 'Parnell's Funeral,'" *English Studies* 34.6 (Dec. 1958), 257–8; F.A.C. Wilson writes, "I think it is very likely that he [Yeats] wanted an ideal reader to pick up the reminiscence of Sordello. And I think one strand of his meaning is, very likely, that the tie of almost feudal allegiance binding Parnell's followers to their leader was or should have been as adamant as that binding Sordello to Sir Blancatz"; see "Yeats' PARNELL'S FUNERAL, II," *Explicator* 27.9 (May 1, 1969), 40–1.
98. "Forty Years," in David R. Clark, ed., *"Parnell's Funeral and other poems" from "A full moon in March": Manuscript Materials* (Ithaca, NY: Cornell University Press, 2003), 45; Peter Ure observes that Sordello's *planh* (funeral poem) is the model, and he suggests that Pound's translation in *The Spirit of Romance* gives Yeats "the structure and figure"; see Ure, "A Source," 257–8.
99. W.B. Yeats, *The King of the Great Clock Tower, Commentaries and Poems* (Dublin: Cuala, 1934); see also the 1935 Macmillan edition of same. In their *Variorum Edition*, Allt and Alspach incorrectly state that lines 16–23 of

"Parnell's Funeral" were published in "Introduction to 'Fighting the Waves'" in *Dublin Magazine* (April–June 1932), *VP*, 541; their dating is presumably based on Wade's *Letters*, 338. Clark follows Wade, Allt and Alspach in the dating of his manuscript materials, cf., Clark, *"Parnell's Funeral"*, page 3. However, the lines did not appear in the introduction in *Dublin Magazine*; Yeats heavily revised his "Introduction to *Fighting the Waves*" for *Wheels and Butterflies* (1934), and this is where lines 16–24 from "Parnell's Funeral" first appear. The "Introduction to *Fighting the Waves*" is discussed further in Chapter 5.

100. W.B. Yeats, *A Full Moon in March* (London: Macmillan, 1935), 45–7.
101. Ure, "A Source," 257.
102. Pound, *Spirit of Romance*, 45; Pound also mentions Yeats in his chapter on Dante, "Il Maestro": "There are also epithets of 'emotional apparition,' transensuous, suggestive: thus in Mr Yeats' line: 'Under a bitter *black*wind that blows from the left hand,'" *Spirit of Romance*, 167.
103. *VP*, 541. This is O'Connell's tomb; for a discussion of O'Connell and Parnell as emblems of Comedy and Tragedy, see R.F. Foster, "The Ghost of Parnell," in Lauren Arrington and Matthew Campbell, eds., *The Oxford Handbook of W.B. Yeats*, forthcoming.
104. Aldington, *Eaten Heart*, 15.
105. MBY 545, p. 368 in Clark, *"Parnell's Funeral"*, 5.
106. Whelpton, *Richard Aldington*, 311.
107. Whelpton, *Richard Aldington*, 311.
108. MBY 545, p. 369 in Clark, ed. *"Parnell's Funeral"*, 13.
109. Aldington, *Life for Life's Sake*, 188.
110. Aldington, *Life for Life's Sake*, 195; his "nervous malady and insomnia" persisted after he left the army, *Life for Life's Sake*, 207.
111. Aldington, *Life for Life's Sake*, 207.
112. Aldington, *Life for Life's Sake*, 343.
113. WBY wrote to Gregory that he was "knocked up in Rome for a few days (constant fateague)"; *CL InteLex* Acc #5213.
114. George Yeats to MacGreevy (Dec. 6, 1928) in Susan Schreibman, ed., *The Thomas MacGreevy Archive*, http://www.macgreevy.org.
115. WBY to Gregory (Dec. 28, 1928), *CL InteLex* Acc #5206.
116. WBY to Gregory (Dec. 28, 1928), *CL InteLex* Acc #5206.
117. MacGreevy to George Yeats (Jan. 13, 1929), MacGreevy Archive. Geoffrey Phibbs was married to the artist Norah McGuinness who designed scenes for the Abbey Theatre; in a letter to George Yeats on March 9, MacGreevy reports gossip that Phibbs had left McGuinness for Laura Riding and was living with her in London, with Robert Graves "as No 1 lover" still occupying the house; that letter concludes, "love to E.P. as well as yourselves."
118. MacGreevy to George Yeats (Jan. 13, 1929), MacGreevy Archive; in this letter, MacGreevy includes Alfred Peyron's translation of "Sailing to Byzantium" into

French; MacGreevy assisted with aspects of the translation and explains some of the decisions.
119. Schreibman follows MacGreevy's dating of his meeting with Aldington; see Susan Schreibman, ed., *The Collected Poems of Thomas MacGreevy: An Annotated Edition* (Dublin: Anna Livia, 1991), 154.
120. Aldington, *Life for Life's Sake*, 342–3; Whelpton opts for the Joyce locale but provides no reference; see *Richard Aldington*, 316; see also MacGreevy, "Richard Aldington as a Friend," TCD.
121. Novel A (and Novels B–E) survey the cultural life of Dublin and include political debates over the dinner table that are strongly evocative of Joyce's *Portrait*; MacGreevy's short story "For Emma" has the protagonist aspire to be a writer, though MacGreevy's character meanders through his thoughts without the epiphany Joyce gives Stephen: "It would be nice to be a writer though. And there was a line to follow to be mid-way between the splendor of Yeats and the darkness of Synge, to be human. No that wasn't the word. They were human in their own ways. To be what? ~~There was this new man that people were talking about~~ It was very difficult."
122. Aldington to Patmore (n.d.), HRHRC; in *Life for Life's Sake*, Aldington describes academic work as "literary vomit," evoking his letter to Patmore, who is otherwise omitted from the memoir; *Life for Life's Sake*, 343.
123. MS Outline, Early Typescripts, "Stillborn / A Novel," TCD.
124. MS Outline, Early Typescripts, "Stillborn / A Novel," TCD.
125. On 4v there is a translation of Rafael Alberti's *Sobre los ángeles*, which was published in 1929, suggesting MacGreevy's draft could be dated as early as the first year of his friendship with Aldington.
126. MacGreevy Papers MS 8052/3–4, TCD.
127. MacGreevy 8039 (3v), TCD; in an essay on MacGreevy's war writing, Gerald Dawe observes: "It was as if the writing of poetry became in MacGreevy's inner self *associated* with war; that the two experiences were interdependent." MacGreevy strove to sequester the association, indicated by his relegating two poems, "Nocturne" and "De Civitate Hominum" in the section "1917–1918" in *Poems* (1934), with the rest of the contents in the long section "1920–1930." Gerald Dawe, "Nocturnes: Thomas MacGreevy and World War One," in Susan Schreibman, ed., *The Life and Work of Thomas MacGreevy: A Critical Reappraisal* (London: Bloomsbury, 2013), 3–16, 3–4.
128. See Dawe, "Nocturnes," 3–4.
129. MS fragment, MacGreevy 8054/4–5, TCD.
130. MS fragment, MacGreevy 8054/4–5, TCD.
131. For the Imagist influence, see Michael Smith, "A Talent for Understanding," in Schreibman, *Critical Reappraisal*, 269; for George Yeats as reader for MacGreevy, see Saddlemyer "Friendship with George and W.B. Yeats" in Schreibman, *Critical Reappraisal*, 219.

132. George Yeats to MacGreevy (July 26, 1926), MacGreevy Archive.
133. Aldington to MacGreevy (Nov. 30, 1930), TCD.
134. W.B. Yeats, ed., *Oxford Book of Modern Verse* (Oxford: Oxford University Press, 1936), xxv (hereafter *OBMV*). For a discussion of Yeats's editorship, see Lucy McDiarmid, "Yeats and the Oxford Book of Modern Verse," in Declan Foley, ed., *Yeats 150: William Butler Yeats 1865–1939* (Dublin: Lilliput, 2015).
135. *OBMV*, xxiiv–xxxvi.
136. *OBMV*, 360. In the 1936 essay, "Modern Poetry," Yeats writes: "It was in Eliot that certain revolutionary War poets, young men who felt they had been dragged away from their studies, from their pleasant life, by the blundering frenzy of old men, found the greater part of their style. There were too near their subject-matter to do, as I think, work of permanent importance, but their social passion, their sense of tragedy, their modernity have passed into young influential poets of today"; Yeats, *Essays and Introductions* (London: Macmillan, 1961), 491–508, 499–500. Pound's thoughts were similar: "undigested war is no better for poetry than undigested anything else"; see "The Hard and Soft in French Poetry," discussed further in Chapter 4.
137. *OBMV*, xxvii, xxxv; Pound also admired *A Farewell to Arms*; in a letter to Zukofsky, he judged "a good deal of it is First Class and deserves serious attention, not merely a pop. novel. I had nothing to say re/ Sun Also Rises" (Feb. 9, 1930), HRHRC; Zukofsky reported to Carl Rakosi, "Pound says his *Farwell to Arms* is good—haven't read it and as you see I'm not crazy to. His influence much more detrimental than he himself—so much for litchrachoor": Zukofsky to Rakosi (Jan. 7, 1931), HRHRC.
138. In *Pages from a Diary Written in Nineteen Hundred and Thirty*, WBY implies that he disapproves of British regard for Sassoon as a war hero; cf., *Pages from a Diary* (Dublin: Cuala, 1945), 45.
139. Philip Hoare, *Serious Pleasures: The Life of Stephen Tennant* (London: Hamish Hamilton, 1990), 147. See also Rupert Hart-Davis, ed. *Siegfried Sassoon: Letters to Max Beerbohm: With a Few Answers* (London: Faber, 1986), 7.
140. Saddlemyer, *Becoming George*, 422; cf., George Yeats to Lennox Robinson (Nov. 30, 1929) in The Huntington.
141. The Yeats Library (NLI) copy of Sassoon's *The Heart's Journey* is the 1935 printing.
142. *OBMV*, 259.
143. *OBMV*, xxxiv.
144. See Chapter 5.
145. Thomas MacGreevy, "W.B. Yeats: A Generation Later," 12–13; TCD.
146. Aldington, *Life for Life's Sake*, 178, 339.
147. Aldington, *Life for Life's Sake*, 215.
148. MacGreevy, *Richard Aldington*, 6.

Chapter 3

1. EP to Aldington (Nov. 3, [1926]), HRHRC.
2. EP to Aldington (Jan. 31, 1927), HRHRC.
3. EP to Aldington (Jan. 23, [1928]), HRHRC.
4. Eric Bulson, *Little Magazine, World Form* (New York: Columbia University Press, 2017), 2. Pound guest-edited the *Little Review* from 1917 to 1919; for a discussion of his editorship and Yeats's contributions to the magazine, see Clare Hutton, "Yeats, Pound, and the *Little Review*, 1914–1918," *International Yeats Studies* 3.1 (2018), https://tigerprints.clemson.edu/iys/vol3/iss1/7.
5. Adrian Stokes, *Stones of Rimini* (London: Faber, 1934); see Pound's copy in HRHRC.
6. After the Second World War, Duncan became famous as author of the libretto for Benjamin Britten's *The Rape of Lucretia* (1946). EP to Ronald Duncan (July 17, 1937 "anno xi"), HRHRC. Pound promoted Bunting and Zukofsky to Duncan for inclusion in *Townsman*: "If you haven't six pages of ENGLISH poetry/you will have to go/cummings/Bunting (Northumbrian) Zukofsky, to get the GIST and Pith" (July 1, 1937), HRHRC. When *Townsman* was launched, Pound puffed it in *Il Mare*, reporting on the front page that the first issue included contributions from Rudge, Pound, Duncan, and Reid; *Il Mare* (Dec. 18, 1937) ["anno XXX"], HRHRC.
7. Pound, *ABC of Reading*, 30.
8. EP to *Contempo* (Sept. 3, 1932), HRHRC.
9. EP to *Contempo* (Feb. 23, [n.d.]), HRHRC. Pound refers to the importance of educating white voters, given the racist disproportionate representation of the electorate, with words that ventriloquize a Southern, racist accent: "every voter votes for five nigguhs, thereby swilling the hauls of congress with the lowest types of amurikum legislator." When *Contempo* covered the Scottsboro trial—in what was probably the magazine's most important issue—Bunting congratulated the editors: "I shall begin to believe that Contempo has found a place for itself after all" (Feb. 5, 1932), HRHRC.
10. See Moody, *Pound*, ii, 102–3 and Wayne Pounds, "Toward the Rapallo Vortex: 'Il Mare: Supplemento Letterario,' 1932–1933," *Paideuma* 29.3 (Winter 2000) 255–9; long version at https://www.academia.edu/224590/Toward_the_Rapallo_Vortex_Il_Mare_Supplemento_Letterario_1932-1933 (accessed June 7, 2019). Vittori's introduction to the bound reprint of the literary supplement positions *Il Mare* in the context of the Italian literary reviews of the thirties; see Verdino, introduction to *Il Mare: Literary Supplement*, vii. Trans. Bruna.
11. Bulson summarizes: "He wanted to help transform Italy into an international center for literature and the arts [....] Italy needed to import more foreign books, overcome its Francophilia, translate modern literature from other

countries, and create a critical conversation about contemporary Italian literature"; "Journalism," in Ira B. Nadel, ed., *Ezra Pound in Context* (Cambridge: Cambridge University Press, 2010), 85–95, 89.
12. Moody, *Pound*, ii, 103.
13. Undated but before May 21, 1927, since Ezra responds to Dorothy's comments on WBY's "Neon Tom" (i.e., Neo-Thomist) obsession; WBY was in London most of that month; see DP to EP (n.d. [1927]), Lilly.
14. See Sueellen Campbell, "The Enemy Attacks: Wyndham Lewis versus Ezra Pound," *Journal of Modern Literature* 10.2 (June 1983), 247–56.
15. *The Enemy: A Review of Art and Literature* 1 (Jan. 1927), ix–xii.
16. The first volume of *The Enemy*, published in January 1927, included essays on Beethoven by J.W.N. Sullivan; Giorgio de Chirico by W. Gibson; and "A Note on Poetry and Belief" by Eliot. But by the next volume, the contents consisted wholly of Lewis's self-publication, barring a short excerpt of "Towards Reintegration" by a "promising catholic student," Henry John. After Yeats's argument with Ezra in 1934 over *The King of the Great Clock Tower*, he incorporated Lewis's slight into "A Packet for Ezra Pound" in *AVB* while—as Paul notes—making the "critique of Pound...more oblique." Paul, "A Vision of Ezra Pound," 259. Yeats's uncertainty about Pound is evident from the beginning of their friendship; Yeats wrote to Harriet Monroe in 1913, "His experiments are perhaps errors, I am not certain; but I would always sooner give the laurel to vigorous error than to any orthodoxy not inspired." WBY to Harriet Monroe (Nov. 7, 1913), *CL InteLex* Acc #2284.
17. For a detailed discussion of Lewis's depiction of Pound, see Campbell, "The Enemy Attacks"; Campbell sums up, "Pound puts his energies into advertising for others while Lewis advertises only himself."
18. I am grateful to Debra Rae Coen for suggesting that I think about "periodical Pound" in my analysis of *The Exile*.
19. EP to DP (May 21, 1927) and DP to EP (June [24], 1927), Lilly. The letter about Bunting also asks, "When is No II Exile likely to appear? How many copies are being printed?"
20. DP to EP (n.d. [1927]), Lilly.
21. DP to EP (May 29, 1927), Lilly.
22. EP to DP (May 21, 1927), Lilly. Pound appears to suggest that he thought that Lewis's attack was a means of selling copies; Campbell's "The Enemy Attacks" shows how Lewis's castigation of Pound was necessary for Lewis to establish himself as an individual, outsider voice; she also notes that the attack in *The Enemy* is exceptional—Lewis praised Pound in other venues, immediately before and after his editorial in *The Enemy*.
23. The timing was fortuitous; Pound's letter is dated Mar. 20, 1927 so appeared as a riposte even though the composition predates the controversy; see *Poetry* 30.3

(June 1927), 174–5, https://www.poetryfoundation.org/poetrymagazine/browse?volume=30&issue=3&page=57.
24. Bulson comments in *Little Magazine, World Form* that "exile [appears to be] a necessary precondition for magazine making," 151.
25. See Bulson, *Little Magazine*, for a detailed discussion of editors who sourced paper from Italy, taking advantage of the devalued lira; Milan was the center of English-language publishing-for-export. Ultimately, import duty scuppered Pound's magazine, which was classed as a book rather than a periodical and was therefore subject to a higher tax.
26. Tim Redman, *Ezra Pound and Italian Fascism* (Cambridge: Cambridge University Press, 1991), 7; also see Roxana Preda, *Ezra Pound's Economic Correspondence, 1933–1940* (Gainesville: University Press of Florida, 2007).
27. Quoted in Torrey, *Roots of Treason*, 134.
28. "National Culture: A Manifesto 1938," in William Cookson, ed., *Ezra Pound, Selected Prose: 1909–1965* (New York: New Directions, 1975), 131–6, 132. Pound here is in agreement with Eliot who wrote, "genuine nationality depends upon the existence of a genuine literature, and you cannot have a nationality worth speaking of unless you have a national literature"; quoted in Bulson, *Little Magazine*, 103.
29. For a discussion of the issue of copyright and complications regarding the printing and importation of *The Exile* to the United States, see chapters 2 and 3 of Robert Spoo, *Without Copyrights: Piracy, Publishing, and the Public Domain* (Oxford: Oxford University Press, 2013).
30. See Mike Cronin, "Catholicising Fascism, Fascistising Catholicism? The Blueshirts and the Jesuits in 1930s Ireland," *Totalitarian Movements and Political Religions* 8.2 (June 2007), 401–11; Mike Cronin, "The Blueshirt Movement, 1932–4: Ireland's Fascists?" *Journal of Contemporary History* 30.2 (April 1995), 311–32. For Fitzgerald's participation in debates about the Italian Blackshirts, see, for example, the Oireachtas (Irish parliament) debate of March 1934. In session, Deputy Norton condemned the Blackshirts for "the stifling of individual liberty, and the stifling of democratic liberty." Norton asked, do Deputy MacDemot and the Opposition Deputies "want to see established here the same tyranny that has disgraced Germany, disgraced Italy and disgraced Austria in later years?" Desmond Fitzgerald replied, "Deputy Norton made a gratuitous and wanton attack upon Italy, Germany and Austria. Such attacks are a disgrace to this House. It is not our business how other people manage their affairs […]. Deputy Norton misuses the word 'democracy.' I could describe myself as a democrat." *Dail Eireann* debate (Mar. 1, 1934), "Wearing of Uniform (Restriction) Bill, 1934—Second Session (Resumed)," https://www.oireachtas.ie/en/debates/debate/dail/1934-03-01/9/.
31. *Paideuma* 12, 384. Pound's refusal of a "subsidy" (although it was very unlikely one would be proffered) is probably informed by difficulties that arose between

Yeats and his fellow directors of the Abbey Theatre and the Irish state after the Abbey accepted a subsidy from the Free State government; see my *W.B. Yeats, the Abbey Theatre, Censorship, and the Irish State* (Oxford: Oxford University Press, 2010).

32. *Paideuma* 12, 382. Examples of Fitzgerald's poetry are printed in *Paideuma* 12, 394–6; for a facsimile of Pound's rejection letter and Anderson's judgement, see 397–8.
33. *Paideuma* 12, 384.
34. *Paideuma* 12, 385–6.
35. Jacqueline Vaught Brogan, *Part of the Climate: American Cubist Poetry* (Berkeley: University of California Press, 1991), 114–15. See also Quartermain's description: "The juxtapositions of which this text is build [sic] are thereby rendered both obvious and yet fluid, uncertain, ambiguous, bordering on indeterminacy [....] It is a visual flattening of surface, and it renders that surface opaque, and thus the writing draws attention to itself as writing, as medium, in a manner directly analogous to that of Cubism"; Peter Quartermain, *Disjunctive Poetics: From Gertrude Stein and Louis Zukofsky to Susan Howe* (Cambridge: Cambridge University Press, 1992), 178–9.
36. Pierre Joris, quoted in Ross Hair's chapter "Luminous Detail: Ezra Pound and Collage," in Hair, *Ronald Johnson's Modernist Collage Poetry* (New York: Palgrave, 2010), 51–64, 51.
37. Hair, *Ronald Johnson*, 55.
38. Hair, *Ronald Johnson*, 52.
39. There is precedent for thinking about Periodical Pound and Pedagogical Pound in terms of the "ideogrammic method," with reference to what Furlani describes as "the prose ideograms" of Guy Davenport. Davenport said of his own work, "the mind gets into the habit of finding cross-references among subjects. This is the best way in the world to make my assemblages, as I call them. I don't think I've ever written a story. If Henry James wrote stories, if Dostoevski wrote stories, I don't write stories." See A. Furlani, "'When Novelists became Cubists': The Prose Ideograms of Guy Davenport," *Style* 36.1 (2002), 111–31.
40. See Bush, *Genesis of Ezra Pound's Cantos*, 10; also Ezra Pound and Ernest Fenollosa, *The Chinese Written Character as a Medium for Poetry: A Critical Edition* (New York: Fordham University Press, 2008 [1919]).
41. For a lucid discussion of the development of Pound's method, see Hair, *Ronald Johnson*, 55–7.
42. Peter Makin, ed., *Ezra Pound's Cantos: A Casebook* (Oxford: Oxford University Press, 2006), 6; see also Girolamo Mancuso, "The Ideogrammic Method in *The Cantos*," in Makin, *Ezra Pound's Cantos*, 65–80.
43. Moody, *Pound*, ii, 98.
44. Thinking about the composition of a magazine as a collage can advance what Sean Latham has theorized as "emergence," the idea that "a particular kind of

complexity" emerges from the "interaction" of elements; see Sean Latham, "Unpacking My Digital Library: Programs, Modernisms, Magazines," in *Making Canada New: Editing Modernism and New Media*, ed. Dean Irvine, Vanessa Lent, and Bart Vautour (Toronto: University of Toronto Press, 2017), 31–60, discussed in relation to Pound and Yeats in Hutton, "Yeats, Pound, and the *Little Review*."

45. Quoted in Carroll F. Terrell, *A Companion to the Cantos of Ezra Pound* (Berkeley: University of California Press, 1980), 83 n. 43.
46. In a letter to Dorothy, Ezra advises, "Tell W.B. neo Thomism is mere hogwash" (May 21, 1927), Lilly.
47. *The Exile* 1, 89.
48. *The Exile* 1, 90–1. The death of Henri Gaudier-Brzeska, among others, in the First World War prompted Pound's reading in the economic causes of war, specifically the manufacturing and financial industries.
49. *The Exile* 1, 92. Pound's "method" is discussed at length in *How to Read*.
50. William Bird to EP (Apr. 26, 1928), Lilly.
51. Pound, "Date Line," 9. Pound misspells Borgo Santo Sepolcro, the eleventh-century town in Arrezo, eastern Tuscany.
52. EP to Homer Pound, de Rachewiltz, *Pound to His Parents* (Dec. 1, 1927), 644.
53. E.P., "Desideria," *The Exile* 3 (Spring, 1928), 108.
54. Zukofsky had sent Pound an essay on Antheil, but Pound preferred to print "Poem Beginning 'The' " first: "If I print 'em together our detractors wd. say you broke in by boosting young George or wd. suspect me of being influenced by gang feeling. Which I am not. (at least in this case)"; EP to Zukofsky (Aug. 18, 1927), in Ahearn, *Pound/Zukofksy*, 3.
55. For a close reading of "Sailing to Byzantium" and "Blood and the Moon" in relation to their publication in *The Exile*, see my essay, "Feeding the Cats: Yeats and Pound at Rapallo, 1928," in Senia Pašeta, ed., *Uncertain Futures: Essays about the Irish Past for Roy Foster* (Oxford: Oxford University Press, 2016), 188–98.
56. The second issue of *The Exile* did not include any poems by Pound, enhancing the correspondences between issues one and three.
57. Louis Zukofsky, "Poem Beginning 'The,' " *Exile* 3 (Spring 1928), 7–8.
58. Terrell, *Companion to the Cantos*, 94 n. 18.
59. My own translation.
60. EP to Aldington (Nov. 19, [?1926]), HRHRC.
61. EP to Zukofsky (Oct. 16, [1934]), HRHRC.
62. EP to Zukofsky (Feb. 12, [1929]), HRHRC. DuPlessis reads Pound and Zukofksy's correspondence in terms of "mentorship within patriarchal poetics"; see Rachel Blau DuPlessis, *Purple Passages: Pound, Eliot, Zukofsky, Olson, Creeley, and the Ends of Patriarchal Poetry* (Iowa City: University of Iowa Press, 2012), 61 and *passim*. Glancing at the contents of *The Exile*, a reader might be misled to believe that there is an outlier in the second number: a "prose

narrative" by Stella Breen entitled "My Five Husbands." However, in that issue's editorial, Pound clarifies that the piece is by "George Steele Seymour of Chicago," who was trying his hand at impersonating a "feminine" mode; see *Exile* 2, 119. Jacqueline Vought Brogan's *Part of the Climate: American Cubist Poetry* (Berkeley: University of California Press, 1991) discusses *The Exile*, reading it as a partially cubist if not a "strictly cubist" journal, and describes Breen's "prose narrative [...] as a modern analogue to 'The Wife of Bath's Tale,'" 114–15.

63. "Do you think Zuk really dislikes the griffin...!? Category v. different from equine!" DP to EP (Sept. 28, 1932), Lilly.
64. Hugh Kenner, *The Pound Era* (Berkeley: University of California Press, 1973), 104; also quoted in Matthew Hart, *Nations of Nothing but Poetry: Modernism, Transnationalism, and Synthetic Vernacular Writing* (Oxford: Oxford University Press, 2010), 213 n 44.
65. Pound's valorization of a hard, "masculine" quality to poetry avers from acknowledging important influences on his musicality: Olivia Shakespear and Olga Rudge. Paterson notes that Bunting thought that Olivia Shakespear's evenings of Elizabethan music "influenced [...] the looser metrics of Pound and Yeats." See Paterson, "Words for Music Perhaps," 145 and Peter Makin, ed., *Basil Bunting on Poetry* (Baltimore: Johns Hopkins University Press, 1999), 35, 122.
66. *A Packet for Ezra Pound*, 7–8 quoted in Paul, "A Vision of Ezra Pound," 261. This praise was omitted from the version of "A Packet" that appeared in *A Vision*, in favor of more abstract reflections on modernism and the Rapallo group; see Paul, "A Vision of Ezra Pound," 48.
67. F.R. Higgins, "Yeats as Irish Poet," 149.
68. See Barbara Spackman, *Fascist Virilities: Rhetoric, Ideology, and Social Fantasy in Italy* (Minneapolis: University of Minnesota Press, 1996); for Yeats's sexuality, see R.F. Foster, "Family Values: Gender, Sexuality, and Crisis in Yeats's Anglo-Irish Aristocracy," in Jonathan Allison, ed., *Yeats's Political Identities: Selected Essays* (Ann Arbor: University of Michigan Press, 1996) and Marjorie Howes, *Yeats's Nations: Gender, Class, and Irishness* (Cambridge: Cambridge University Press, 1996).
69. Quoted in Torrey, *Roots of Treason*, 128. Zukofsky puns on the generative power of the penis in the "Peter Out" section of "Poem Beginning 'The'"; for a reading, see Du Plessis, *Purple Passages*, 65. For D'Annunzio's interest in the ambiguity of gender identity, see Hughes-Hallett, *The Pike*, 159–60; for Yeats and gender, see Elizabeth Butler Cullingford, *Gender and History in Yeats's Love Poetry* (Cambridge: Cambridge University Press, 1993), Howes, *Yeats's Nations*, and more recently Zsuzsanna Balázs, "Yeats's Queer Dramaturgies," *International Yeats Studies* 4.1 (Nov. 2019), https://doi.org/10.34068/IYS.04.01.02.
70. Pound, *ABC of Reading*, 39–40. A notable exception here is Sappho, whom Pound goes on to discuss, though he qualifies that "Catullus was in some ways a better writer than Sappho"; *ABC of Reading*, 47–8.

71. See Barbara Spackman, *Fascist Virilities: Rhetoric, Ideology, and Social Fantasy in Italy* (Minneapolis: Minnesota University Press, 1996).
72. "Date Line," 10. In the same essay, he argues that writers' success in the American market is "not the *vox populi*. One is inclined to talk of popular taste, when one should hunt for the chaps working the oracle."
73. "Date Line," 15, translation my own.
74. Pound's notes from 1930, quoted in Rainey, *Institutions of Modernism*.
75. Harper and Paul, *AVB*, xxxiii. For Yeats's discussion of the relationship between Spengler and Frobenius, see section XIII of "'The Great Year of the Ancients" in Harper and Paul, *AVB*, 189–90. Pound met Frobenius in May 1930, at the premiere of Antheil's *Transatlantic*; see Moody, *Pound*, ii, xv. Gibson writes that Rapallo Notebook E shows Yeats's reading of Frobenius's *The Voice of Africa*: "Yeats knew no German and this essay [i.e., the Ghanian tale of Samba Gana and Anallja Tu-Bari in *Paideuma*] was never translated, and so he was dependent on either Ezra Pound's or George Yeats's ad hoc translation." See Matthew Gibson, "'Timeless and Spaceless?' Yeats's Search for Models of Interpretation in Post-Enlightenment Philosophy, Contemporary Anthropology and Art History, and the Effects of These Theories on "The Completed Symbol," "The Soul in Judgment," and "The Great Year of the Ancients," in Neil Mann et al., *W.B. Yeats's "A Vision": Explications and Contexts* (Liverpool: Liverpool University Press, 2012).
76. For Zukofksy, see Du Plessis, *Purple Passages*, 71; for Ford, see *The Cantos: Some Testimonials*, 13 in Bunting Archive, Durham. For an example of the embeddedness of this idea in Pound's thought, in *ABC of Reading* he remarks, "Writers as such have a definite social function exactly proportioned to their ability AS WRITERS. This is their main use. All other uses are temporary, and can be estimated only in relation to the views of a particular estimator," 32; see also "A graver issue needs biological analogy [....] A nation which neglects the perceptions of its artists declines. After a while it ceases to act, and merely survives," *ABC of Reading*, 82.
77. See Bette H. Kirschstein, "The Remasculinization of the Artist and Author in Ford Madox Ford's Life Writing," *Biography* 21.2 (Spring 1998), 153–74.
78. "Madox Ford in Rapallo," *Il Mare*, 11–12. Trans. Bruna. This interview also appears, in translation by Olga Rudge, in Britta Lindberg-Seyersted, ed., *Pound/Ford, the Story of a Literary Friendship* (London: Faber, 1982), 108–10. Elizabeth Madox Roberts's first novel *The Time of Man* (1926) was received to critical acclaim; for a recent reappraisal of her work, see Matthew Nickel, "Elizabeth Madox Roberts: Modernist," *Mississippi Quarterly* 69.4 (Fall 2016), 413–33. Caroline Gordon won the O. Henry award in 1934 for the short story "Old Red." She was twice married to Allen Tate, with whom she hosted F. Scott Fitzgerald, Hemingway, Faulkner, Flannery O'Connor, Eliot, Robert Penn Warren, and Ford; she wrote two important works of criticism, *The House of*

Fiction and How to Read a Novel; see Frederick P. W. McDowell, Caroline Gordon—American Writers 59: University of Minnesota Pamphlets on American Writers (Minneapolis: University of Minnesota Press, 1966), www.jstor.org/stable/10.5749/j.ctttvbmw.1.

79. Andrzej Gąsiorek, "Exiles," The Oxford Critical and Cultural History of Modernist Magazines: Volume II: North America 1894–1960 (Oxford: Oxford University Press, 2012), DOI: 10.1093/acprof:osobl/9780199545810.001.0001, 708–709.
80. From the second preface to Jefferson and/or Mussolini, quoted in Bulson, "Journalism," in Nadel, Ezra Pound in Context, 94.
81. Gąsiorek, "Exiles," 711.
82. See Bulson, Little Magazine, 148.
83. Catherine E. Paul and Barbara Zaczek, "Margherita Sarfatti & Italian Cultural Nationalism," Modernism/modernity 13.1 (Jan. 2006), 889–916. DOI: 10.1353/mod.2006.0004.
84. "Da Marinetti [From Marinetti]" Il Mare, 316. Trans. Bruna. Marinetti refers specifically to Benedetta Cappa's paintings Viaggio di Gararà and Forze Umane.
85. Du Plessis, Purple Passages, 32–3 and the chapter "Pound Edits Loy and Eliot" in Purple Passages, 32–58.
86. Antheil to EP (n.d. [?May 1924]), Lilly.
87. Rainey, Institutions of Modernism, 141.
88. Pound, Jefferson and/or Mussolini, 33–4; see Catherine E. Paul, Fascist Directive: Ezra Pound and Italian cultural nationalism (Clemson, SC: Clemson University Press, 2017), 136 for a discussion of Pound's idea of Mussolini as builder.
89. For the institutions of fascist culture, see Philip V. Cannistraro, "Mussolini and the Italian Intellectuals," in Guido Bonsaver and Robert S.C. Gordon, eds., Culture, Censorship and the State in Twentieth-Century Italy (London: Routledge, 2005), 34–41.
90. Rarely one to abandon an analogy, Pound continued in the same vein in Il Mare's literary supplement, where he suggested that a handful of books could be "useful as an apparatus for weight and measurement, and, perhaps, as galvanometers to estimate the different virtues and qualities of literature and poetry"; Ezra Pound, "Foreign Affairs/Notes," Il Mare, 32. Trans. Bruna.
91. Quoted and translated in Bulson, "Journalism," in Nadel, Ezra Pound in Context, 88.
92. "Da Marinetti [From Marinetti]," Il Mare, 316. Trans. Bruna. Where Marinetti, unsurprisingly, argued for the continuity of Futurism in Italian fascism, Monotti regarded them as two distinct phases: "It is by accident, a fortunate accident, that our best artists started from Futurism more or less unconsciously, embracing it (or perhaps denying it)." See Francesco Monotti, "Dal Futrismo al Fascismo [From Futurism to Fascism]," Il Mare, 342. Trans. Bruna. Moody notes Pound's interview with L'Indice where "he went so far as to say that had he been living in Italy in 1912 to 1924 he would have made common cause with

the Futurists, at least on the need, in Italy, to clean out the dead past and to have a live contemporary perception precedent to the work of art"; *Pound*, ii, 103.
93. "Da Marinetti [From Marinetti]," *Il Mare*, 316. Trans. Bruna.
94. Ezra Pound, "Terra Italica," in Cookson, *Selected Prose: 1909–1965*, 54–60, 54.
95. Translation my own. The pun is an example of what Pound describes in *How to Read* as "Logopœia, 'the dance of the intellect among words' […] ironical play"; *How to Read*, 25–6. Pound instructed Stanley Nott to visit Fascio de Londra at 15 Greek Street, giving them permission to quote from *Jefferson and/or Mussolini* and referring to the book as "REALLY the most important piece of Italian propaganda yet printed in English or in England." Pound to Stanley Nott (Feb. 19, 1937), HRHRC.
96. DP to EP (Sept. 12, 1931), Lilly.
97. For literary magazines and exile, see Bulson, *Little Magazine* and Gaşiorek, "Exiles."
98. "Da Marinetti [From Marinetti]," *Il Mare*, 316. Trans. Bruna.
99. *How to Read*, 13–4. For the publication of the essay "How to Read" in periodicals, see Bulson, "Journalism," in Nadel, *Ezra Pound in Context*, 85.
100. Pound, *ABC of Reading*, 42.
101. Verdino, intro to *Il Mare*, x. Trans. Bruna. Verdino notes that the winner of the competition, Francesco Orlando, "a young futurist writer," was only ever locally famous.
102. EP to Zukofsky (Sept. 21, 1932), HRHRC. Dated 1932 in HRHC but probably 1931, since Pound continued, "Your incomprehensible pome will be in nex[t] number [of *Il Mare*]. You will snort at my adjective. What indeed IS comprehensible. Basil's latin is poss. more so."
103. Emanuel Gazzo, "The Literary Fortnightly," *Il Mare*, 16–17. Trans. Bruna.
104. Hughes-Hallett writes that early in the regime, "It suits Mussolini that the Italian public should believe that d'Annuzio is wholeheartedly behind the new regime, but in truth they are suspicious of one another. The poet is a maverick"; *The Pike*, 43.
105. Salvator Gotta, "Confessioni di Scrittori," *Il Mare*, 2–4. Trans. Bruna.
106. P.M. Bardi, "Poesia Poplare Fascista [Fascist Popular Poetry]," *Il Mare*, 332. Trans. Bruna.
107. Burton, *Strong Song*, 181. For Bunting's important role in the Vivaldi performances by Rudge—and their fascist aesthetics—see Paul, *Fascist Directive*, appendix.
108. Julia Boyd, *Travellers in the Third Reich* (London: Elliott and Thompson, 2018), 205–6.
109. Bunting to Zukofsky (Nov. 16, 1935), HRHRC.
110. Bunting to Zukofsky (May 9, 1943), HRHRC. Mussolini chose "Me ne frego" as one of the slogans for the regime, alluding to D'Annunzio's fearless attitude to the possibility of his own death in battle during the First World War.

111. Burton, *Strong Song*, 397; Julian Stannard, *Basil Bunting* (Tavistock: Northcote, 2014), 83–5. Bunting wrote to Zukofsky about the work: "I am no hand at Italian," and in any case, Pound "intends to print it [...] seeing that most edicated Eyetalians read Latin alright" (Sept. 1932), HRHRC.
112. EP to DP (Sept. 5, [1932]), Lilly.
113. EP to DP ([Dec. 28, 1932]), Lilly.
114. Bunting, "Diagnosi [Diagnosis]," *Il Mare*, 53. Trans. Bruna.
115. Bunting, "Diagnosi [Diagnosis]," *Il Mare*, 53. Trans. Bruna.
116. *How to Read*, 17.
117. Ezra Pound, "Nota in luogo d'Appunti [A footnote in lieu of Notes]," *Il Mare*, 77. Trans. Bruna.
118. Pound, *ABC of Reading*, 36.
119. Bunting to M. Bacigalupo (Mar. 20, 1985), Bunting MS 385/1–2. Durham.
120. For further similarities, see Bunting's article "How to acquire a style" which—in Poundian fashion—consists almost entirely of epigraphs. Bunting, "Come acquistare uno stile," *Il Mare*, 177–8. Also see Monotti's "Acqua Acestosa," where he condemns the quantity of bad criticism circulating: "the critic is mostly the person who, not being able to handle a machine gun, decided to buy a pea-shooter at the fair. And he shoots," *Il Mare*, 145–6. Trans. Bruna. Monotti's analogy anticipates (and maybe even inspired) Bunting's response to Zukofsky's question, in 1941, what do you "feel with a machine gun?" to which Bunting replied, "I criticise a machine by nearly the same criteria as I do a work of art. A Lee-Enfield rifle, a Hotchkiss machine-gun, have nothing superfluous or fancy about them. They are utterly simple—having reached that simplicity via complications & sophistications galore. The kind of people who, if they had literary minds at all, would like euphemism or thickness, prefer Lewis guns or Remington or Ross rifles. My machine-gun is a Hotchkiss, & I feel towards it something similar to what I feel for Egyptian sculpture [....] I think Holbein or Bach or Praxiteles, as well as Alexander, would have appreciated a Hotchkiss gun: whereas a lot of our own machines might <u>merely</u> have astonished them" (Sept. 22, 1941), HRHRC.
121. *Poetry Information* 19 (Autumn 1978), 4.
122. *Active Anthology*, 11. For a discussion of how Pound's *Active Anthology* sits within his prolific anthological projects, see Charlotte Estrade, "Transatlantic Crossroads: Ezra Pound's 1933 *Active Anthology*," *Caliban: French Journal of English Studies* 33 (2013), 123–32, https://journals.openedition.org/caliban/121.
123. *How to Read*, 9.
124. *How to Read*, 10.
125. John G. Nichols writes, "In their educative roles, Pound's anthologies enacted revisionist attempts to combat prior compilations that stressed established literary traditions and a homogenous literary culture." See "Ezra Pound's Poetic

Anthologies and the Architecture of Reading," *PMLA* 121.1 (Jan. 2006), 170–85, 173.
126. Beach, *ABC of Influence*, 18. Nichols writes, "Pound's anthologies implicitly argue that an awareness of how one reads should be crucial in the encounter with modernist literature, outstripping readers' reliance on editorial supervision, historical formations, and biographical backgrounds," "Ezra Pound's Poetic Anthologies," 175.
127. EP to Zukofsky (Nov. 8, [1932]), HRHRC.
128. James Longenbach, *Modernist Poetics of History: Pound, Eliot and the Sense of the Past* (Princeton, NJ: Princeton University Press, 1987), 143.
129. Hair, *Ronald Johnson*, 60.
130. Paul, *Fascist Directive*, 199, 83–140; see also Pound, *Guide to Kulchur* (New York: New Directions, 1938).
131. Nichols, "Ezra Pound's Poetic Anthologies," 174.
132. *How to Read*, 8.
133. Quoted in Paul, *Fascist Directive*, 200.
134. Nichols, "Ezra Pound's Poetic Anthologies," 181.
135. EP to DP (July [5], 1935) and (July 19, 1935), Lilly.
136. EP to Dorothy Pound (July 30, 1935), Lilly.
137. Pound, *ABC of Reading*, 38.
138. Bunting, "Open Letter to Louis Zukofsky," *Il Mare*, 72–3. Trans. Bruna. Although the term "Objectivist" was not established until 1931, it has retrospectively colored scholars' discussion of some of Zukofsky's earliest work; Ruth Jennison describes "Objectivism" as "a high modernism, but it was also a modernism whose practitioners remained in constant contact with the diverse and radical cultures that sprouted from crisis-driven cracks in the edifice of capitalism," *The Zukofsky Era: Modernity, Margins, and the Avant-Garde* (Baltimore, MD: Johns Hopkins University Press, 2012), 147–79. Scroggins shows how the term was imposed due to editorial demands; Harriet Monroe, on Pound's suggestion, invited Zukofsky to edit an issue of *Poetry*, and she insisted that Zukofsky identify a "new group" that would give a sense of unity to his selections. Zukofsky was reluctant to comply, but when he was pressed, he settled on "Objectivist," an idea derived from his essay "Sincerity and Objectification" about the poet Charles Reznikoff. See Mark Scroggins, *Poem of a Life: A Biography of Louis Zukofsky* (Emeryville, CA: Shoemaker & Hoard, 2007), 105–10.
139. EP, "The New English Weekly," *Contempo* (Apr. 22, 1933), HRHRC; Pound, *ABC of Reading*, 95, 131, 134, *passim*.
140. Pound, *ABC of Reading*, 96.
141. The title demarcates the difference between the chronological structure of *Workers Anthology* and the chronological organization of anthologies that are instrumental in canon-formation, which are discussed by John G. Nichols in "Editor, Anthologist," in *Ezra Pound in Context*, 66.

142. *Workers Anthology*, Bunting MS 54, Durham.
143. See Chapter 4.
144. Pound, *ABC of Reading*, 95.
145. For some of Pound's "tests," see *ABC of Reading*, 66–70.
146. *Test of Poetry*, xi.
147. Bunting to Zukofsky (Nov. 3, 1948), HRHRC.
148. EP to Isabel Pound (Nov. 22, [1927]), de Rachewiltz, *Pound to His Parents*, 641.
149. Forrest Reid writes, "Pound considered his prose and his poetry to be complementary versions of a synthetic digest, like *Ulysses*"; *Pound/Joyce: Letters of Ezra Pound to James Joyce with Pound's Essays on Joyce* (London: Faber, 1968), 245.
150. Quoted in Verdino, intro. to *Il Mare*, ix. Trans Bruna.
151. Pound, "Date Line," 5.

Chapter 4

1. Quoted in Foster, *Yeats*, ii, 395.
2. Foster, *Yeats*, ii, 395.
3. Foster, *Yeats*, ii, 396–7.
4. Foster, *Yeats*, ii, 379.
5. W.B. Yeats, *Pages from a Diary Written in Nineteen Hundred and Thirty* (Dublin: Cuala Press, 1944), 1.
6. Foster, *Yeats*, ii, 400–1.
7. Foster, *Yeats*, ii, 412.
8. Yeats, *Pages from a Diary*, 7. See Matthew Gibson, *Yeats, Coleridge and the Romantic Sage* (New York: St. Martin's Press, 2000) for discussion of the drafts of the diary and the published edition.
9. Pound, "The Hard and Soft in French Poetry," *Poetry* 11.5 (Feb. 1918), 264–71, http://www.jstor.org/stable/20571567. The terms are drawn from Théophile Gautier.
10. F.R. Higgins, "Yeats and Poetic Drama in Ireland," *The Irish Theatre: Lectures Delivered to the Abbey Theatre Festival held in Dublin in August 1938*, ed., Lennox Robinson (London: Macmillan, 1939), 65–88, 71; the phrase is repeated in F.R. Higgins, "Yeats as Irish Poet," in Stephen Gwynn, ed., *Scattering Branches: Tributes to the Memory of W.B. Yeats* (London: Macmillan, 1940), 147–55, 148.
11. Yeats, *Pages from a Diary*, 7.
12. Yeats, *Pages from a Diary*, 7.
13. T.W. Henley, *The Complete Poetical Works of Robert Burns* (Boston, MA: Houghton Mifflin, 1897), xxxii.
14. Wit Pietrzak, *The Critical Thought of W.B. Yeats* (London: Palgrave, 2017), 13.
15. Quoted in Pietrzak, *Critical Thought*, 13.

16. Pietrzak, *Critical Thought*, 15; cf., Frayne and Johnson, *Uncollected Prose*, i, 105.
17. Richard Aldington, "Everyman's Poets—V: Robert Burns: The Natural Man," *Everyman* (June 17, 1933), 152. Also see TS with emendations, HRHRC.
18. Aldington, "Everyman's Poets," 152.
19. Basil Bunting to George Marion O'Donnell (1934) in Dale Reagan, "Basil Bunting obiter dicta," in Carroll F. Terrell, ed., *Basil Bunting: Man and Poet* (Orono, ME: National Poetry Foundation, 1983), 239–40.
20. Yeats, *Pages from a Diary*, 7.
21. See also Harry Gilonis, "Soiled Mosaic: Bunting's Horace Translations," in James McGonigal and Richard Price, eds., *The Star You Steer By: Basil Bunting and British Modernism* (Amsterdam: Rodopi, 2000), 205–31, 207.
22. Yeats, *Pages from a Diary*, 7–8. Dorothy sent Ezra a review from *TLS* criticizing Bunting's form: "his poetry suggests rather that he is still too intoxicated by a sense of liberty to accept the discipline which poetry, no less than journalism, demands"; "Form," *TLS* (July 3, 1930), encl. DP to EP (n.d. [July 9, 1930]), Lilly.
23. Basil Bunting to Louis Zukofsky (Nov. 10, 1964), HRHRC.
24. For a discussion of "In Memory of Eva Gore Booth and Con Markiewicz" in the context of Rapallo, see my essay "Fighting Spirits: Yeats, Pound, and the Ghosts of *The Winding Stair* (1929)," in *Yeats Annual* 21 (2018), 269–93, https://books.openedition.org/obp/5657?lang=en.
25. Zukofsky to EP (Dec. 12, 1930), in Ahearn, *Pound/Zukofsky*, 78. Yeats described Browning as a "dangerous influence"; see WBY to Olivia Shakespear (Mar. 2, [1929]), *CL InteLex* Acc #5221.
26. For the controversy over Pound's "translation," see Donald Davie, *Ezra Pound: Poet as Sculptor* (Oxford: Oxford University Press, 1964), 78–81.
27. Thomas Drew-Bear, "Ezra Pound's "Homage to Sextus Propertius," *American Literature* 37.2 (May 1965), 204–10, 207.
28. The "literal translation" to which Drew-Bear refers is by H.E. Butler, published in Loeb Classical Library and reprinted in 1916.
29. Ezra Pound, *Active Anthology* (London: Faber, 1933), 11.
30. They met in late December 1932; EP to DP (n.d. [Dec. 27, 1932]), Lilly.
31. Pound, *Active Anthology*, 130.
32. Pound, *Active Anthology*, 140.
33. *VPl*, 809–10.
34. *VPl*, 851.
35. Yeats, *Pages from a Diary*, 13–14.
36. Aldington, "Everyman's Poets," 152.
37. Henley, *Poetical Works of Robert Burns*, xiii–xiv.
38. EP to Homer Pound (Dec. 2, [1928]) and (Dec. 8, [1928]), de Rachewiltz, *Pound to His Parents*, 674–5. Pound hoped Yeats would use the academy to "bust censorship" but worried it might be "merely for frivvle"; see EP to DP ([Sept. 25, 1932]), Lilly.

39. *Paideuma* 12, 388.
40. EP to Fitzgerald (Oct. 24, [1928]), *Paideuma* 12, 388.
41. Fitzgerald to EP (Dec. 13, 1928), *Paideuma* 12, 389–90.
42. EP to Fitzgerald (Dec. 20, 1928), *Paideuma* 12, 391.
43. Pound similarly conjoins the form of the Limerick and Cockney dialect in "Formalism," a poem enclosed in a letter to James Laughlin, in December 1933, a few months after Laughlin's visit to Rapallo: "There was once a barbary ape / who was jailed for arson and rape / His fyce 'ad th' look / Of Milford Beaverbrook / But you mustn't judge things by the shape?" in David M. Gordon, ed. *Ezra Pound and James Laughlin: Selected Letters* (New York: Norton, 1994), 10.
44. Reid, *Pound/Joyce*, 241. On one of Pound's evenings with the Joyces in Paris, "Nora insist[ed] on my swallowing 25 fr. worth of caviar—no expense to be spared. Giorgio really fine voice if interested 'in nothing but Bel Canto'"; EP to DP (Apr. 30, [1930]), Lilly.
45. Reid, *Pound/Joyce*, 244. Joyce's somber tone is inflected with the news he shared at the close: "I hope you had a pleasant *ceppo* [*Ceppo di Natale*]. Ours was saddened by the death of my father in Dublin. He loved me deeply."
46. EP to Homer Pound (Dec. 28, [1928]), de Rachewiltz, *Pound to His Parents*, 677; MacGreevy may have seen Pound in Rapallo, Rome, or both; he left his calendar in Rome and asked Pound to find it and return it to him; see EP to MacGreevy (Oct. 29, [1929]), TCD.
47. EP to Thomas MacGreevy (n.d.), TCD.
48. Fitzgerald to Pound (Dec. 13, 1928), *Paideuma* 12, 389–90.
49. EP to MacGreevy (Oct. 29, [1929]), TCD.
50. EP to MacGreevy (Oct. 29, [1929]), TCD.
51. W.B. Yeats, "The Censorship and St Thomas Aquinas," in Colton Johnson, ed., *W.B. Yeats: Later Articles and Reviews, Collected Works of W.B. Yeats, Volume X* (New York: Scribner, 2000); see also Warwick Gould, "'Satan Smut & Co' Yeats and Suppression of Evil Literature in the Early Years of the Free State," *Yeats Annual* 21 (2018), https://doi.org/10.11647/OBP.0135.05. Compare also Yeats's Thomism to Aldington's ideas about sex and divinity, discussed in Chapter 2.
52. WBY to Olivia Shakespear ([Nov. 22, 1931]), *CL InteLex* Acc #5539.
53. ballad, n. 2nd definition; *OED*. For the connection between another of Yeats's ballads, "Those Dancing Days are Gone," and Pound's *Cantos*, see Paterson, "Words for Music Perhaps," 151–2.
54. Pound, *ABC of Reading*, 14; Pound later asks, "What was there to the Celtic movement? Apart from, let us say, the influence of Irish ballad rhythm on Yeats's metric?" *ABC of Reading*, 80.
55. "Crazy Jane and Jack the Journeyman" and "Crazy Jane Talks with the Bishop" were written in November 1931; for the dating of the composition, see Norman A. Jeffares, *A New Commentary on the Poems of W.B. Yeats* (Stanford, CA: Stanford University Press, 1984), 307–12.

56. Pierre Longuenesse notes the similarity of the First Attendant's song in *A Full Moon in March* (1935) to medieval ballads. This may be a legacy of collaboration with Pound. See Longuenesse, "Playing with Voices and with Doubles in Two of Yeats's Plays: *The Words upon the Window-pane* and *A Full Moon in March*," *Yeats Annual* 19 103–17, 109, doi: 10.11647/OBP.0038.05.
57. NLI 13,580, 37ʳ in David R. Clark, ed., *Words for Music Perhaps and Other Poems: Manuscript Materials* (Ithaca, NY: Cornell University Press, 1999), 329 (hereafter *WMP*); this line was dropped in Yeats's first revision. Where I read "dreepy" as Burnsian, I'm grateful to Declan Kiberd for suggesting that it may also evoke Synge's use of the demotic. In *Pages from a Diary*, 13, Yeats reflects on Synge and dialect.
58. Helen Vendler, *Our Secret Discipline: Yeats and Lyric Form* (Oxford: Oxford University Press, 2007), 116. Jane speaks the closing refrain of "Crazy Jane and the Bishop" and pits Jack "the solid man" against the vain priest. Yeats's initial line for the second refrain was "the learned man & the knave," but the potential confusion for readers who might mistake "the learned man" for the priest was resolved by a revision made prior to the fourth (existing) draft, which is the galley proof for Yeats's planned *Collected Works*; Clark, *WMP*, 335. A related experiment is "Mad as the Mist and Snow," where, Paterson notes, the "consistency of stress, 4-3-4-3-4-3, extending the ballad stanza by half […] made it singable"; Paterson, "Words for Music Perhaps," 149.
59. Paterson writes in regard to the refrain of "Three Things," "Refrains are hardly a new feature in Yeats's verse, but their extensive use in this period is unprecedented, even taking into account his early ballads. This refrain gives the poem its bite." Paterson, "Words for Music Perhaps," 144.
60. *VP*, 511.
61. WBY to Margot Collis (Nov. 23, [1934]), *CL InteLex* Acc #6134.
62. For a study of *Michael Robartes and the Dancer* and the history of the ballad, see Edna Longley, "*Michael Robartes and the Dancer*: Helicon and Houlihan" in Jacqueline Genet, ed. *Studies on W.B. Yeats* (Caen: Universite de Caen, 1989), 119-143. https://books.openedition.org/puc/383?lang=en#text
63. *CL InteLex* Acc #5221.
64. Paterson, "Words for Music Perhaps," 143.
65. Foster, *Yeats*, ii, 386.
66. Ellmann, quoted in Clark, *WMP*, 581.
67. WBY to Shakespear, *CL InteLex* Acc #5221.
68. Pound, "The Later Yeats," *Poetry* 4.2 (May 1914), 64–49, http://www.jstor.org/stable/20570064.
69. Other late modernist poets also used the ballad form ironically; Claude McKay in *Constab Ballads* represented Jamaican patois, "sometimes by subversion, irony and disguise—tools of the dispossessed and subaltern—to voice a creolized modern verse"; Paul Peppis, "Salvaging Dialect and Cultural

Cross-Dressing in McKay's *Constab Ballads*," *Twentieth-Century Literature* 59.1 (2013), 37–48, 40. Auden's "As I Walked Out One Evening" (1940) begins as a visionary ballad anticipating natural harmony and personal fulfillment before undermining that possibility in the sixth stanza "O stand, stand at the window / As the tears scald and start; / You shall love your crooked neighbour / With your crooked heart."

70. A generation of critics read "Easter, 1916" as a "celebration of blood sacrifice," a view that was complicated by Jonathan Allison, among others. See "The Attack on Yeats," *South Atlantic Review* 55.4 (Nov 1990), 61–73. Nonetheless, Allison maintains that "The Rose Tree" stands in contrast to "Easter, 1916" whereas I argue here that its ironies are more deeply embedded. For some of the most recent reappraisals of "Easter, 1916," see the round of essays in *International Yeats Studies* 1.1 (2016), https://tigerprints.clemson.edu/iys/vol1/iss1/.
71. *A Broadside* 5 (May 1935).
72. Charles Gavan Duffy, *The Ballad Poetry of Ireland* (Dublin: J. Duffy, 1846), 248. In "Popular Ballad Poetry of Ireland," a review of Duffy's anthology, Yeats cites his work as emblematic of the power of literature to shape a national consciousness; see Pietrzak, *Critical Thought*, 17.
73. The order of old and new poems was not consistent in the 1935 *Broadside* series; the "traditional" ballad could occupy the first or second position.
74. Matthew Campbell discusses Richard Milliken's "The Groves of Blarney" and reception of the ballad by Ferguson and others in *Irish Poetry Under the Union, 1801–1924* (Cambridge: Cambridge University Press, 2013), 49–50.
75. The poem was published in the *Spectator* (Feb. 1934), *Poetry* (Dec. 1934), and collected in *A Full Moon in March* (1935).
76. For the Blueshirts' reception of the songs, see Foster, *Yeats*, ii, 477–9.
77. *VP*, 543.
78. *VP*, 544.
79. W.B. Yeats and F.R. Higgins, "Anglo-Irish Ballads," *Broadsides: A Collection of Old and New Songs* (Dublin: Cuala Press, 1935), n.p.; Boston College.
80. Campbell writes that Yeats and Higgins "work from an understanding of the quarter tones of Japanese music, which 'permit speech to rise imperceptibly into song' [….] the melismatic performance of the *sean nós* singer [is] cast unavoidably into the modes of the music of antiquity"; *Irish Poetry Under the Union*, 28.
81. WBY to Hilaire Belloc (July 6, 1936), *CL InteLex* Acc #6602; the letter corresponds to Yeats's request for Belloc's ballad "Mrs Rees," which he had sung at a party at Wilfred Blunt's "before the war," and which Yeats hoped Belloc would allow him to publish in the second series of 1937, which Yeats co-edited with Dorothy Wellesley; *CL InteLex* Acc #6584.
82. WBY to Dorothy Wellesley (Oct. 9, [1935]), *CL InteLex* Acc #6383. Campbell writes, "MacDonagh's fine distinction between Yeats being 'tune-deaf' but not

'tone-deaf' is borne out by [the *Broadsides'*] wilful restriction of musical possibility"; Campbell, *Irish Poetry Under the Union*, 28.
83. In their introduction to the series, Yeats and Higgins write: "If what is called the gapped scale, if the wide space left unmeasured by the mathematical ear where the voice can rise wavering, quivering, through its quarter-tones, is necessary if we are to preserve in song the natural rhythm of words, one understands why the Greeks murdered the man who added a fourth string to the lyre"; Yeats and Higgins, "Anglo-Irish Ballads" in *Broadsides* (1935), n.p.
84. *AVA*, xlv.
85. "F.R. Higgins," 180.
86. W.H. Auden, "The Public v. the Late Mr William Butler Yeats," *Partisan Review* 6.3 (Spring 1939); repr. in W.H. Pritchard, ed., *W.B. Yeats: A Critical Anthology* (London: Penguin, 1972), 136–42, 142.
87. Auden, "The Public v. the Late Mr William Butler Yeats," 142.
88. The scholarship on Pound and music is extensive; for brief surveys, see Michael Ingham, "Pound and Music," in Ira B. Nadel, *The Cambridge Companion to Ezra Pound* (Cambridge: Cambridge University Press, 1999), 236–48; Mark Byron, "A Defining Moment in Ezra Pound's *Cantos*: Musical Scores and Literary Texts," in Michael J. Meyer, ed., *Literature and Music* (Amsterdam: Rodopi, 2002), 157–82; Ann Saddlemyer, "William Butler Yeats, George Antheil, Ezra Pound Friends and Music," *Studi Irlandesi: A Journal of Irish Studies* 2.2 (2013), 55–71; and, more fulsomely, R. Murray Schafer, ed., *Ezra Pound and Music: The Complete Criticism* (London: Faber, 1978) and Conover, Olga Rudge, and Ezra Pound.
89. EP to DP (July 7, [1934]), Lilly; and EP to Ronald Duncan (Aug. 4, 1939), HRHRC.

Chapter 5

1. *Il fascism fa la storia, non la scrive*, quoted and translated by Paul, *Fascist Directive*, 131.
2. EP to Homer Pound (Jan. 8, 1927), de Rachewiltz, *Pound to His Parents*, 616. Pound's friendship with Stokes helped him to develop the idea of the quattrocento as a touchstone for the rejuvenation of contemporary civilization; in *How to Read*, Pound refers to "Italy, around the year 1300, [when] there were new values established, things said that had not been said in Greece, or in Rome or elsewhere"; *How to Read*, 31. Privately, Pound cautioned Thomas MacGreevy that Stokes's work "might at first sight appear somewhat fantastic, but it is based on sound archaeological knowledge"; EP to Thomas MacGreevy, TCD.
3. For Stokes and Pound, see two articles by Stephen Kite: "Architecture at Virtù: Adrian Stokes, Ezra Pound, and the Ethics of 'Patterned Energy,'" discussed below, and "Architecture as Techne: Adrian Stokes, Ezra Pound and the Art of

the Machine," *Paideuma* 33.1 (1), 33–55. See also Richard Read, *Art and Its Discontents: The Life of Adrian Stokes* (Farnham: Ashgate, 2002).
4. Read, *Art and Its Discontents*, 90; see also Janet Sayers, *Art, Psychoanalysis and Stokes: A Biography* (London: Karnac, 2015).
5. Adrian Stokes, *Sunrise in the West: A Modern Interpretation of Past and Present* (London: Keegan, Paul, Trench, Trubner, 1926), 151; see also Read, *Art and Its Discontents*, 92–3. Stokes later dismissed *Sunrise in the West* as juvenilia, but as Read has shown, the book laid the groundwork for Stokes's most important writing, including *The Quattro Cento*. George Yeats's ideas are masked by her collaborations with W.B., but their work together on *A Vision* indicates that the couple had common thoughts on the aristocracy of art; for their collaborations on *A Vision*, see Margaret Mills Harper, *Wisdom of Two: The Spiritual and Literary Collaboration of George and W.B. Yeats* (Oxford: Oxford University Press, 2006).
6. D'Annunzio is a key figure in understanding the metaphysical dimension to Italian fascism, and he was remembered in these terms in an article by Enzo de Leone for *Il Mare*'s literary supplement: "Gabriele D'Annunzio defines the volume [Conti's *La Beata Riva*] as a '…love treatise of an enthusiastic exegete, to whom the work of art is but religion made tangible in a living form…'"; Enzo de Leone, "Men of Italy," *Il Mare*, 25–8. Trans. Bruna. The metaphysical idea of art and the state was described succinctly elsewhere in *Il Mare*, "real art belongs to all epochs"; see "Noterelle [Little Notes]," *Il Mare*, 63–4. Trans. Bruna.
7. Quoted in Foster, *Yeats*, ii, 398. Olivia Shakespear wrote to Thomas MacGreevy in 1926, "I am struggling with O. Spengler—Have you read him? The translation is vile [….] I wish the earth would bust up & have done with it." Olivia Shakespear to Thomas MacGreevy (n.d. [postmarked Nov. 1926]), TCD. Shakespear provided Yeats with reading material during his illness in the winter of 1927–8, Yeats wrote to Shakespear asking her to send him "translation of one of Prousts novels [….] a book called 'the Idea of the Holy' by some German Theologian," remarking, "I want something read a little more sollid than detection." WBY to Olivia Shakespear, *CL InteLex* Acc #5062.
8. See, for example, "The value of Yeats is nothing but the sum of his expressed moments of reality: the value of Communism, or the value of Fascism, is the sum of its working truth or realities [….] *All things fall and are built again*. How comfortable! We have no right to listen to Yeats, no right at least to stay outside [….] we must recognise, and not evade, realities of the present [….] or else Beauty in view becomes a beast"; quoted in Foster, *Yeats*, ii, 398; *AVB*, xliv.
9. Quoted in *AVB*, xlv.
10. Bunting MS 305/52, Durham. In *How to Read* (1931), Pound criticized Spengler for "attempt[ing] a synthesis […] before [having] attained sufficient knowledge of detail"; for "stuff[ing] expandable and compressible objects into rubberbag categories" and for "limit[ing] reference and interest by supposing that the pedagogic follies which they [i.e., he] encountered constitute an error universally

distributed," *How to Read*, 7. The reference to Toynbee points to Bunting's own interest; in a letter to Zukofsky in 1940, he recommended Toynbee's *Study of History*, although "badly written," for the superiority of its ideas in comparison to "any of the other historical philosophers—not excluding Marx." See Bunting to Zukofsky (Mar. 19, 1940), HRHRC.
11. Bunting MS 305/52. Durham. Bunting gives the example of Pound's likening of Eleanor and Helen to each other.
12. Peter Nicholls, "Lost Object(s): Ezra Pound and the Idea of Italy" in Richard Taylor and Claus Melchior, eds., *Ezra Pound and Europe* (Amsterdam: Rodopi, 1993), 165–76, 170. Nicholls's reading is contextualized in his interpretation of Adorno and Habermas's theories of memory, mourning, modernism, and national culture after Auschwitz. For Nicholls, this frame provides a way of understanding how Pound writes about Italy after the collapse of the fascist regime as "a sort of *inability* to mourn," 172. Nicholls's reading also clarifies how Pound's belief in Italian fascism is encoded in the form of the *Cantos*, even when the objects are not explicitly politicized. Elsewhere, Nicholls "suspects" that as European politics were increasingly destabilized, Pound "was hastening to produce a body of materials which might provide guidance in the crisis to come. In fact there are signs that Pound conceived these Cantos [i.e., 52–71] as an act of direct political intervention"; Peter Nicholls, "A Metaphysics of the State," in Peter Makin, ed., *Ezra Pound's Cantos: A Casebook* (Oxford: Oxford University Press, 2006), 149–64, 151.
13. Hughes-Hallett, *The Pike*, 447.
14. Hughes-Hallett, *The Pike*, 447.
15. Quoted in Walter L. Adamson, "Modernism and Fascism: The Politics of Culture in Italy, 1903–1922," *American Historical Review* 95.2 (1990), 359–90, 359.
16. Yeats cites Gentile's *The Theory of Mind as Pure Act* in *AVB*: "our thoughts and emotions have duration and quality" and exist outside of time; although this statement seems banal, Yeats's reading of Gentile (whose philosophy draws from Kant) support Yeats's idea of the poet's access to universal knowledge and, therefore, the special role that the poet plays in guiding the state; see *AVB* 52 and 350 n. 21.
17. Giovanni Gentile, "The Philosophic Basis of Fascism," in *Readings on Fascism and National Socialism*, ed. Alan Swallow (Chicago, IL: Swallow Press, 1952), 48–61.
18. Yeats, *Pages from a Diary*, 55.
19. Yeats, *Pages from a Diary*, 53.
20. For the importance of homosociality in the Rapallo poets' pre-history, see McDiarmid, *Poets and the Peacock Dinner*.
21. Bonnie K. Scott, *Refiguring Modernism*, vol. 1 (Bloomington and Indianapolis: Indiana University Press, 1995), 84. That is not to say that Ezra actively

discouraged Dorothy from pursuing her talents as an artist. Scott quotes from a letter from Dorothy to Ezra in which she reports "doing some new early Vict[orian] wool work"; Ezra replies: "I am not in the least sure that you ought to embroider. It kills time but it also draws off a lot of little particles of energy, that ought to be dammed up until they burst out into painting." There is an argument to be made here, beyond the parameters of my study, about the unequal weighting of "domestic" and "public" art forms in Ezra Pound's thought.
22. Moody, *Pound*, ii, 118.
23. DP to EP (July 30, 1924), Lilly.
24. Similarly, she advised that he read G.D.H. Cole on industrial and political organization; DP to EP (Sept. 20, 1932), Lilly.
25. That's not to say that relations were always easy; Dorothy wrote to Ezra in August 1934, "I hope O[lga]. won't be in Rapallo when I get back? Its such a depressing start for the winter: & I suppose she'll be there most of the time, for concerts?" DP to EP (Aug. 29, 1934), Lilly.
26. WBY to Mabel Beardsley [Jan. 7, 1915], *CL InteLex* Acc #2574.
27. WBY to Mabel Beardsley [Jan. 7, 1915], *CL InteLex* Acc #2574.
28. Shakespear Pound, *Etruscan Gate*, 11.
29. For Ezra Pound, Fernand Léger, and the Return to Order, see Beasley, *Ezra Pound*.
30. "Leger in gd. form—dining tonight"; EP to DP (n.d. [May 16, 1933]), Lilly. Another notable constellation of Leger, the Pounds, Antheil, and W.B. Yeats is the film *Mechanical Ballet* on which Leger, Pound, and Antheil collaborated; Adrian Paterson notes that Yeats's phrase "mechanical song" referring to "Mad as the Mist and Snow" gestures to Antheil's influence. Antheil had been approached by Lennox Robinson in Paris to write the score for Yeats's play *Fighting the Waves*, and Antheil came to Rapallo to collaborate. Yeats told Robinson, "When you selected Antheil I think it was <a piece of> divination." See Paterson, "Words for Music Perhaps," 149–50.
31. Olivia Shakespear to Dorothy Shakespear (Mar. 1902), http://contentdm6.hamilton.edu/cdm/compoundobject/collection/poupos/id/32/rec/11.
32. Beasley, *Ezra Pound*, 75. The importance of quattrocento art and architecture to Pound's *Cantos* has been examined in fine detail in Lawrence Rainey's essay on patronage and the Malatesta cantos, and in Richard Read's *Art and its Discontents*, about the mutual influence of Pound and Stokes.
33. DP to EP (Dec. 20, 1925), Lilly.
34. DP to EP (Sept. 3, 1931), Lilly. Maintaining a semblance of intellectual life with a young child wasn't easy: "Nursery life is hell—one's spare time is spent collecting ones wits for the next session: I've no spare time except after dinner, when I read the paper"; DP to EP (Sept. 7, 1931), Lilly.
35. Michaelangelo Sabatino, "Space of Criticism: Exhibitions and the Vernacular in Italian Modernism," *Journal of Architectural Education* 62.3 (Feb. 2009), 35–52.

36. Dorothy Shakespear to EP (begun Mar. 16, 1914) in Omar Pound and A. Walton Litz, eds., *Ezra Pound and Dorothy Shakespear: Their Letters 1909–1914* (New York: New Directions, 1984), 356–7; quoted in David A. Lewis, ed., *Dorothy Shakespear, 1886–1973* (Nacogdoches, TX: SFA Gallery, Stephen F. Austin State University, 1997), 7.
37. See https://www.tate.org.uk/press/press-releases/vorticists-manifesto-modern-world; https://www.hamilton.edu/news/story/shakespear-exhibit-opens-at-hamiltons-emerson-gallery; https://www.hamilton.edu/wellin/wellinformed/my-year-with-the-dorothy-shakespear (accessed Mar. 13, 2019).
38. Lewis, *Dorothy Shakespear*, 2.
39. Francesco Monotti, "Dal Futurismo al Fascismo [From Futurism to Facism]," *Il Mare*, 342. Trans. Bruna.
40. Gentile, "The Philosophic Basis of Fascism," quoted in Rainey, *Institutions of Modernism*, 127.
41. Antonio Negri, "Ideas, Quotations, Controversies," in *Post zang tumb tuuum: Art Life Politics Italia 1918–1943*, ed. Germano Celant (Milan: Fondazione Prada, 2018), 116.
42. Negri, "Ideas, Quotations, Controversies," in Celant, *Post zang*, 116.
43. D. Medina Lasansky, *The Renaissance Perfected: Architecture, Spectacle, and Tourism in Fascist Italy* (University Park: Pennsylvania State University Press, 2004), 141.
44. Lasansky, *Renaissance Perfected*, xxviii.
45. *Pittura metafisica* was reconceptualized as Il Novecento Italiano in 1922 by Margherita Grassini Sarfatti, Mario Sironi, Anselmo Buccia, and Lino Pesaro. Some of these artists exhibited with Carrà, De Chirico, and Arturo Martini at the Galleria Arts in Milan in March–April of 1920, showing the convergence of the metaphysical and Novecento movements. De Chirico joined the 1926 exhibition "La Mostra del Novecento Italiano" in Milan; see Paola Pettenella, "Marguerite Sarfatti and Novecento," in Celant, *Post zang*, 130. For Mussolini's remarks, see Negri, "Ideas, Questions, Controversies," in Celant, *Post zang*, 117. The Novecento movement also had a literary articulation, in the journal *900*, which was published in French for the first two years of its circulation; the editorial board included James Joyce, Georg Kaiser, and Ilya Eherenburg; see Ruth Ben-Ghiat, *Fascist Modernities: Italy 1922–1945* (Berkeley: University of California Press, 2001), 27–8. For the relationship of the Novecento group's exhibitions to syndicalist exhibitions, see Sileno Salvagnini, "Art in Action: The Organisation of Italian Artistic Culture," in Celant, *Post zang*, 79.
46. Marilisa Castura, "A Context for Fascist Art and Culture: An Examination of Debates in *Critica fascista* (1923–1943)," unpublished Ph.D. thesis, University of East Anglia, 2008, 46. Bottai was a Member of the Chamber of Fasci and Corporations from 1929 to 1943, rising quickly through the ranks as Governor of Rome from 1935 to 1936, simultaneously serving as Governor of Addis Ababa

for just three weeks in May of 1936 and Education Minister from November 1936 to February 1943.
47. Quoted in Ben-Ghiat, *Fascist Modernities*, 25.
48. Casturà, "Context for Fascist Art and Culture," 46.
49. Casturà, "Context for Fascist Art and Culture," 141.
50. "Plastic values" developed from Berenson's emphasis on "tactile values," that is, the idea that art was not something to be passively observed; rather "conscious seeing" could excite pleasure and imaginative change in the viewer. Early Renaissance art was a touchstone for the kind of solid architectural forms that was valued by artists and theorists in the 1920s and 1930s; see Paul, *Fascist Directive*, 53–8.
51. Ian Chilvers and John Glaves-Smith, "Novecento Italiano," *A Dictionary of Modern and Contemporary Art*, 3rd edn. (Oxford: Oxford University Press, 2015), online. Mussolini made it clear that no accolades would be given to "fascist art" that was not also *good* art: "The party card does not give talent to those who don't already possess it." Quoted in Ben-Ghiat, *Fascist Modernities*, 23.
52. Pound, *Jefferson and/or Mussolini*, 92.
53. Lewis, *Dorothy Shakespear*, 2. The work in *Etruscan Gate* perhaps finds most affinity with some of the paintings of Giorgio Morandi, a Novecento artist whose "Still Life with Very Fine Hatching" (1933) brings architectural sensibilities to bear on domestic materials in a style that is very like Dorothy Pound's. My thanks to Sophie Dess for her research assistance on Novecento exhibitions documented in catalogues held in the New York Public Library.
54. For examples of Dorothy Pound's Vorticist work, see her illustrations for the Three Mountains editions of *Elimus: A Story by B.C. Windeler, with Twelve Designs by D. Shakespear* (1923), and her drawings for *A Draft of XVI Cantos* (1924). My interpretation varies from Moody, who describes Dorothy Pound's illustrations for the Hours Press edition as "vorticist." Cunard published 212 copies, superseding the Rodker and Bird editions of the Cantos; Moody, *Pound*, ii, 78. *Elimus* can be viewed at http://www.flashpointmag.com/Elimus_Gallery/Elimus/content/_5663332079_large.html.
55. EP to DP (n.d. [Apr, 1, 1929]), Lilly.
56. See Paul, *Fascist Directive*, chapter 3, especially 119–40.
57. John Champagne, *Aesthetic Modernism and Masculinity in Fascist Italy* (London: Routledge, 2012), 1.
58. Moody, *Pound*, ii, 40.
59. "Cortona: Lampodario Etrusco," Dorothy Pound to Olivia Shakespear (May 6, [1922]), Pound Family Postcards, Hamilton College. Shakespear responded by sending a copy of the Frazer [probably a volume of *Golden Bough*], for which Dorothy thanked her in a postcard of May 25. Leo Frobenius also discusses the Etruscans, specifically Etruscan mythology and numerology; for a discussion of WBY's reading of Frobenius, see Gibson, "'Timeless and Spaceless,'" 127; see also *AVB*, 259.

60. Ben-Ghiat, *Fascist Modernities*, 34.
61. Lasanksy, *Renaissance Perfected*, 53.
62. Paul, "A Vision of Ezra Pound," 254.
63. "Ascoli Piceno: Porta del Palazzo Bonaparte," DP to Olivia Shakespear (Oct. 5, [1928]), Pound Family Postcards, Hamilton College.
64. See Paul, *Fascist Directive*, 120–1 and Pound, *Jefferson and/or Mussolini*, 85.
65. Lasansky notes that the language of the regime was of "rediscovery" not "redesign" of architectural ruins: "Thanks to Fascist intervention these structures had been freed from the detritus of the intervening centuries to reemerge with renewed vigour and vitality"; *Renaissance Perfected*, 141.
66. Paul, *Fascist Directive*, 120 and 307 n. 110.
67. "Teramo: Porta Romana (Mon. Naz.)," DP to Olivia Shakespear, Pound Family Postcards, Hamilton College.
68. Quoted and translated in Negri, "Ideas," in Celant, *Post zang*, 121.
69. "Bastioni e antico acquedotto," n.d., Pound Family Postcards, Hamilton College.
70. David A. Lewis suggests that *Portofino from Hillside* inspired Dorothy Pound's scheme for an illuminated "A." See Lewis, *Dorothy Shakespear*, 17–18 and back jacket copy. In 1932, Dorothy asked Ezra to see if Olga Rudge could bring back "postcards or photos of Orsanmichele [in Florence]? I want the Madonna, and the interlacing arches on the outside walls. Anything almost might be useful" for the Cavalcanti canto; DP to EP (Dec. 27, 1932), Lilly.
71. In "Yeats in the Senate," David Fitzpatrick notes the lack of education among TDs (representatives in the lower house of the Irish parliament) in comparison with Yeats's fellow Senators: "To every Protestant there were ten Catholic members, hardly three-fifths of the T.D.s had completed secondary school, and in the course of the twenties the commercial classes gained representation at the expense of professional men [....] It was soon evident that enlightened "authoritative" government through such a legislature would be an up-hill task"; *Studia Hibernica* 12 (1972), 7–26, 21.
72. Pound, *Jefferson and/or Mussolini*, 127.
73. The technique of collapsing time is similar to what Yeats does in his essay, "Commentary on a Parnellite at Parnell's Funeral."
74. W.B. and George Yeats owned Gentile's *The Reform of Education* in its 1922 translation by Dino Bigongiari. Harper and Paul summarize, "Gentile proposes education of the individual as an aspect of the whole"; they observe, drawing from Paul Scott Stanfield, that WBY misattributed Gentile's ideas about education to Croce; *AVB* 352 n. 35.
75. Cronin, "The State on Display," 50–1.
76. Stone writes, "The cult of display in interwar Italy had produced a cultural moment in which modernism, monumentality, and the public sphere intersected in the name of Fascism"; see "Exhibitions and the Cult of Display," in Celant, *Post zang*, 191.
77. Ben-Ghiat, *Fascist Modernities*, 35.

78. I'm grateful to Catherine Paul for pointing me to these changes in her reading of a draft of this chapter.
79. WBY to Dorothy Wellesley (Aug. 12, [1937]), *CL InteLex* Acc #7039. The poem continues for a further two stanzas; in a postscript he writes, "First stanza goes better thus. (I hate writing for the eye): Because there's more to bite on / In sunlight or in wind, / I have bid you turn / From the cavern of the mind." The turn in Yeats's thought is also indicated in the way that his *Broadside* series with Wellesley in 1936 for Cuala Press lacks the political tenor of his 1935 series with Higgins, discussed later in this chapter.
80. Saddlemyer, *Becoming George*, 479. George's skill as a linguist meant she could be critical of WBY's professional translators; Ezra wrote to Dorothy in June 1928, "W.B.Y's translator turned up night before I left Wien. Have write G.Y. to let the feller git on with his work," Lilly.
81. Stone gives the figure as "over 1,800,000 visitors;" see Marla Stone, "Staging Fascism: The Exhibition of the Fascist Revolution," *Journal of Contemporary History* 28.2 (April 1993), 215–43, 215, https://www.jstor.org/stable/260709 (accessed Mar. 7, 2019).
82. I'm grateful to John Kelly for confirming the absence of information about the program in surviving Yeats correspondence and for affirming the probability of W.B. and/or George's attendance at the Exhibition.
83. Ben-Ghiat, *Fascist Modernities*, 35.
84. Stone, "Staging Fascism," 218.
85. A "rather impressive, if one have of *senso storico*"; quoted in Paul, *Fascist Directive*, 103.
86. EP to DP ("Xmas" [1932]), Lilly.
87. "Gabriele D'Annunzio and Luigi Pirandello," *National Committee for the IV Centenary of the Foundation of the Academy of the Lincei*, http://www.lincei-celebrazioni.it/volta/i4pirandello.html (accessed Jan. 31, 2018). Cf., *Prima pagina della Lettera manoscritta, indirizzata a Marpicati in occasione della preparazione del quarto convegno Volta, firmata con una sigla non identificata*. Roma, Accademia Nazionale dei Lincei, Archivio storico Fondo Reale Accademia d'Italia, Titolo VIII, B. 22, Fasc. 46, S. fasc. 1, cc. 6–9 and *Minuta del Promemoria del Cancelliere della Reale Accademia d'Italia, Arturo Marpicati, indirizzato a Benito Mussolini*. Roma, Accademia Nazionale dei Lincei, Archivio storico Fondo Reale Accademia d'Italia, Titolo VIII, B. 22, Fasc. 46, S. fasc. 1, c. 4.
88. Salvagnini, "Art in Action," in Celant, *Post zang*, 84.
89. EP to Homer Pound (Mar. 21, [1928]), de Rachewiltz, *Pound to His Parents*, 652. Sem Benelli (1877–1949) was an Italian dramatist, most of whose plays are imitative of D'Annunzio. He was "an adherent" of fascism from 1921 to 1924, but after the socialist politician Matteotti was assassinated by fascists, Benelli "distanced himself from the regime and concentrated on writing plays with philosophical themes," emigrating to Switzerland until after the Second World War; see Luca Zopelli, "Sem Benelli," *Grove Music Online* (Oxford: Oxford

University Press, 2002), https://doi-org.liverpool.idm.oclc.org/10.1093/gmo/9781561592630.article.0009009.
90. Reale Accademia D'Italia, *Convegno di Lettere: Il Teatro Drammatico* (Roma: Reala Accademia D'Italia, 1935–XIII), n.p. (hereafter *Volta*). Yeats Library, NLI.
91. Lino Pertile writes that the Academy, founded in 1927, "offered the highest accolades—and a good salary—to Italian scientists, scholars and artists in exchange for support or even simple acquiescence [to the regime]. Again many respected intellectuals, with the exclusion of the Crocean hard core, yielded to the temptation. Marinetti, ironically enough, the old arch-enemy of all academies, was one of the first to be appointed." Lino Pertile, "Fascism and Literature," in *Rethinking Italian Fascism: Capitalism, Populism, and Culture*, ed. David Forgacs (London: Lawrence and Wishart, 1986), 162–84, 172–3. For Marinetti's ideas about radio, see Timothy C. Campbell, "Marinetti, *Marconista*: The Futurist Manifesto and the Emergence of Wireless Writing" in Debra Rae Cohen, Michael Coyle, and Jane Lewty, eds., *Broadcasting Modernism*, 51–67. Marinetti, as discussed above, was invested in the idea of theatricality, but—as discussed later in this chapter—his ideas about the mechanisms of theatricality differed significantly from Pirandello and Yeats. For Marinetti's early "realization of a new theatricality," see Martin Puchner, *Stage Fright: Modernism, Anti-Theatricality, and Drama* (Baltimore, MD: Johns Hopkins University Press, 2002), 12. Pound was invited to speak at the Florence book fair in 1932, where—he bragged to Zukofsky—Stefan Zweig and Pirandello would also be speaking; EP to Zukofsky (May 4, 1932), HRHRC.
92. Translations my own.
93. For a discussion of Yeats's involvement in the Group Theatre in London and its connection to the Volta Conference in Rome, see my essay, "Toward a Late Modernist Theatre," *Modernism/modernity*, forthcoming.
94. ([Oct. 11, 1934]) *CL InteLex* Acc #6110.
95. ([Oct. 11, 1934]) *CL InteLex* Acc #6110. Aldington recalls being part of a group who took "the Italian Futurist" Marinetti to see WBY in London: "Sturge Moore, Ezra, and I acted as interpreters, for Marinetti spoke no English and Yeats would not talk a language of which he was not a master. Yeats read some of his own poems, which Marinetti would have thought disgustingly *passéistes* if he had understood them; and then Yeats through Sturge Moore asked Marinetti very politely to recite something of his. Whereupon Marinetti sprang up and in a stentorian Milanese voice began bawling:

> "Automobile,
> Ivre d'espace,
> Qui piétine d'angoisse," etc.

until Yeats had to ask him to stop because neighbours were knocking in protest on the floor, ceiling, and party walls"; Aldington, *Life for Life's Sake*, 108.
96. For a succinct summary of theories of theater's relation to the public sphere, see Puchner, *Stage Fright*, 10–1.

97. For Tairoff, see Oliver M. Sayler, *The Russian Theatre* (London: Brentano's, 1922), 141.
98. Sayler, *Russian Theatre*, 142.
99. For a discussion of these examples, and a qualifying statement about the parallel of Nazi and Soviet theaters, see Puchner, *Stage Fright*, 12. The Volta conferences, of which the conference on theater was just a part, has its counterpart on the political left with the Frankfurt School, which sought to bring Marxist critical theory to bear on artistic praxis, especially Walter Benjamin's theorization of tragedy. The crucial difference between the two institutions—and a major difference on which their legacies rely—is that the Frankfurt School was grounded in a body of theoretical writing that superseded any particular national context. Italian fascism, on the other hand, did not have recourse to such a unifying theory. The failure of Italian fascism to theorize itself, historians argue, was largely to blame for the difficulty in establishing and disseminating Italian fascism; for this argument, see, for example, Duggan, *Force of Destiny*, passim.
100. Guido Bonsaver, *Censorship and Literature in Fascist Italy* (Ontario: University of Toronto Press, 2007), 159. For Mussolini's censorship of Pirandello's libretto for the opera *La favola del figlio cambiato* by Gian Francesco Malipiero, see Bonsaver, Censorship and Literature, 74–5.
101. Mussolini, quoted in Emil Ludwig, *Talks with Mussolini*, Trans. Eden and Cedar Paul (London: G. Allen & Unwin, 1932), 214. Stanley Weintraub notes that Shaw visited Italy four times between 1926 and 1931, when he believed "what he was told, and what he read in the British press, which repeated fascist propaganda about an imperial revival"; see Weintraub, "GBS and the Despots."
102. WBY to Wyndham Lewis (Aug. 7, 1930), *CL InteLex* Acc #5371.
103. For discussions of Starkie's fascism, see Emilie Morin, *Beckett's Political Imagination* (Cambridge: Cambridge University Press, 2017) and Jacqueline Hurtley, *Walter Starkie, 1894–1976: An Odyssey* (Dublin: Four Courts, 2013).
104. Walter Starkie, *Luigi Pirandello* (London: Dent, 1926), 134–5.
105. Starkie, *Pirandello*, 135.
106. Hurtley, *Water Starkie*, 122.
107. Quoted in Hurtley, *Walter Starkie*, 136–7.
108. Quoted in Hurtley, *Walter Starkie*, 137. For a discussion of Yeats's radio broadcasts as a means of bringing Greek theater to life, see Emily Bloom, *The Wireless Past: Anglo-Irish Writers and the BBC, 1931–1968* (Oxford: Oxford University Press, 2016).
109. WBY to Margot Collis, *CL InteLex* Acc #6134.
110. See, for example, "At Parnell's Funeral," in *VP*, 541.
111. *Volta*, 386. The Irish Civil War as referent in the Volta speech is further underlined by Yeats's discussion of Lady Gregory's heritage, her life spent "in two Galway houses; the house where she was born, since burnt down in a year of trouble."
112. *Volta*, 388.

113. *Volta*, 391.
114. *Volta*, 391.
115. For an important reading of this poem and the long essay, see Donald Childs, *Modernism and Eugenics: Woolf, Eliot, Yeats, and the Culture of Degeneration* (Cambridge: Cambridge University Press, 2001), 208–10.
116. Mary Ann Frese Witt, *The Search for Modern Tragedy: Aesthetic Fascism in Italy and France* (Ithaca, NY: Cornell University Press, 2001), 2.
117. WBY to Edmund Dulac (n.d. [Dec. 10, 1934]), *CL InteLex* Acc #6145.
118. Croce may have mediated Hegel for Yeats; in "The Great Wheel," Yeats notes, "Though reality is not logical it becomes so in our minds if we discover logical refutations of the writer or movement that is going out of fashion. There is always error, which has nothing to do with 'the conflict' which creates all life. Croce in his study of Hegel identifies error with negation." Harper and Paul note that Yeats owned a copy of Croce's *What is Living and What is Dead of the Philosophy of Hegel*. Yeats also owned Croce's *Logic as the Science of the Pure Concept*, translated by Douglas Ainslie, a book that he "read carefully"; see *AVB*, 53 and 350 n. 25.
119. See Paterson, "Words for Music Perhaps," 149–51.
120. For a discussion of WBY's framing of his drama, see Charles I. Armstrong's chapter "Disputing *The Resurrection*," in *Reframing Yeats: Genre, Allusion, and History* (London: Bloomsbury, 2013), 63–76.
121. *VPl*, 560, 562.
122. "Introduction to Fighting the Waves," *Dublin Magazine* (Apr.–June 1932), 7–11, 8.
123. The image of the mirror may owe something to Yeats's reading of Strzygowski, whose "view of the West [was] as a 'mirror' of all other compass points," and Yeats links this to his classification of space and time in *AVB*; see Gibson, "'Timeless and Spaceless,'" 129.
124. EP, "Appunti [Notes]," *Il Mare*, 163–5. Trans. Bruna.
125. Nally, "Political Occult," 341.
126. Nally, "Political Occult," 338 and Mike Cronin, *Blueshirts and Irish Politics* (Dublin: Four Courts, 1997), 197–8.
127. Fitzpatrick, "Yeats in the Senate," 19.
128. Oswald Spengler, *The Decline of the West, or The Downfall of the Occident*, Trans. Charles Francis Atkinson (London: George Allen & Unwin, [1918–23], 1932), 38; see also Nally, "Political Occult," 333.
129. Spengler, *Decline of the West*, 249.
130. Spengler, *Decline of the West*, 432. Nally's "The Political Occult" first alerted me to the connection between Yeats's Caesar and Spengler's Caesarism. I record that debt here. Nally briefly develops Yeats's reading of Spengler in terms of WBY's 1934 "Commentary on Three Songs," before making a further connection with his play *Purgatory*.

131. Spengler, *Decline of the West*, 310 n. 1.
132. "Introduction to Fighting the Waves," *Dublin Magazine*, 9–10.
133. Quoted in Catherine E. Paul, *In the Museums of Modernism: Yeats, Pound, Moore, Stein* (Ann Arbor: University of Michigan Press, 2002), 13. For a discussion of Yeats's 1937 poem "The Municipal Gallery Revisited," see Paul, *Museums of Modernism*, 39–64.
134. For a detailed discussion of Yeats's reading of Berkeley, as mediated by Joseph Hone who collaborated with Mario Rossi on translations of Berkeley's philosophy, see W.J. McCormack, *"We Irish" in Europe: Yeats, Berkeley and Joseph Hone* (Dublin: University College Dublin Press, 2010). There is a notable similarity between Yeats's interest in Berkeley's philosophy of immaterialism and Pound and Bunting's ideas about "active" speech; in the article "Definire I nostri termini [Defining our terms]" for *Il Mare*, Bunting critiques Bergson's philosophy and writes, "No word lies exclusively in the power of man. You can assign any value you like to an algebraic term, but you cannot treat a number in the same way. A word is much more animated and resistant compared to a number, and derives its life and adaptability from usage, not the usage of one man in one book only, but of thousands of generations of billions of speakers"; *Il Mare*, 227–8. Trans. Bruna.
135. Sterling P. Lamprecht, "Review of Hone, Rossi, and Yeats, *Bishop Berkeley: His Life, Writings, and Philosophy*," *Journal of Philosophy* 29.19 (Sept. 15, 1932), 528–30, 528.
136. Lamprecht, "Review of *Bishop Berkeley*," 528.
137. Spengler, *Decline of the West*, 459.
138. Spengler, *Decline of the West*, 465.
139. Paul, *Fascist Directive*, 126.
140. Paul, *Fascist Directive*, 126–32.
141. Paul, *Fascist Directive*, 139.
142. EP to DP (June 25, 1933) and (June 29, 1933), Lilly.
143. DP to EP (June 29, 1933), Lilly.
144. EP to DP (June 26, 1934), Lilly.
145. EP to DP (June 29, 1934), Lilly.
146. EP to DP (Aug. 28, [1934]), Lilly.
147. For the composition of *The King of the Great Clock Tower* in Rapallo, see Richard Allen Cave, *The King of the Great Clock Tower: and a Full Moon in March: Manuscript Materials* (Ithaca, NY: Cornell University Press, 2007), xliii–xliv (hereafter *KOGCT*).
148. WBY to Olivia Shakespear (Aug. 7, [1934]), *CL InteLex* Acc #6080.
149. Cave, *KOGCT*, xlvi.
150. Cave, *KOGCT*, xlvii.
151. Cave arrives at the same conclusion, via a different route: "The strength of *The King of the Great Clock Tower* theatrically lies in its heightened abstraction,

which enables the play to move effortlessly toward its conclusion through dance, mime, tableau, and choric song"; *KOGCT*, xlvii.
152. *VP* 1309–10. Yeats's frustration with Pound emerges through his revisions of *A Packet for Ezra Pound*; see Catherine E. Paul, "Compiling *A Packet for Ezra Pound*," *Paideuma* 38 (2011), 29–53.
153. *AVB*, 301–2; see also Nally, "Political Occult," 340.

Chapter 6

1. Nancy Cunard, These Were the Hours: Memories of my Hours Press, Reanville and Paris, 1928–1931 ed. Hugh Ford (Carbondale: Southern Illinois University Press, 1969), 52. Cunard enjoyed drives in the countryside; after a particularly raucous party in Rome, Aldington met Cunard for the first time when he burst into her bedroom "and announced, 'I've come instead of Ezra.' Then, covering his testicles with his hand for protection, he 'pounced.' 'Oh no no! Not this!' Nancy protested, and persuaded him to come for 'a nice talk and a drive in the country instead.'" Torrey, Roots of Treason, 125.
2. Lois Gordon, Nancy Cunard: Heiress, Muse, Political Idealist (New York: Columbia University Press, 2007), 121, 123, 180. Aldington and Patmore also visited Pound in Rome, but that was in 1930, a year after Cunard published Aldington's long poem, The Eaten Heart. Cunard writes that the Hours Press published The Eaten Heart "about a year and a half before his greatly acclaimed war novel, Death of a Hero appeared," but both Death of a Hero and The Eaten Heart were published in 1929.
3. Burton writes, "Pound's incarceration in St Elizabeth's psychiatric hospital after the Second World War effectively finished him off as a poet and, more damaging yet, as an editor"; Strong Song, 260–1. More recently, in The Bughouse, Daniel Swift shows how Pound continued to be an important touchstone for mid-century poets, including Elizabeth Bishop and Robert Lowell; see The Bughouse: The Poetry, Politics, and Madness of Ezra Pound (London: Harville Secker, 2017). David Moody's three-volume biography has recovered in extensive detail Pound's vibrant and varied literary and political pursuits in Rapallo.
4. Cunard, These Were the Hours, 52.
5. H.D. wrote about the fisherman in Pound's poem, "The Goodly Fere": "He is the center of some kind of communal integration-disintegrating toward rebirth, as personally Ezra severed me (psychically) from friends and family. If having been severed, painfully reintegrated, we want only to forget the whirlwind or the forked lightning that destroyed our human, domestic serenity and security, that is natural"; End to Torment, 48.
6. H.D. End to Torment, 6.
7. H.D. End to Torment, 32.

8. Rattray was an undergraduate at Dartmouth; he went on to have an esteemed career as translator and poet, with degrees from the Sorbonne and Harvard. His essay "Weekend with Ezra Pound" is reprinted in William Van O'Connor and Edward Stone, eds., A Casebook on Ezra Pound (Cornwall, NY: Cornwall Press, 1959), 104–17.
9. H.D. End to Torment, 9.
10. Aldington lecture on Eliot and Pound, dated 1953 but delivered in 1939; HRHRC.
11. Aldington, Life for Life's Sake, 106.
12. Aldington, Life for Life's Sake, 323–4.
13. W.H. Auden and John Garrett, The Poet's Tongue (London: G. Bell & Sons, 1935), ix; also quoted in Samuel Hynes, The Auden Generation: Literature and Politics in England in the 1930s (London: Faber, 1976), 14. Aldington and Garrett include five poems by Yeats, but none by Aldington, Pound, or Bunting.
14. Aldington, Life for Life's Sake, 133, 135.
15. Aldington, Life for Life's Sake, 133.
16. Longenbach writes, "although Pound felt the impulse to address the European conflict in verse, he worried that without any firsthand experience of the war, his poetry would seem facile and opportunistic, the emotion literary and false"; Stone Cottage, 115.
17. Aldington, Life for Life's Sake, 104.
18. Aldington to MacGreevy (May 31, 1931), TCD.
19. Aldington to MacGreevy (June 4, 1959), TCD; see Canto LXXX in Cantos of Ezra Pound (New York: New Directions, 1996), 514; this canto would have been of particular interest to Aldington since it also contains some of Pound's most famous lines on Yeats: "the problem after any revolution is what to do with / your gunmen / as old Billyum found out in Oireland / in the Senate, Bedad! Or before then / Your gunmen thread onmoi drreams"; 516.
20. Pound sometimes saw himself as Aldington's peer; he signed a letter, "yr. disobliged and disobt. shall we say 'contemporary' (no other relationship being conceivable"; Pound to Aldington (Mar. 31, 1928), HRHRC; the next letter chastises Aldington for not writing a more favorable review of Remy de Goncourt: "meditate on yr prore ole farver's wordz."
21. Marius Hentea compares Henry Green and H.E. Bates, for example, as proof against "generation" as a reliable means of constructing literary history; see "The Problem of Literary Generations: Origins and Limitations," Comparative Literature Studies 50.4 (2013), 567–88.
22. Hemingway, A Moveable Feast, 27.
23. Aldington, Life for Life's Sake, 107.
24. Aldington to MacGreevy (Feb. 11, 1962), TCD; Aldington discounts the proposition, saying he thought Dorothy was about nine years old when the affair happened, and besides "she was remarkably like Hope and utterly unlike W.B."

25. VPl, 1010.
26. VPl, 1009; Salomé was one of the books Pound asked his mother to pack and bring to Rapallo when he wrote to her in February 1925 from Palermo; see de Rachewiltz, Pound to His Parents, 555.
27. VPl, 712.
28. MacGreevy, "W.B. Yeats: A Generation Later," 5, http://www.macgreevy.org/style?style=text&source=art.ur.002.xml&action=show.
29. MacGreevy, "W.B. Yeats: A Generation Later," 3.
30. See MacGreevy MS 8000/6 (12) and 8000/6b (10–11), TCD.
31. MacGreevy, "W.B. Yeats: A Generation Later," 9.
32. CL InteLex Acc #2153.
33. Kelly and Schuchard, Collected Letters of W.B. Yeats, ii, 500.
34. MacGreevy, "W.B. Yeats: A Generation Later," 9.
35. MacGreevy, "W.B. Yeats: A Generation Later," 9.
36. Aldington to MacGreevy (June 15, 1932), TCD.
37. Aldington to MacGreevy (Sept. 21, 1932), TCD.
38. MS 8003/10, TCD; the typescript is undated; Rhiannon Moss writes that the piece was "probably written in the late 1930s," but the proposed amendment was not brought before the Dail until 1958; for her dating, see "Thomas MacGreevy, T.S. Eliot and Catholic Modernism in Ireland," in Edwina Keown and Carol Taaffe, eds., Irish Modernism: Origins, Contexts, Publics (Bern; Oxford: Peter Lang, 2009), 131–44, 141.
39. MS 8003/10 (2), TCD.
40. Steve Shoemaker, "Between Contact and Exile: Louis Zukofsky's Poetry of Survival," in Mark Scroggins, ed., Upper Limit Music: The Writing of Louis Zukofsky (Tuscaloosa: University of Alabama Press, 1997), 23–43, 40. Shoemaker's title refers to the magazines—William Carlos Williams's Contact and Pound's Exile—in which Zukofsky published.
41. Zukofsky to Carl Rakosi (Jan. 7, 1931), HRHRC. William Carlos Williams later wrote, "Z. is a Jew who had a devout father not exclusively concerned with the formal minutiae of his religion, a father whom he loved while he found himself unwilling to follow into the details of his ancient religion according, we'll say, to Leviticus. Z is also a poet, a poet devoted to working out by the intelligence the intricacies of his craft; he is embedded in a matrix of his art and the multiple addictions which govern him, make him, of this time"; William Carlos Williams, "Louis Zukofksy," Agenda 3.6 [Louis Zukofsky Special Issue, ed. Charles Tomlinson] (Dec. 1964), 1–4, 3.
42. Bunting to Zukofsky (Aug. 6, 1945), HRHRC.
43. Bunting to Zukofsky (Aug. 6, 1945), HRHRC.
44. Cf., Ahearn, Pound/Zukofsky, 9 and Tim Woods, The Poetics of the Limit: Ethics and Politics in Modern and Contemporary American Poetry (Basingstoke: Palgrave, 2002), 118–30.

45. Bunting uses this racist word even when purporting to formulate an argument against racism; see his use of the term in the letter to Pound on Dec. 16, 1938, quoted in Burton, Strong Song, 263.
46. Bunting to Zukofsky (May 5, 1947), HRHRC.
47. Bunting to Pound (Dec. 16, 1938), quoted in Burton, Strong Song, 262.
48. Quoted in Burton, Strong Song, 262.
49. Richard Burton writes, "Bunting and Pound had been corresponding about economics, communism, anti-Semitism and Fascism since 1934 and the correspondence had become increasingly fractious"; Strong Song, 259.
50. Charles Norman, The Case of Ezra Pound (New York: Bodley, 1948), 55.
51. Louis Zukofsky to Charles Norman (Nov. 14, 1945), with revisions and a note by William Carlos Williams, HRHRC.
52. Norman, Case, 10.
53. F.O. Matthiessen took issue with this view; in his statement for the book he stated clearly, "Pound cannot be considered as a poet withdrawn from the world, like Emily Dickinson or Rilke, for instance"; Norman, Case, 57.
54. Norman, Case, 31.
55. Norman, Case, 35.
56. Norman, Case, 55.
57. Norman, Case, 56. Italian fascism was not coterminous with anti-Semitism; see, for example, D.P. Tryphonopoulos and L. Surette, eds., "I Cease not to Yowl": Ezra Pound's Letters to Olivia Rosetti Agresti (Urbana: University of Illinois, 1998).
58. Scroggins, Poem of a Life, 220.
59. Norman, Case, 56–7.
60. Keith Green, "Forgiveness, Pardon, and Punishment in Spinoza's Ethical Theory and 'True Religion,'" Journal of Early Modern Studies 5.1 (Spring 2016), 65–87; DOI: 10.5840/jems2016513.
61. Bunting to Zukofsky (Sept. 28, 1953), HRHRC.
62. Louis Zukofsky, "Work/Sundown," in Prepositions: The Collected Critical Essays of Louis Zukofsky, Expanded Edition (Berkeley: University of California Press, 1967), 165–6.
63. n.d. [May Day, 1939]), HRHRC.
64. (Nov. 3, 1939), HRHRC.
65. (Aug. 9, 1940), HRHRC.
66. Quoted in Burton, Strong Song, 178; as Burton makes clear this was "wide of the mark" since Pound's audience with Mussolini occurred eight months before the Buntings left Rapallo; "Perhaps Marion was trying to protect her ex-husband from the toxic effect of association with Pound in post-war America"; Burton, Strong Song, 179.
67. Postcard from Marion Bunting to Mr and Mrs Homer Pound, April 1935; Durham.

68. Burton takes a different view: "Bunting never failed to acknowledge his debt to Pound although he was always careful to contextualise it"; Strong Song, 218.
69. In the Preface to the Collected Poems, Bunting writes about his influences, "it was mostly from poets long dead whose names are obvious: Wordsworth and Dante, Horace, Wyat and Malherbe, Manuchehri and Ferdosi, Villon, Whitman, Edmund Spenser; but two living men also taught me much: Ezra Pound and in his sterner, stonier way, Louis Zukofsky. It would not be fitting to collect my poems without mentioning them"; Collected Poems (London: Fulcrum Press, 1968), n.p. In a special issue of Agenda published to mark Pound's eightieth birthday in 1965, Charles Tomlinson registered that "Pound still calls forth ['distrust'] in academic circles [....] Fourteen years have done something, however, to habilitate the poet's presence in the academy"; Charles Tomlinson, "The Tone of Pound's Critics," Agenda 4.2 (Oct.–Nov. 1965), 46–9, 46. This habilitation was tempered by the tone of the obituaries; for example, Time magazine concluded, "Increasingly in the 1930s, the Cantos reflected the poet's fondness for Mussolini's Fascism, his zany theories about usury and money [...] and finally, vicious anti-Semitic doggerel. War came [....]"; Time 100.20 (Nov. 13, 1972), 75. Pound's death made the front page of The New York Times, which printed a full-page obituary, including the now famous picture of Pound giving the fascist salute as he set sail for Italy after his release from St. Elizabeth's; "There is little question that Pound was one of the half dozen most important figures in the English literature of this century [....] At the same time, he was known to many Americans solely as an eccentric, a drum-beater for Hitler and Mussolini, a persistent anti-Semite and a traitor to the country of his birth"; Paul L. Montgomery: Ezra Pound: A Man of Contradictions," New York Times (Nov. 2, 1972), 39. The Times (London) extensively covered Pound's funeral and was sympathetic and not a little racist: "He encouraged Yeats [....] He helped Joyce [....] His own anti-Jewishness was simplistic and ideological, based on ideas about usury. Jews tend to be open-minded and intelligent, and Pound tended to like individual Jews"; "Mr Ezra Pound: Poet who Helped to Create Modernism," Times (London) (Nov. 2, 1972), 18.
70. Williams and Meyer, "A Conversation with Basil Bunting," 38.
71. Jonathan Williams, Descant on Rawthey's Madrigal (Frankfort, KY: gnomen press, 1968), n.p.; quoted in Burton, Strong Song, 170; in interview in October 1982, Bunting said something similar, while admitting to closer proximity: "I didn't on the whole work with Pound. I did some odd jobs for him. Proof-reading, things of that sort. Otherwise we met very frequently, I dare say, four times a week, and we'd spend several hours together in the afternoon or evening. That was always instructive and useful. Pound was very willing to impart whatever help he could"; quoted in Burton, Strong Song, 173.

72. Basil Bunting, "Yeats Recollected," Agenda 12.2 (Summer 1973), 36–47, 36.
73. Peter Makin, Bunting: The Shaping of his Verse (Oxford: Clarendon Press, 1992), 37.
74. When Basil and Marion's first child was born, they only had the serendipitous award of $50 from Poetry to pay the hospital bill; the Pounds gave the Buntings another $300 to help cover the costs of Marion's complicated delivery and extended hospitalization; see Burton, Strong Song, 170.
75. Eric Mottram, "Conversation with Basil Bunting on the Occasion of His 75th Birthday," Poetry Information 19 (Autumn 1978), 3–10, 4.
76. Mottram, "Conversation," 4.
77. Mottram, "Conversation," 8.
78. Quoted in Burton, Strong Song, 218. Bunting claims that the article was not sincere: "I perceive in it bits that sound like me and bits that are certainly Ezra shifted over into my words; and it has none of the things that I would have said if I'd been writing for, for instance, the Criterion which might have irritated EP. In short it's a joint performance of a chore neither of us fancied."
79. The word "silly" recurs when Bunting describes his concerns about ageing: "I would like to write another thing before I get too old to be credible. Old men become silly, so I've begun distrusting myself"; perhaps insinuating Pound's "silly" views had come after he passed into literary irrelevance; Williams and Meyer, "A Conversation with Basil Bunting," 37–46.
80. Bunting, "Yeats Recollected," 37.
81. Alasdair Clayre in Jonathan Williams, ed. Madeira & Toasts for Basil Bunting's 75th Birthday (Highlands, N.C.: Jargon Society, 1975), n.p.
82. Bunting, "Yeats Recollected," 45.
83. Bunting, "Yeats Recollected," 45–6.
84. Bunting, "Yeats Recollected," 46.
85. Virginia Woolf, Three Guineas (London: Hogarth, 1938), 259.
86. Woolf, Three Guineas, 260.
87. Quoted in Humphrey Carpenter, A Serious Character: The Life of Ezra Pound (Boston, MA: Houghton Mifflin, 1988), 816–17.
88. Samuel Hynes, "Meeting E.P.," The New Yorker (June 12, 2006), 74–100, 93.
89. H.D., End to Torment, 31; H.D. quotes Canto 93; Leucothea also appears in Canto 96.
90. H.D., End to Torment, 41.
91. Patmore 1.5, HRHRC.
92. Patmore 3.5, HRHRC.
93. Patmore diary, HRHRC.
94. Patmore's essay shares the page with an article proposing that there were few successful English "actresses" because British culture did not permit women to express emotion, while male English actors were uninhibited; Diana Bourbon,

"Just for the Sake of Argument...written to provoke...," The Sphere (Feb. 8, 1930), 228. Below Patmore's article are pictures from the World Beauty Contest in Galveston, Texas, showing "Miss Juogslavia," "Miss Germany," and "Miss Russia" (a Parisianne émigrée since "Russia forbade an official entry").
95. Brigit Patmore, "A traveller's lament on things one is never told," The Sphere (Feb. 8, 1930), 228.
96. Patmore 1.5, HRHRC.
97. Patmore, "traveller's lament."
98. Rebecca Wisor, "About Face: The Three Guineas Photographs in Cultural Context," Woolf Studies Annual 21 (2015), 1–49.
99. Saddlemyer, Becoming George, 631. Saddlemyer follows here Donald Pearce's remembrance of George: "In marrying Yeats she had, in fact, and by her own admission, put her directly at the service of a great poet for the rest of her life, a commitment that continued, without stint, not merely to the end of his life, but for thirty more years after that, to the end of her own"; see Donald Pearce, "Hours with the Domestic Sybil: Remembering George Yeats," Southern Review 28.3 (Summer 1992), 485.
100. Saddlemyer, Becoming George, 644.
101. Harper Wisdom of Two.
102. AVB 301–2, quoted in Harper, Wisdom of Two, 339.
103. Paul Corner, "Collaboration, Complicity, and Evasion," in Alf Lüdtke, ed., Everyday Life in Mass Dictatorship: Collusion and Evasion (London: Palgrave, 2016), 75–93, 83.
104. Aldington to MacGreevy (Nov. 15, 1958), TCD.
105. Bunting, "Yeats Recollected."
106. Pearce, "Hours with the Domestic Sybil," 485.
107. Saddlemyer, Becoming George, 583. For the texts of Pound's radio broadcasts, both those delivered and planned, see Leonard Doob, Ezra Pound Speaking (Westport, CT: Greenwood Press, 1978) and Matthew Feldman, Ezra Pound's Fascist Propaganda, 1935–45 (London: Palgrave, 2013).
108. Saddlemyer, Becoming George, 603.
109. Saddlemyer, Becoming George, 622; cf., George Yeats to Richard Ellmann (Nov. 19, 1945), McFarlin Library, University of Tulsa.
110. Saddlemyer, Becoming George, 630, citing "unpublished memoir by David Clark," Saddlemyer, Becoming George, 790 n. 58.
111. Saddlemyer, Becoming George, 630; Saddlemyer cites Patricia Greacen to George Yeats (Sept. 11, 1956); Paul de Man to George Yeats (Feb. 11, 1957); see also Virginia Moore to George Yeats (July 27, 1953), Becoming George, 790 n. 58. For a recent and unevenly regarded appraisal of Paul de Man's collaboration with the Nazis in Belgium, see Evelyn Barish, The Double Life of Paul de Man (New York: Liveright, 2014).

112. Richard Ellmann, "Ez and Old Billyum," in Eva Hesse, New Approaches to Ezra Pound (London: Faber, 1969), 55–85 and Saddlemyer, Becoming George, 645. This is at variance with Anne Yeats's recollection of meeting Pound at the airport and ferrying him to meet George at the Royal Hibernian Hotel; she said of Pound, "he'd talk your head off." With thanks to Roy Foster for the vignette.

Select Bibliography

Adamson, Walter L. "Modernism and Fascism: The Politics of Culture in Italy, 1903–1922," *American Historical Review* 95.2 (1990), 359–90.
Ahearn, Barry, ed. *Pound/Zukofsky: Selected Letters of Ezra Pound and Louis Zukofsky* (New York: New Directions, 1987).
Aldington, Richard. *Life for Life's Sake: A Book of Reminiscences* (New York: Viking, 1941).
Allt, Peter and Russell K. Alspach. *The Variorum Edition of the Poems of W.B. Yeats* (London: Macmillan, 1966).
Alspach, Russell K. and Catherine C. Alspach, eds. *The Variorum Edition of the Plays of W.B. Yeats* (London: Macmillan, 1966).
Antheil, George. *Bad Boy of Music*, int. Charles Amirkhanian (New York: Da Capo Press, 1981).
Arrington, Lauren. "Feeding the Cats: Yeats and Pound at Rapallo, 1928," in Senia Pašeta, ed., *Uncertain Futures: Essays about the Irish Past for Roy Foster* (Oxford: Oxford University Press, 2016), 188–98.
Arrington, Lauren. "Fighting Spirits: Yeats, Pound, and the Ghosts of *The Winding Stair* (1929)," in *Yeats Annual* 21 (2018), 269–93. https://books.openedition.org/obp/5657?lang=en.
Auden, W.H. "The Public v. the Late Mr William Butler Yeats," *Partisan Review* 6.3 (Spring 1939); repr. in W.H. Pritchard, ed., *W.B. Yeats: A Critical Anthology* (London: Penguin, 1972), 136–42.
Beach, Christopher. *ABC of Influence: Ezra Pound and the Remaking of American Poetic Tradition* (Berkeley: University of California Press, 1992).
Beasley, Rebecca. *Ezra Pound and the Visual Culture of Modernism* (Cambridge: Cambridge University Press, 2007).
Ben-Ghiat, Ruth. *Fascist Modernities: Italy 1922–1945* (Berkeley: University of California Press, 2001).
Blanton, C.D. *Epic Negation: The Dialectical Poetics of Late Modernism* (Oxford: Oxford University Press, 2015).
Blau DuPlessis, Rachel. *Purple Passages: Pound, Eliot, Zukofsky, Olson, Creeley, and the Ends of Patriarchal Poetry* (Iowa City: University of Iowa Press, 2012).
Boase, Roger. *The Origin and Meaning of Courtly Love: A Critical Study of European Scholarship* (Manchester: Manchester University Press, 1977).
Bonsaver, Giudo. *Censorship and Literature in Fascist Italy* (Ontario: University of Toronto Press, 2007).
Bradford, Curtis, ed. *W.B. Yeats: The Writing of "The Player Queen"* (DeKalb: Northern Illinois University Press, 1977).
Bridge, Ursula, ed. *W.B. Yeats and T. Sturge Moore: Their Correspondence, 1901–1937* (New York: Oxford University Press, 1953).

Bulson, Eric. *Little Magazine, World Form* (New York: Columbia University Press, 2017).
Burton, Richard. *A Strong Song Tows Us: The Life of Basil Bunting* (Oxford: Infinite Ideas, 2013).
Bush, Ronald. *The Genesis of Ezra Pound's Cantos* (Princeton, NJ: Princeton University Press, 1976).
Butler Cullingford, Elizabeth. *Gender and History in Yeats's Love Poetry* (Cambridge: Cambridge University Press, 1993).
Campbell, Matthew. *Irish Poetry Under the Union, 1801–1924* (Cambridge: Cambridge University Press, 2013).
Campbell, Timothy C. "Marinetti, *Marconista*: The Futurist Manifesto and the Emergence of Wireless Writing," in Debra Rae Cohen, Michael Coyle, and Jane Lewty, eds., *Broadcasting Modernism* (Gainesville: University Press of Florida, 2013), 51–67.
Cannistraro, Philip V. "Mussolini and the Italian Intellectuals," in Guido Bonsaver and Robert S.C. Gordon, eds., *Culture, Censorship and the State in Twentieth-Century Italy* (London: Routledge, 2005), 34–41.
Carpenter, Humphrey. *A Serious Character: The Life of Ezra Pound* (Boston, MA: Houghton Mifflin, 1988).
Casturà, Marilisa. "A Context for Fascist Art and Culture: An Examination of Debates in *Critica fascista* (1923–1943)," unpublished Ph.D. thesis, University of East Anglia, 2008.
Celant, Germano, ed. *Post zang tumb tuuum: Art Life Politics Italia 1918–1943* (Milan: Fondazione Prada, 2018).
Champagne, John. *Aesthetic Modernism and Masculinity in Fascist Italy* (London: Routledge, 2012).
Clark, David R., ed. *"Parnell's Funeral and other poems" from "A full moon in March": Manuscript Materials* (Ithaca: Cornell University Press, 2003).
Clark, David R. *Words for Music Perhaps and Other Poems: Manuscript Materials* (Ithaca, NY: Cornell University Press, 1999).
Conover, Ann. *Olga Rudge and Ezra Pound: "What thou lovest well—"* (London: Yale University Press, 2001).
Corner, Paul. "Collaboration, Complicity, and Evasion," in Alf Lüdtke, ed., *Everyday Life in Mass Dictatorship: Collusion and Evasion* (London: Palgrave, 2016), 75–93.
Cronin, Mike. "The State on Display: The 1924 Tailteann Art Competition," *New Hibernia Review* 9.3 (Autumn 2005), 50–71; doi:10.1353/nhr.2005.0050.
Cunard, Nancy. *These Were the Hours: Memories of my Hours Press, Reanville and Paris, 1928–1931*, ed. Hugh Ford (Carbondale: Southern Illinois University Press, 1969).
Davie, Donald. *Ezra Pound: Poet as Sculptor* (Oxford: Oxford University Press, 1964).
Davis, Thomas. *The Extinct Scene: Late Modernism and Everyday Life* (Columbia: Columbia University Press, 2016).
Drew-Bear, Thomas. "Ezra Pound's 'Homage to Sextus Propertius,'" *American Literature* 37.2 (May 1965), 204–10.
Duggan, Christopher. *The Force of Destiny: A History of Italy Since 1796* (London: Penguin, 2008).

Ellmann, Richard. "Ez and Old Billyum," in Eva Hesse, ed., *New Approaches to Ezra Pound* (London: Faber, 1969), 55–85.
Estrade, Charlotte. "Transatlantic Crossroads: Ezra Pound's 1933 *Active Anthology*," *Caliban: French Journal of English Studies* 33 (2013), 123–32; https://journals.openedition.org/caliban/121.
Finneran, Richard J., George Mills Harper, and William M. Murphy, eds. *Letters to W.B. Yeats*, Volume 2 (London: Macmillan, 1977).
Fischer, Hartwig and Sean Rainbird. *Wassily Kandinksy: The Path to Abstraction* (London: Tate, 2006).
Fitzgerald, Mary. "Pound and Irish Politics," *Paideuma* 12.2 (Fall/Winter 1983), 377–418.
Fitzpatrick, David. "Yeats in the Senate," *Studia Hibernica* 12 (1972), 7–26.
Foster, R.F. *W.B. Yeats: A Life*, Volume 2 *The Arch Poet* (Oxford: Oxford University Press, 2001).
Furlani, A. "'When Novelists became Cubists': The Prose Ideograms of Guy Davenport," *Style* 36.1 (2002), 111–31.
Fussell, Paul. *The Great War and Modern Memory*, int. Jay Winter (Oxford: Oxford University Press, 2013).
Gates, Norman T. *Richard Aldington: An Autobiography in Letters* (University Park: Pennsylvania State University Press, 1992).
Gentile, Giovanni. "The Philosophic Basis of Fascism," in *Readings on Fascism and National Socialism*, ed. Alan Swallow (Chicago, IL: Swallow Press, 1952), 48–61.
Gibson, Matthew. "'Timeless and Spaceless?' Yeats's Search for Models of Interpretation in Post-Enlightenment Philosophy, Contemporary Anthropology and Art History, and the Effects of These Theories on 'The Completed Symbol,' 'The Soul in Judgment' and 'The Great Year of the Ancients,' in Neil Mann, Matthew Gibson, and Claire Nally, eds., *W.B. Yeats's "A Vision": Explications and Contexts* (Liverpool: Liverpool University Press, 2012).
Gibson, Matthew. *Yeats, Coleridge and the Romantic Sage* (New York: St. Martin's Press, 2000).
Gilonis, Harry. "Soiled Mosaic: Bunting's Horace Translations," in James McGonigal and Richard Price, eds., *The Star You Steer By: Basil Bunting and British Modernism* (Amsterdam: Rodopi, 2000), 205–31.
Gordon, David M., ed. *Ezra Pound and James Laughlin: Selected Letters* (New York: Norton, 1994).
Gordon, Lois. *Nancy Cunard: Heiress, Muse, Political Idealist* (New York: Columbia University Press, 2007).
Gould, Warwick. "'Satan Smut & Co': Yeats and Suppression of Evil Literature in the Early Years of the Free State," *Yeats Annual* 21 (2018), https://doi.org/10.11647/OBP.0135.05.
Green, Keith. "Forgiveness, Pardon, and Punishment in Spinoza's Ethical Theory and 'True Religion,'" *Journal of Early Modern Studies* 5.1 (Spring 2016), 65–87; doi:10.5840/jems2016513.
Hair, Ross. *Ronald Johnson's Modernist Collage Poetry* (New York: Palgrave, 2010).
Harper, Margaret Mills and Catherine Paul, eds. *A Vision: The Revised 1937 Edition* in *The Collected Works of W.B. Yeats Volume XIV* (New York: Scribner, 2015).

Harper, Margaret Mills and Catherine Paul. *Wisdom of Two: The Literary and Spiritual Collaboration of George and W.B. Yeats* (Oxford: Oxford University Press, 2006).
Hart-Davis, Rupert, ed. *Siegfried Sassoon: Letters to Max Beerbohm: With a Few Answers* (London: Faber, 1986).
H.D. *End to Torment: A Memoir of Ezra Pound*, ed. Norman Holmes Pearson and Michael King (New York: New Directions, 1979).
Hemingway, Ernest. *A Moveable Feast* (London: Vintage, 2000 [1964]).
Hentea, Marius. "The Problem of Literary Generations: Origins and Limitations," *Comparative Literature Studies* 50.4 (2013), 567–88.
Higgins, F.R. "Yeats and Poetic Drama in Ireland," *The Irish Theatre: Lectures Delivered to the Abbey Theatre Festival held in Dublin in August 1938*, ed. Lennox Robinson (London: Macmillan, 1939), 65–88.
Hoare, Philip. *Serious Pleasures: The Life of Stephen Tennant* (London: Hamish Hamilton, 1990).
Hora, Kevin. *Propaganda and Nation Building: Selling the Irish Free State* (London: Routledge, 2016).
Hughes-Hallett, Lucy. *The Pike: Gabriele D'Annunzio: Poet, Seducer and Preacher of War* (London: Fourth Estate, 2013).
Hurtley, Jacqueline. *Walter Starkie, 1894–1976: An Odyssey* (Dublin: Four Courts, 2013).
Hynes, Samuel. "Meeting E.P.," *The New Yorker* (June 12, 2006), 74–100.
Hynes, Samuel. *The Auden Generation: Literature and Politics in England in the 1930s* (London: Faber, 1976).
Ingelbien, Raphael. "Metres and the Pound: Taking the Measure of British Modernism," *European Review* 19.2 (2003), 285–97.
Jeffares, Norman A. *A New Commentary on the Poems of W.B. Yeats* (Stanford, CA: Stanford University Press, 1984).
Jennison, Ruth. *The Zukofsky Era: Modernity, Margins, and the Avant-Garde* (Baltimore, MD: Johns Hopkins University Press, 2012).
Kelly, John and Ronald Schuchard, eds. *The Collected Letters of W.B. Yeats. Volume 3: 1901–1904* (Oxford: Oxford University Press, 1994).
Kindellan, Michael. "Ownership and Interpretation: On Ezra Pound's Deluxe First Editions," *Reconnecting Aestheticism and Modernism: Continuities, Revisions, Speculations*, ed. Bénédicte Coste, Catherine Delyfer, and Christine Reynier (London: Routledge, 2017), 187–202.
Kirschstein, Bette H. "The Remasculinization of the Artist and Author in Ford Madox Ford's Life Writing," *Biography* 21.2 (Spring 1998), 153–74.
Lasansky, D. Medina. *The Renaissance Perfected: Architecture, Spectacle, and Tourism in Fascist Italy* (University Park: Pennsylvania State University Press, 2004).
Lewis, David A., ed. *Dorothy Shakespear, 1886–1973* (Nacogdoches, TX: SFA Gallery, Stephen F. Austin State University, 1997).
Lindberg-Seyersted, Britta, ed. *Pound/Ford, the Story of a Literary Friendship* (London: Faber, 1982).
Longenbach, James. *Stone Cottage: Pound, Yeats, and Modernism* (Oxford: Oxford University Press, 1988).

Longuenesse, Pierre. "Playing with Voices and with Doubles in Two of Yeats's Plays: *The Words upon the Window-pane* and *A Full Moon in March*," *Yeats Annual* 19 (2013), 103–17; doi:10.11647/OBP.0038.05.

MacGreevy, Thomas. *Richard Aldington: An Englishman* (London: Chatto & Windus, 1931).

McCormack, W.J. *"We Irish" in Europe: Yeats, Berkeley and Joseph Hone* (Dublin: University College Dublin Press, 2010).

McDiarmid, Lucy. *Poets and the Peacock Dinner: The Literary History of a Meal* (Oxford: Oxford University Press, 2014).

McDowell, Frederick P.W. *Caroline Gordon—American Writers 59: University of Minnesota Pamphlets on American Writers* (Minneapolis: University of Minnesota Press, 1966), www.jstor.org/stable/10.5749/j.ctttvbmw.1.

Makin, Peter. *Bunting: The Shaping of his Verse* (Oxford: Clarendon Press, 1992).

Makin, Peter, ed. *Ezra Pound's Cantos: A Casebook* (Oxford: Oxford University Press, 2006).

Miller, Henry. *Tropic of Cancer* (New York: Modern Library, 1983 [1961]).

Moody, A. David. *Ezra Pound: Poet*, 3 vols (Oxford: Oxford University Press, 2015).

Moss, Rhiannon. "Thomas MacGreevy, T.S. Eliot and Catholic Modernism in Ireland," in Edwina Keown and Carol Taaffe, eds., *Irish Modernism: Origins, Contexts, Publics* (Bern; Oxford: Peter Lang, 2009), 131–44.

Mottram, Eric. "Conversation with Basil Bunting on the Occasion of His 75th Birthday," *Poetry Information* 19 (Autumn 1978), 3–10.

Murphy, Russell Elliott. "'Old Rocky Face, look forth': W.B. Yeats, the Christ Pantokrator, and the Soul's History (The Photographic Record)," in *Yeats: An Annual of Critical and Textural Studies* XIV, ed. Richard Finneran (Ann Arbor: University of Michigan Press, 1996), 69–117.

Nally, Claire. "The Political Occult: Revisiting Fascism, Yeats and 'A Vision,'" in Neill Mann, Matthew Gibson, and Claire Nally, *W.B. Yeats's "A Vision": Explications and Contexts* (Liverpool: Liverpool University Press, 2012), 329–43.

Nicholls, Peter. "A Metaphysics of the State," in Peter Makin, ed., *Ezra Pound's Cantos: A Casebook* (Oxford: Oxford University Press, 2006), 149–64.

Nicholls, Peter. "Lost Object(s): Ezra Pound and the Idea of Italy," in Richard Taylor and Claus Melchior, eds., *Ezra Pound and Europe* (Amsterdam: Rodopi, 1993), 165–76.

Nickel, Matthew. "Elizabeth Madox Roberts: Modernist," *Mississippi Quarterly* 69.4 (Fall 2016), 413–33.

Norman, Charles. *The Case of Ezra Pound* (New York: Bodley, 1948).

O'Connor, William Van and Edward Stone, eds., *A Casebook on Ezra Pound* (Cornwall, NY: Cornwall Press, 1959).

Paige, D.D., ed. *The Letters of Ezra Pound 1907–1941* (London: Faber, 1950).

Paterson, Adrian. "Words for Music Perhaps," in *Essays on Music and Language in Modernist Literature*, ed. Katherine O'Callaghan (London: Routledge, 2018), 140–58.

Patmore, Brigit. *My Friends When Young: The Memoirs of Brigit Patmore*, ed. Derek Patmore (London: Heinemann, 1968).

Paul, Catherine E. "A Vision of Ezra Pound," in Neil Mann, Matthew Gibson, and Claire Nally, eds., *W.B. Yeats's "A Vision": Explications and Contexts* (Liverpool: Liverpool University Press, 2012), 252–68.

Paul, Catherine E. *Fascist Directive: Ezra Pound and Italian Cultural Nationalism* (Clemson, SC: Clemson University Press, 2017).

Paul, Catherine E. *In the Museums of Modernism: Yeats, Pound, Moore, Stein* (Ann Arbor: University of Michigan Press, 2002).

Paul, Catherine E. and Margaret Mills Harper, eds. W.B. Yeats, *A Vision (1925)*, in *Collected Works of W.B. Yeats* 13 (New York: Scribner, 2008).

Paul, Catherine E. and Barbara Zaczek, "Margherita Sarfatti & Italian Cultural Nationalism," *Modernism/modernity* 13.1 (Jan. 2006), 889–916; doi:10.1353/mod.2006.0004.

Pearce, Donald. "Hours with the Domestic Sybil: Remembering George Yeats," *Southern Review* 28.3 (Summer 1992), 485–501.

Peppin, Brigid. "Women that a Movement Forgot," *Tate Etc.* 22 (Summer 2011), https://www.tate.org.uk/context-comment/articles/women-movement-forgot.

Peppis, Paul. "Salvaging Dialect and Cultural Cross-Dressing in McKay's *Constab Ballads*," *Twentieth-Century Literature* 59.1 (2013), 37–48.

Pertile, Lino. "Fascism and Literature," in *Rethinking Italian Fascism: Capitalism, Populism, and Culture*, ed. David Forgacs (London: Lawrence and Wishart, 1986), 162–84.

Pietrzak, Wit. *The Critical Thought of W.B. Yeats* (London: Palgrave, 2017).

Pound, Omar and A. Walton Litz, eds. *Ezra Pound and Dorothy Shakespear: Their Letters 1909–1914* (New York: New Directions, 1984).

Pounds, Wayne. "Toward the Rapallo Vortex: 'Il Mare: Supplemento Letterario,' 1932–1933," *Paideuma* 29.3 (Winter 2000), 255–9.

Preda, Roxanna. *Ezra Pound's Economic Correspondence, 1933–1940* (Gainesville: University Press of Florida, 2007).

Puchner, Martin. *Stage Fright: Modernism, Anti-Theatricality, and Drama* (Baltimore, MD: Johns Hopkins University Press, 2002).

Quartermain, Peter. *Disjunctive Poetics: From Gertrude Stein and Louis Zukofsky to Susan Howe* (Cambridge: Cambridge University Press, 1992).

de Rachewiltz, Mary. *Ezra Pound to His Parents: Letters 1895–1929* (Oxford: Oxford University Press, 2010).

Rainey, Lawrence. *Institutions of Modernism: Literary Elites and Public Culture* (New Haven, CT: Yale University Press, 1998).

Read, Richard. *Art and Its Discontents: The Life of Adrian Stokes* (Farnham: Ashgate, 2002).

Redman, Tim. *Ezra Pound and Italian Fascism* (Cambridge: Cambridge University Press, 1991).

Reid, Forrest. *Pound/Joyce: Letters of Ezra Pound to James Joyce with Pound's Essays on Joyce* (London: Faber, 1968).

Sabatino, Michaelangelo. "Space of Criticism: Exhibitions and the Vernacular in Italian Modernism," *Journal of Architectural Education* 62.3 (Feb. 2009), 35–52.

Saddlemyer, Ann. *Becoming George: The Life of Mrs. W.B. Yeats* (Oxford: Oxford University Press, 2002).

Saddlemyer, Ann. "Friendship with George and W.B. Yeats," in Susan Schreibman, ed., *The Life and Work of Thomas MacGreevy: A Critical Reappraisal* (London: Bloomsbury, 2013), 212–26.
Sanderson, Rena, Sandra Spanier, and Robert W. Trogdon, eds. *The Letters of Ernest Hemingway, Volume 3 1926–1929* (Cambridge: Cambridge University Press, 2015).
Sayler, Oliver M. *The Russian Theatre* (London: Brentano's, 1922).
Schreibman, Susan, ed. *The Life and Work of Thomas MacGreevy: A Critical Reappraisal* (London: Bloomsbury, 2013).
Scott, Bonnie K. *Refiguring Modernism*, vol. 1 (Bloomington and Indianapolis: Indiana University Press, 1995).
Scroggins, Mark. *Poem of a Life: A Biography of Louis Zukofsky* (Emeryville, CA: Shoemaker & Hoard, 2007).
Shakespear Pound, Dorothy. *Etruscan Gate: A Notebook with Drawings and Watercolours*, ed. Moelwyn Merchant (Exeter: Rougemont Press, 1971).
Shoemaker, Steve. "Between Contact and Exile: Louis Zukofsky's Poetry of Survival," in Mark Scroggins, ed., *Upper Limit Music: The Writing of Louis Zukofsky* (Tuscaloosa: University of Alabama Press, 1997), 23–43.
Spanier, Sandra, Albert J. Defazio III, and Robert W. Trogdon, eds. *The Letters of Ernest Hemingway, Volume 2 1923–1925* (Cambridge: Cambridge University Press, 2013).
Stanfield, Paul Scott. "The Irish Free State and the European Crisis," in David Holdeman and Ben Levitas, eds., *W.B. Yeats in Context* (Cambridge: Cambridge University Press, 2010), 57–68.
Stannard, Julian. *Basil Bunting* (Tavistock: Northcote, 2014).
Swift, Daniel. *The Bughouse: The Poetry, Politics, and Madness of Ezra Pound* (London: Harville Secker, 2017).
Terrell, Carroll F. *A Companion to the Cantos of Ezra Pound* (Berkeley: University of California Press, 1980).
Terrell, Carroll F., ed. *Basil Bunting: Man and Poet* (Orono, ME: National Poetry Foundation, 1981), 145–59.
Tomlinson, Charles. "The Tone of Pound's Critics," *Agenda* 4.2 (Oct.–Nov. 1965), 46–9.
Torrey, E. Fuller. *The Roots of Treason: Ezra Pound and the Secret of St. Elizabeths* (San Diego, CA: Harcourt Brace Jovanovich, 1984).
Ure, Peter. "A Source of Yeats's 'Parnell's Funeral,'" *English Studies* 34.6 (Dec. 1958), 257–8.
Vaught Brogan, Jacqueline. *Part of the Climate: American Cubist Poetry* (Berkeley: University of California Press, 1991).
Vendler, Helen. *Our Secret Discipline: Yeats and Lyric Form* (Oxford: Oxford University Press, 2007).
Weintraub, Stanley. "GBS and the Despots," *TLS* (Aug. 22, 2011), https://www.the-tls.co.uk/articles/public/george-bernard-shaw-and-the-despots/.
Wertham, Frederic. "The Road to Rapallo: A Psychiatric Study," *American Journal of Psychotherapy* 3.4 (1949), 585–600.
Whelpton, Victoria. *Richard Aldington: Poet, Soldier and Lover 1911–1929* (Cambridge: Lutterworth, 2013).

Williams, Jonathan and Tom Meyer. "A Conversation with Basil Bunting [1976]," *Poetry Information* 19 (Autumn 1978), 37–48.

Williams, William Carlos. "Louis Zukofksy," *Agenda* 3.6 [Louis Zukofsky Special Issue, ed. Charles Tomlinson] (Dec. 1964), 1–4.

Wilson, F.A.C. "Yeats' PARNELL'S FUNERAL, II," *Explicator* 27.9 (May 1969), 40–1.

Wisor, Rebecca. "About Face: The *Three Guineas* Photographs in Cultural Context," *Woolf Studies Annual* 21 (2015), 1–49.

Witt, Mary Ann Frese. *The Search for Modern Tragedy: Aesthetic Fascism in Italy and France* (Ithaca, NY: Cornell University Press, 2001).

Index

For the benefit of digital users, indexed terms that span two pages (e.g., 52–53) may, on occasion, appear on only one of those pages.

aesthetic(s) 79, 105, 107, 116, 133, 138–9
   architectural 113, 154
   arguments 77–8
   Byzantine 116
   of death 49
   of Dorothy Pound 118–20
   of Ezra Pound and W.B. Yeats 5–6
   fascist 12–13, 17, 74–5, 112–14, 116, 120–2, 126–30, 134–5, 144, 153, 156–7
   objectivist 82
   politics of 114
   positive 44–5
   quattrocento 110–11
   revolution 60
   totalitarian 122
   of violence 141
   Vorticist 110
Aldington, Richard 10, 13, 45, 48–9
   correspondence from Pound 20–1, 55, 66
   The Colonel's Daughter 47
   Death of a Hero 30–5, 39–40, 47–8, 52
   Decameron (translation) 40–1
   The Eaten Heart 40–5, 137
   and Imagism 50
   Life for Life's Sake 33–4, 45, 52, 138–9
   and lyric form 36–8
   and relationship with Brigit Patmore 27–30, 155
   and Robert Burns 83, 88–9, 93
   and Thomas MacGreevy 143–4, 157
   and W.B. Yeats 140–1
Antheil, George 10–11, 33, 71, 104, 127
   Bel Esprit 10, 21
   Fighting the Waves 104, 107–8, 120, 127–31, 134–5, 175n.99, 198n.30
   see also Yeats, W.B.
   Mechanical Ballet 10, 198n.30

architecture 7, 15–16, 110–13, 123, 131
   fascist 105
   Italian 110–11
   Norman 110–11
   Renaissance 110–11
   Roman 110–11
   see also aesthetic(s)
   see also fascism (fascist)
Auden, W.H. 103–4, 138
   The Poet's Tongue 139
   see also Garrett, John
D'Annunzio, Gabriele 17, 69, 74–5, 77, 106–7, 124–5, 135, 158, 196n.6, 202nn.87,89

ballad(s) 91, 94
   broadside 18, 86–7, 100–4
   form 88–90, 95–100
   lyric 103–4
   meter 97
Beckett, Samuel 9, 143
Beerbohm, Max 1–2, 23, 30, 50, 132
Bird, William 8, 13, 63–6
   The Three Mountains Press 8
Bowen, Stella 11
Bunting, Basil 172n.61, 174n.73, 179nn.6,9
   correspondence with Pound 10
   and *Il Mare* 75–9
   and Pound 104, 106–7, 206n.134
   and Robert Burns 89–92, 96
   Workers Anthology 80–4
   and Yeats 157–9
   and Zukofsky 22–3, 39, 56–7, 144–54, 178n.137
Bunting, Marion 154
Burton, Richard 77, 159

Carrà, Carlo 111–13
De Chirico, Giorgio 111–14
Cox–McCormack, Nancy 11–12, 71
Cunard, Nancy 40, 66–7, 137
  These Were the Hours: Memories of my Hours Press 137

Dante 38, 82–3, 90, 93, 133, 153
  Purgatorio 40
Delehanty, Elizabeth 19–20
depression 1, 45
  economic 62, 115–16

Eliot, T.S. 8–10, 21, 41
  Bunting on 146, 151, 153
  memorial service of 158–9
  and "poetic inheritance" 80–1
  and Pound 34, 37, 55, 91, 138
  W.B. Yeats on 49
  The Waste Land 1
Ernst, Max 22

fascism (fascist) 11–12, 21–2, 72–3, 81–2, 101, 103–4, 149–51
  and *Il Mare* 74–8
  anti-fascist 11
  and anti-intellectualism 107
  and architecture 105
  and art 112–14, 118, 134–5, 141, 143, 153, 156–7
  Doctrine of Fascism 101
  influence of 12–19, 25, 58
  fascio 12
  fascismo 63–4
  Fascist National Institute of Culture 72
  Fascist Revolution 120–2
  methodology 81
  movement(s) 56, 59, 70–1, 107, 110, 112, 114–16, 123, 126–7, 131–2, 149, 154–7
  National Fascist Party 17–18, 36
  and Pound 137–8, 144, 147–51, 153
  and rediscovery 117–20
  theory 106
  thought 70, 105, 108
  and the Volta Conference 124–5
  W.B. Yeats on 120–1, 128–30
Fitzgerald, Desmond 19, 59–60, 93–5
Ford, Ford Madox 10, 70, 139, 174n.80
Fordism 92
Frobenius, Leo 16–17, 66–7, 70–1

Garrett, John 139
  The Poet's Tongue 139
  see also W.H. Auden
Gaudier-Brzeska, Henri 12–13, 183n.48
Gentile, Giovanni 15–16, 105, 107–8, 112–13, 120–2
Gonne, Iseult 5
Gonne, Maude 5–6
Grierson, H.J.C. 9

Hammond, Douglas 154
Hauptmann, Gerhart 1–2, 23, 55, 85
Hemingway, Ernest 11–13, 50, 62, 70, 140, 149–50
  A Moveable Feast 10
  A Farewell to Arms 50
O'Higgins, Kevin 6
Hitler, Adolf 22–3, 66, 77, 133–4, 141, 147, 149, 153
Hynes, Samuel 3, 154–5

Irish Statesman 95, 125

James, Henry 70, 182n.39
  Daisy Miller 34
Jefferson, Thomas 18–19, 21–2, 108
Joyce, James 47, 94, 101
  Ulysses 1, 94, 134

Lawrence, D.H. 31, 40, 52
Lees, George Hyde 5, 29, 111
Leger, Fernand 10, 110
  Mechanical Ballet 10, 198n.30
  see also Antheil, George
Lewis, Wyndham 55
  correspondence with W.B. Yeats 8–9
  and Pound 12–13, 16–17, 56–7, 110–11, 124–5, 149, 156

MacGreevy, Thomas 1, 8–9, 16–17, 31, 35, 37
  and Aldington 45–9, 52, 139–41, 143–4, 157
  and Pound 94
  and W.B. Yeats 50, 52, 95, 141–3
Makin, Peter 61, 151
Malatesta, Sigismondo 11–12, 21, 115–16, 198n.32
Il Mare 12, 56, 66–7, 70–9, 82, 112, 151
  see also Bunting, Basil
  see also fascism (fascist)

Monotti, Francesco 12, 34, 79, 112, 186n.92
Monroe, Harriet
    Poetry 57
Mussolini 106, 113–16, 122, 156–7
    and Bunting 75–7, 153
    Foro Mussolini 118
    government of 12–19, 36, 65, 69, 107,
        131–2, 137–8
    and Hemingway 12
    and Hitler 77
    and MacGreevy 16–17
    and Cox-McCormack 71
    and Pound 11, 72, 81–2, 107, 133–4, 139,
        147, 149–50
    and Sarfatti 70–1
    and the Volta Conference 122–6
    and Yeats 17, 120–1, 127–30, 135, 142

painting 12–13, 24, 63–4, 70–1,
        82, 86–7
    metaphysical 107, 110–15, 143
    see also Pound, Dorothy
Parnell, Charles Stewart 16, 125–6, 129
    see also W.B. Yeats, "Parnell's Funeral"
Patmore, Brigit 13, 27–31, 34–5, 47–9, 137
    and Rapallo 154–6
    This Impassioned Onlooker 27, 29–30
    My Friends When Young 28
Pound, Dorothy (nee Shakespear) 29, 154–7
    aesthetics of 105, 108–9, 118–20
    and Aldington 140–1, 154
    correspondence with Ezra Pound 11, 13,
        19, 56–7, 77, 81–2, 104, 122, 132, 137
    drawings 12–13, 66–7
    Etruscan Gate 12–13, 110, 114–15, 154
    on fascism 73
    and paintings 111–12, 114–16, 118–21
    and Rapallo 110–11
    relationship with Ezra Pound 4–5, 7, 9
Pound, Ezra 1–7, 49, 63–9, 137–41,
        144–56, 158–9
    ABC of Reading 55–9, 69, 74, 78–80,
        82–4, 95–6
    Active Anthology 79–80, 91–3
    and Aldington 27–31, 33–4,
        39–41, 47, 55
    and ballads 93–6, 99–102
    and Dorothy Pound 108–18, 120, 122–3
    A Draft of XVI Cantos 8, 40, 200n.54
    A Draft of XXX Cantos 114, 118–20

The Exile 7–9, 57, 59–63, 73–5
    and fascism 126–9, 131–4
    and Gabriele D'Annunzio 17
    and Gentile 107
    Guide to Kulchur 58, 63–4, 66, 81–2
    How to Read 74, 77–8, 80–2, 84
    Jefferson and/or Mussolini 18–19, 21–2, 72,
        80–2, 108, 113–14, 116, 120, 131–2
    Lustra 90–1
    and MacGreevy 37–8, 46, 50
    and *Il Mare* 70–3, 75–8
    and Nancy Cox-McCormack 12–17
    Personae 90–1
    and Portofino 86–7
    and Rapallo 9–11, 18–23, 25, 103–4
    and Robert Burns 89
    and Spengler 105–7
    The Spirit of Romance 38–40, 43–4
    and Stokes 108
    and Whitman 38–9
    and Zukofsky 78–84, 90–3

Rakosi, Carl 21–2, 151
Rapallo 85, 115–16, 159
    Albergo Rapallo 23, 27
    and Aldington 21, 27–30, 33–5, 40–1,
        44–5, 47
    and Bunting 75–9, 151–2
    and Burns or ballad influence 87–91,
        93–4, 96, 98, 103–4
    and Ezra and Dorothy Pound 9–17, 20–5,
        27–8, 30, 55–8, 60, 63, 66, 69–70,
        72–3, 108, 115–16, 118–20, 137–8
    and plasticity 113–14, 135
    and Stokes 105
    and totalitarian criticism 83–4, 154
    and W.B. and George Yeats 1–2, 4–8,
        16–17, 21–5, 28, 30, 50, 125–6,
        129–30, 132, 134
    and mysticism of 157
    and Zukofsky 22–3, 144, 147
Redimiculum Matellarum 89, 96
Robinson, Lennox 8–9, 50, 85, 127, 198n.30
Ruddock, Margot 97–8, 123–4
Rudge, Olga 4–5, 9, 104, 122,
        187n.107, 201n.70

Sarfatti, Margherita 16–17, 70–1
Shakespear, Dorothy
    see Pound, Dorothy

226 INDEX

Shakespear, Olivia 4–5, 23–4, 95–6, 98, 110–11, 115–16, 132
Shakespeare, William 35, 38, 133, 153
　As You Like It 35
　cult of 88–9
　Shakespearean sonnet 38
Shaw, George Bernard 14–16, 124–5, 142
Sitwell, Osbert 30, 105
Sordello 40, 43–4
Spengler, Oswald 16–17, 70, 105–7, 129–34, 141
　Decline of the West 70, 106–7, 129–31
　Sunrise in the West: A Modern Interpretation of Past and Present 105
Spinoza, Baruch 92, 145–6, 148
Stein, Gertrude 140
Stokes, Adrian 20–1, 55–6, 105, 108, 133
　Stones of Rimini 55–6, 105
Strater, Henry 8

Volta Conference 115–16, 121–7

Wadsworth, Beaumont 20–1
Wallace, George 12
Walpole, Horace 34–5
　The Castle of Otranto 34–5
Wertham, Frederic 13
Whitman, Walt 3–4, 35, 37–9, 52
Wilde, Oscar 16, 141
　Salome 141
William, William Carlos 22–3, 60, 71, 147–8, 209nn.40–41
Woolf, Virginia 70, 134, 153–4, 156
　Three Guineas 153–4, 156
　Waves 134

Yeats, George 1–2, 4–5, 7–9, 85
　and Aldington 27–8, 34–5, 45
　Baedeker's 7
　and MacGreevy 48–50
　and Pound 23–5, 40, 43, 99, 132
　and *A Vision* 105, 116, 156–9
　and the Volta Conference 121–2
Yeats, W.B.
　and Aldington 27–31, 33–5, 37–8, 41–6, 49–52, 85–9
　"Rapallo" 1–2
　and ballads 99–104
　Broadsides: A Collection of Old and New Songs 100
　and Bunting 153
　and the Crazy Jane ballads 95–8
　Crossways 100
　and Dorothy Pound 109
　Early Poems and Stories 9
　and Ezra Pound 4–9, 14–15, 19–21, 40, 56–7, 59, 64, 67–9, 82–3, 93, 132–5, 138–41, 151–3
　Fighting the Waves 104, 107–8, 120, 127–31, 134–5
　see also Antheil, George
　and George Yeats 156–9
　and Joyce 94
　The King of the Great Clock Tower 43–4, 126–7, 130, 132–3, 141
　and MacGreevy 142–3
　Michael Robartes and the Dancer 100–1
　and Mussolini 15–18, 120–2
　Oedipus at Colonus 125–7
　The Oxford Book of Modern Verse 41, 49–51
　Pages from a Diary Written in Nineteen Hundred and Thirty 87–8, 103, 106
　and Patmore 156
　"Parnell's Funeral" 18, 38, 43–5, 107–8
　Playboy of the Western World 126
　and Rapallo 1–2, 23–4
　Responsibilities 97, 99–100
　The Tower 1, 7–8, 25, 29–30, 64
　The Unicorn from the Stars 141
　A Vision 1–2, 7–8, 16–17, 25, 102–3, 105–8, 116, 121, 134, 156–7, 159
　and the Volta Conference 122–31
　Wheels and Butterflies 120, 128, 134
　The Winding Stair and Other Poems 88–9, 95, 103–4
　and Zukofsky 79, 92–3
　see also Rapallo
Ypres, Battle of 1, 30, 51, 65–6

Zukofsky, Louis 21–3, 39
　and the *Active Anthology* 90–3, 104
　and anti-semitism 146, 148–9
　and Bunting 79–84
　Workers Anthology 79, 83
　and fascism 144–52
　and Jewishness 65–6
　and Pound 56, 60, 65–7, 70, 74–5, 77
　Prepositions 149
　A Test of Poetry 83–4